A PLUME BOOK

THE SECRET HISTORY OF THE AMERICAN EMPIRE

JOHN PERKINS is the author of *Confessions of an Economic Hit Man*, which spent more than a year on the *New York Times* bestseller list. He is a founder and board member of Dream Change and The Pachamama Alliance, two nonprofit organizations dedicated to creating a stable, sustainable, and peaceful world. Visit www.johnperkins.org.

**Praise for *Confessions of an Economic Hit Man* and
*The Secret History of the American Empire***

"Reading *The Secret History of the American Empire* is like finding the key that unlocks a mystery. It simultaneously confirms your suspicions and inspires you to hope. I wouldn't say it's good news, but it's important news . . . about where America's gone wrong, and what it will take for us to make things right."
—Marianne Williamson

"John Perkins' new book is both an eye-opening exposé of global corruption and a fascinating story of adventure and intrigue. This devastating indictment of current economic policies also offers hope by showing the power of the growing movement toward a caring economics worldwide."
—Riane Eisler, author of *The Chalice and the Blade* and
The Real Wealth of Nations

"A significant contribution to the new universal way of searching for innovative and better approaches to coexistence."
—Dr. Rafael Correa Delgado, President of Ecuador

"A highly readable—and shocking—book. It's difficult to accept that U.S. and corporate policies can be so brutal and greedy, but knowing John Perkins personally, I have come to understand the importance of disclosing this uncomfortable truth. Only by confronting the truth can we eventually create a world that works for all of us. John Perkins inspires us to get up and take action to create a more just and equitable world."

—Jack Canfield, cocreator of the
Chicken Soup for the Soul® series

"[E]ntertaining but disturbing accounts of the American government wreaking havoc around the world in support of American business."

—*Publishers Weekly*

"This is a book that gives us hope. Its secrets not only reveal the urgency of our global crisis but help us understand what we can do to create a sustainable, peaceful world."

—John Gray, author of
Men Are from Mars, Women Are from Venus

"Perkins has written about the dark underbelly of our global system and reveals in a riveting and compelling narrative what we need to know to be truly responsible citizens in a world gone mad with greed, secrecy, and avarice. You won't want to put this book down, and you will be inspired to act as a result of reading it."

—Lynne Twist, author of the national bestseller
The Soul of Money

"Perkins has ripped open the belly of the financial buccaneers from his unique place on the inside. Here are the real-life details—nasty, manipulative, plain evil—of international corporate skullduggery spun into a tale rivaling the darkest espionage thriller."

—Greg Palast, author of *Armed Madhouse* and
The Best Democracy Money Can Buy

"Perkins combines the brilliance and suspense of a Graham Greene thriller with the authority of his insider vantage point to tell a true, powerful, revealing, and bone-chilling personal story that names names, and connects the dots."

—David C. Korten, author of the bestselling
When Corporations Rule the World

"[A] gripping tell-all book."   —*Rocky Mountain News*

"Astonishing."   —*Boston Herald*

"This riveting look at a world of intrigue reads like a spy novel . . . Highly recommended."   —*Library Journal*

"One of the most important nonfiction works of the year, if not the decade . . . a gripping page-turner."   —*New York Spirit*

The Truth About Economic Hit Men, Jackals,

and How to Change the World

JOHN PERKINS

The Secret History
of the
American Empire

A PLUME BOOK

PLUME
Published by the Penguin Group
Penguin Group (USA) Inc., 375 Hudson Street, New York, New York 10014, U.S.A.
Penguin Group (Canada), 90 Eglinton Avenue East, Suite 700, Toronto, Ontario,
Canada M4P 2Y3 (a division of Pearson Penguin Canada Inc.) • Penguin Books
Ltd., 80 Strand, London WC2R 0RL, England • Penguin Ireland, 25 St. Stephen's
Green, Dublin 2, Ireland (a division of Penguin Books Ltd.) • Penguin Group
(Australia), 250 Camberwell Road, Camberwell, Victoria 3124, Australia (a divi-
sion of Pearson Australia Group Pty. Ltd.) • Penguin Books India Pvt. Ltd., 11
Community Centre, Panchsheel Park, New Delhi – 110 017, India • Penguin
Group (NZ), 67 Apollo Drive, Rosedale, North Shore 0632, New Zealand (a divi-
sion of Pearson New Zealand Ltd.) • Penguin Books (South Africa) (Pty.) Ltd., 24
Sturdee Avenue, Rosebank, Johannesburg 2196, South Africa

Penguin Books Ltd., Registered Offices: 80 Strand, London WC2R 0RL, England

Published by Plume, a member of Penguin Group (USA) Inc. Previously published
in a Dutton edition.

First Plume Printing, May 2008

10 9 8 7 6 5 4 3 2

 REGISTERED TRADEMARK—MARCA REGISTRADA

The Library of Congress has catalogued the Dutton edition as follows:
Perkins, John, 1945–
    The secret history of the American empire : economic hit men, jackals, and the
truth about global corruption / John Perkins.
        p. cm.
    ISBN 978-0-525-95015-8 (hc.)
    ISBN 978-0-452-28957-4 (pbk.)
    1. United States—Foreign economic relations.   2. United States—Foreign
relations—2001– 3. Corporations, American—Foreign countries.
4. Corporations, American—Corrupt practices.   5. Globalization—Social aspects.
    6. Imperialism.   I. Title.
    HF1455.P46 2007
    337.73—dc22   2007010604

Printed in the United States of America
Original hardcover design by Carla Bolte

*To you who are committed to
creating a stable, sustainable, and peaceful world.*

Contents

Part 3: The Middle East

Part 4: Africa

Part 5: Changing the World

Acknowledgments

This book would have been impossible without the courageous men and women who stepped forward from the ranks of economic hit men and jackals to share their stories; in doing so they took personal risks and were forced to confront the darkest aspects of their lives. I owe them my deepest gratitude.

It could not have been written without the people who envisioned and manage the NGOs that are changing corporatocracy policies; they, their staffs, and volunteers light a path for the rest of us to follow. Some play a prominent role in the pages of this book, but many remain anonymous—as do those who donate their money to these important organizations. I thank all of them.

And also the people around this planet who stand up to the corporatocracy, the few whose names make the news and the many who walk the picket lines, hang banners, speak out, send e-mails, run for office, vote for positive change, and shop consciously. They are the true heroes of the history that is being written today.

Without Paul Fedorko's encouragement, neither *Confessions of an Economic Hit Man* nor this book would have been published. In addition to being my tireless agent, Paul has "watched my back," been my confidant and sounding board.

Emily Haynes, my editor, has been a tenacious advocate, helping me transform a raw manuscript into a book aimed at honoring the request expressed by World Bank officials and their children to expose *The Secret History of the American Empire* and propose solutions. In addition to her, I thank all the committed people at the Penguin Group, especially Brian Tart, Trena Keating, Beth Parker, Lisa Johnson, and Melanie Gold.

A special word of gratitude to Peg Booth, my publicist, Debbe Kennedy of the Global Dialogue Center, David Tucker of The Pachamama Alliance, Llyn Roberts of Dream Change, Steve Piersanti of Berrett-Koehler, Stephan Rechtschaffen of the Omega Institute, Amy Goodman of *Democracy Now!*, Sabrina Bologni, Jan Coleman, Josh Mailman, Richard Perl, Howard Zinn, John Mack, and so many others who have dedicated themselves to getting the word out and making this a stable, sustainable, and peaceful world.

My deepest appreciation goes to my family—Winifred, Jessica, and Daniel—for their support, inspiration, and love. And to a cat, Snowball, who takes some of the loneliness out of writing.

A Note from the Author

The people and incidents in this book are real. I have made every effort to present them as accurately as personal records, notes, letters, e-mails, memories, and published documents permit. In some cases I have changed names and details for the sake of anonymity—an important condition for many of the people I interviewed—or combined dialogs to facilitate the flow of the narrative, but only where this does not threaten the book's integrity. Whenever I discuss historical events, I am guided by an obligation to provide as accurate a record as possible, sometimes augmenting a speaker's words with source materials referenced in the endnotes. However, this does not include altering or verifying details behind personal stories; when individuals describe their roles in highjacking a commercial airliner, invading a country to assassinate its president, bribing heads of state, profiteering from natural disasters, seducing and extorting democratically elected officials, and conducting other clandestine activities, I feel that I forfeit my rights to interpret their observations. I do want to emphasize that every major event I participated in has been documented by other authors, historians, and journalists, or within the archives of organizations like the World Bank; the story may be mine, but the episodes are a matter of record.

The Secret History of the
American Empire

Prologue

This book takes up where *Confessions of an Economic Hit Man* left off. Back when I finished writing that book in 2004, I had no idea whether anyone would want to read about my life as an economic hit man (EHM). I chose to describe events that I needed to confess. Subsequently, traveling across the United States and to other countries, lecturing, fielding questions, and talking with men and women who are concerned about the future, I have come to understand that people everywhere desire to know what is really going on in the world today. We all want to be able to read between the lines of the news reports and hear the truths that are glossed over by the self-serving pronouncements of the individuals who control our businesses, governments, and media (collectively, the *corporatocracy*).

As I explained in *Confessions*, I tried to write that book several times. I approached other EHMs and jackals—the CIA-sponsored mercenaries who step in to influence, cajole, bribe, and sometimes assassinate—and asked them to include their stories. Word quickly spread; I myself was bribed and threatened. I stopped writing. After 9/11, when I made the commitment to move forward, I decided that this time I would tell no one until the manuscript was published. At that point it became an insurance policy; the jackals knew that if anything unusual happened to me, sales of the book would skyrocket. Writing *Confessions* without assistance from others with similar experiences might have been difficult, but it was my safest route. Since its publication, people have stepped out from the shadows. EHMs, jackals, reporters, Peace Corps volunteers, corporate executives, and World Bank, International Monetary Fund (IMF), and government officials have come to me with their own confessions.

The stories they share in the following pages expose the facts behind the events that are shaping the world our children will inherit. They underscore the inevitable conclusion: We must act, we must change.

I want to emphasize that you will not find gloom and doom in these pages. I am optimistic. I know that, although serious, our problems are man-made. We are not threatened by a giant meteor. The fire of the sun has not been extinguished. Because we created these problems, we can solve them. By exploring the dark recesses of our past we can develop a light for examining—and changing—the future.

When you finish reading *The Secret History of the American Empire*, you too will, I believe, feel absolutely confident that we will do the right thing. You will have identified a plan of action. Together we will utilize the resources providence has provided to establish human societies that reflect our highest ideals.

One evening a few months into my book tour for *Confessions* I found myself lecturing in a Washington, D.C., bookstore. The woman introducing me had mentioned earlier that she expected a number of World Bank staffers to attend.

Created at Bretton Woods in my home state of New Hampshire in 1944, the Bank was charged with reconstructing countries devastated by the war. Its mission soon became synonymous with proving that the capitalist system was superior to that of the Soviet Union. To further this role, its employees cultivated cozy relationships with capitalism's main proponents, multinational corporations. This opened the door for me and other EHMs to mount a multitrillion-dollar scam. We channeled funds from the Bank and its sister organizations into schemes that appeared to serve the poor while primarily benefiting a few wealthy people. Under the most common of these, we would identify a developing country that possessed resources our corporations coveted (such as oil), arrange a huge loan for that country, and then direct most of the money to our own engineering and construction companies—and a few collaborators in the developing country. Infrastructure projects, such as power plants, airports, and industrial parks, sprang up; however, they seldom helped the poor, who were not connected to electrical grids, never used airports, and lacked the skills required for employment in industrial parks. At some point we EHMs returned to the indebted country and demanded our pound of flesh: cheap oil, votes on critical United Nations issues, or troops to support ours someplace in the world, like Iraq.

In my talks, I often find it necessary to remind audiences of a point that seems obvious to me but is misunderstood by so many: that the World Bank is not really a world bank at all; it is, rather, a U.S. bank. Ditto its closest sibling, the IMF. Of the twenty-four directors on their boards, eight represent individual countries: the United States, Japan, Germany, France, the United Kingdom, Saudi Arabia, China, and Russia. The rest of the 184 member-countries share the other sixteen directors. The United States controls nearly 17 percent of the vote in the IMF and 16 percent in the World Bank; Japan is second with about 6 percent in the IMF and 8 percent in the Bank, followed by Germany, the United Kingdom, and France, each with around 5 percent. The United States holds veto power over major decisions and the president of the United States appoints the World Bank president.

When my formal talk was finished, I was escorted to a table to sign books. The line snaked through the rows of bookcases. It would be another long evening. What I had not expected were the number of men and women in business attire who handed me cards indicating that they held high positions in foreign embassies and the World Bank. There were several ambassadors from other countries; a couple of these asked me to sign books for their presidents, as well as for themselves.

The last people in line were four men: Two wore business suits and ties and two, who were much younger, were dressed in blue jeans and polo shirts. The older men handed me their World Bank business cards. One of the younger men spoke up. "Our fathers gave us permission to tell you this," he said. "We've watched them go off to work every morning at the Bank dressed . . ."—he pointed at them—"like this. But when protesters congregate here in Washington to demonstrate against the Bank, our fathers join them. We watch them go incognito, wearing old clothes, baseball caps, and sunglasses to support those people because they believe they—and you—are right."

Both of the older men shook my hand vigorously. "We need more whistle-blowers like you," one of them said.

"Write another book," the other added. "Include more of the details you presented tonight, about what happened to the countries you worked in, all the damage done by people like us in the name of progress. Expose this empire. Spell out the truth behind places like Indonesia where the statistics look so good and the reality's so bad. And also give us hope. Offer our sons alternatives. Map out a way for them to do a better job."

I promised him I would write such a book.

Before we get into the main text of that book, I would like to examine a word he used. Empire. It has been bandied about in the press and classrooms and at local pubs for the last few years. But what exactly is an empire? Does America, with its magnificent constitution, its Bill of Rights, its advocacy of democracy, really deserve such a label—one that brings to mind a long history of brutal and self-serving rule?

> **Empire:** nation-state that dominates other nation-states and exhibits one or more of the following characteristics: 1) exploits resources from the lands it dominates, 2) consumes large quantities of resources—amounts that are disproportionate to the size of its population relative to those of other nations, 3) maintains a large military that enforces its policies when more subtle measures fail, 4) spreads its language, literature, art, and various aspects of its culture throughout its sphere of influence, 5) taxes not just its own

citizens, but also people in other countries, and 6) imposes its own currency on the lands under its control.

This definition of "Empire" was formulated in meetings I held with students at a number of universities during my book tour in 2005 and 2006. Almost without exception, the students arrived at the following conclusion: The United States exhibits all the characteristics of a global empire. Addressing each of the above points:

Points 1 and 2. The United States represents less than 5 percent of the world's population; it consumes more than 25 percent of the world's resources. This is accomplished to a large degree through the exploitation of other countries, primarily in the developing world.

Point 3. The United States maintains the largest and most sophisticated military in the world. Although this empire has been built primarily through economics—by EHMs—world leaders understand that whenever other measures fail, the military will step in, as it did in Iraq.

Point 4. The English language and American culture dominate the world.

Points 5 and 6. Although the United States does not tax countries directly, and the dollar has not replaced other currencies in local markets, the corporatocracy does impose a subtle global tax and the dollar is in fact the standard currency for world commerce. This process began at the end of World War II when the gold standard was modified; dollars could no longer be converted by individuals, only by governments. During the 1950s and 1960s, credit purchases were made abroad to finance America's growing consumerism, the Korean and Vietnam Wars, and Lyndon B. Johnson's Great Society. When foreign businessmen tried to buy goods and services back from the United States, they found that inflation had reduced the value of their dollars—in effect, they paid an indirect tax. Their governments demanded debt settlements in gold. On August 15, 1971, the Nixon administration refused and dropped the gold standard altogether.

Washington scrambled to convince the world to continue accepting the dollar as standard currency. Under the Saudi Arabian Money-laundering Affair (SAMA) I helped engineer in the early seventies, the royal House of Saud committed to selling oil for only U.S. dollars. Because the Saudis controlled petroleum markets, the rest of OPEC (Organization of Petroleum Exporting Countries) was forced to comply. As long as oil reigned as the supreme resource, the dollar's domination as the standard world currency was assured—and the indirect tax would continue.

A seventh characteristic emerged during my discussions with the students: An empire is ruled by an emperor or king who has control over the government and media, is not elected by the people, is not subject to their will, and whose term is not limited by law.

On first glance, this seems to set the United States apart from other empires. However, the appearance is illusory. This empire is ruled by a group of people who collectively act very much like a king. They run our largest corporations and, through them, our government. They cycle through the "revolving door" back and forth between business and government. Because they fund political campaigns and the media, they control elected officials and the information we receive. These men and women (the corporatocracy) are in charge regardless of whether Republicans or Democrats control the White House or Congress. They are not subject to the people's will and their terms are not limited by law.

This modern empire has been built surreptitiously. Most of its own citizens are not aware of its existence; however, those exploited by it are, and many of them suffer from extreme poverty. On average twenty-four thousand people die of hunger and hunger-related diseases every day. More than half the planet's population lives on less than two dollars a day—often not enough to provide the basic amenities, and about the same in real terms as they received thirty years ago. For us to live comfortable lives, millions must pay a very high price. While we have become aware of the environmental damage engendered by our consumptive lifestyles, the majority of us are either oblivious to or in denial of the costs in human suffering. Our children, however, will have no choice but to take responsibility for the imbalances we have created.

In the process of building this empire, we in the United States have managed to discard our most fundamental beliefs, those that in the past defined the very essence of what it is to be an American. We have denied ourselves and those we colonize the rights so eloquently expressed by our Declaration of Independence. We have forfeited the principles of universal equality, justice, and prosperity.

History teaches that empires do not endure; they collapse or are overthrown. Wars ensue and another empire fills the vacuum. The past sends a compelling message. We must change. We cannot afford to allow history to repeat itself.

The power base of the corporatocracy is its corporations. They define our world. When we look at a globe we see the outlines of slightly less than two hundred countries. Many of the boundaries were established by colonial powers and most of these countries have minimal impact on their neighbors. From a geopolitical viewpoint this model is archaic; the reality of our modern world might better be represented by huge clouds that encircle the planet, each symbolizing a multinational corporation. These powerful entities impact every single country. Their tentacles reach into the deepest rainforests and to the most remote deserts.

The corporatocracy makes a show of promoting democracy and transparency among the nations of the world, yet its corporations are imperialistic dictatorships where a very few make all the decisions and reap most of the profits. In our electoral process—the very heart of our democracy—most of us get to vote only for candidates whose campaign chests are full; therefore, we must select from among those who are beholden to the corporations and the men who own them. Contrary to our ideals, this empire is built on foundations of greed, secrecy, and excessive materialism.

On the positive side, corporations have proven highly efficient at marshaling resources, inspiring collective creativity, and spreading webs of communications and distribution to the most remote corners of the planet. Through them, we have at our disposal everything we need to ensure that those twenty-four thousand people do not die of hunger every day. We possess the knowledge, technologies, and systems required to make this a stable, sustainable, equitable, and peaceful planet.

The founders of this nation recognized that revolution should not lead to anarchy. They freed themselves from tyranny, but they were wise enough to also adopt many of the commercial and legal structures that had proven so successful for the British. We must accomplish something similar. We need to accept the benefits this empire has created and use them to unite, to heal the rifts, and to close the gap between rich and poor. We must take courage, as the founders of this nation did. We must break the mold that has defined human interaction and suffering. We must transform the empire into a model of good stewardship and good citizenry.

The key to making this happen, to creating a world that our children will be proud to inherit, is through transforming the power base of the corporatocracy, the corporations—the way they define themselves, set their goals, develop methods for governance, and establish criteria for selecting their top executives. Corporations are totally dependent on us. We humans provide their brains and muscles. We are their markets. We buy their products and fund their endeavors. As this book will illustrate, we have been extremely successful at changing corporations whenever we have set it as our goal—for example, in cleaning up polluted rivers, halting damage to the ozone layer, and reversing discrimination. Now we must learn from our successes and rise to new levels.

Taking the necessary actions—those presented in this book—will require that we finish a task begun in the 1770s but never completed. We are summoned to pick up the baton carried by our founders and by the men and women who followed after them, who opposed slavery, pulled us out of the Depression, and fought Hitler, and who came to our shores fleeing oppression or simply seeking the better life offered by our most sacred documents. The hour has arrived for us to muster the courage needed to continue the work all of them began. Let us not allow this empire to collapse and be replaced by another; let us instead transform it.

After that evening in the Washington, D.C., bookstore, my thoughts often returned to the request made by the two World Bank executives. I had promised them I would write another book, expose the damage done by men like me, and offer hope for a better world. I needed to do that. I needed to share the stories of people who are ignored by the mainstream media because their words might anger advertisers, and to give voice to those who are shunned for insisting on anonymity because their jobs, pensions, and lives may depend on it. I needed to offer an alternative to the sanitized reports and misleading statistics that pass as "objective" or "scientific" because they include reams of information compiled by researchers who all too often are funded by the corporatocracy. I understood that there would be those who would be quick to criticize my use of quotes from anonymous speakers and from men and women who have experienced news in the making, but who are not invited to appear on the Sunday morning TV talk shows; yet I felt that I needed to honor those experiences and the voices that describe them. I owed it to the people who read *Confessions*, to the sons of those executives, my twenty-three-year-old daughter, and the generation those two young men and she represent around the world. For all of them—and for myself—I had to take the next step.

Part 1: Asia

Mystery Woman of Jakarta

I was ready to rape and pillage when I headed to Asia in 1971. At twenty-six, I felt cheated by life. I wanted to take revenge.

I am certain, in retrospect, that rage earned me my job. Hours of psychological testing by the National Security Agency (NSA) identified me as a potential economic hit man. The nation's most clandestine spy organization concluded that I was a man whose passions could be channeled to help fulfill its mission of expanding the empire. I was hired by Chas. T. Main (MAIN), an international consulting firm that did the corporatocracy's dirty work, as an ideal candidate for plundering the Third World.

Although the causes for my rage are detailed in *Confessions of an Economic Hit Man*, they can be summarized in a few sentences. The son of a poor prep-school teacher, I grew up surrounded by wealthy boys. I was both terrified and mesmerized by women and, therefore, shunned by them. I attended a college I hated because it was what my mother and father wanted. In my first defiant act, I dropped out, landed a job I loved as a copy boy on a big city newspaper, and then, tail between my legs, returned to college in order to avoid the draft. I married too young because it was what the one girl who finally accepted me demanded. I spent three years in the Amazon and Andes as an impoverished Peace Corps volunteer— once again forced to evade the draft.

I consider myself a true and loyal American. This too contributed to my rage. My ancestors fought in the Revolution and most other U.S. wars. My family was predominantly conservative Republican. Having cut my literary teeth on Paine and Jefferson, I thought a conservative was someone who believed in the founding ideals of our country, in justice and equality for all; I was angered by the betrayal of these ideals in Vietnam and by the oil company–Washington collusion that I saw destroying the Amazon and enslaving its people.

Why did I choose to become an EHM, to compromise my ideals? Looking back, I can say that the job promised to fulfill many of my fantasies; it offered money, power, and beautiful women—as well as first-class travel to exotic lands. I was told, of course, that I would be called upon to do nothing illegal. In fact, if I did my job well, I would be lauded, invited to lecture at Ivy League schools, and wined and dined by royalty. In my heart I knew that this journey was fraught with peril. I was gambling with my soul. But I thought I would prove the exception. When I headed for Asia, I figured I would reap the benefits for a few years, and then expose the system and become a hero.

I have to admit, too, that I had developed a fascination for pirates and adventure at an early age. But I had lived the opposite type of life, always doing what was expected of me. Other than quitting college (for a semester), I was the ideal son. Now it was time to rape and pillage.

Indonesia would be my first victim . . .

The earth's largest archipelago, Indonesia consists of more than seventeen thousand islands stretching from Southeast Asia to Australia. Three hundred different ethnic groups speak more than 250 distinct languages. It is populated with more Muslims than any other nation. By the close of the 1960s we knew that it was awash in oil.

President John F. Kennedy had established Asia as the bulwark of anticommunist empire builders when he supported a 1963 coup against South Vietnam's Ngo Dinh Diem. Diem was subsequently assassinated and many people believed the CIA gave that order; after all, the CIA had orchestrated coups against Mossadegh of Iran, Qasim of Iraq, Arbenz of Guatemala, and Lumumba of the Congo. Diem's downfall led directly to the buildup of U.S. military forces in Southeast Asia and ultimately the Vietnam War.

Events did not transpire the way Kennedy had planned. Long after the U.S. president's own assassination, the war turned catastrophic for the United States. In 1969, President Richard M. Nixon initiated a series of troop withdrawals; his administration adopted a more clandestine strategy, focused on preventing a domino effect of one country after another falling under communist rule. Indonesia became the key.

One of the principal factors was Indonesia's President Haji Mohammed Suharto. He had earned a reputation as a stalwart anti-Communist and a man who did not hesitate to use extreme brutality in executing his policies. As head of the army in 1965 he had crushed a Communist-instigated coup; the subsequent bloodbath claimed the lives of 300,000–500,000 people, one of the worst politically engineered mass murders of the century, reminiscent of those of Adolf Hitler, Josef Stalin, and Mao Tse-tung. Another estimated one million people were thrown into jails and prison camps. Then, in the aftermath of the killings and arrests, Suharto took over as president, in 1968.

When I arrived in Indonesia in 1971, the goal of U.S. foreign policy was clear: stop communism and support the president. We expected Suharto to serve Washington in a manner like that of the shah of Iran. The two men were similar: greedy, vain, and ruthless. In addition to coveting its oil, we wanted Indonesia to set an example for the rest of Asia, as well as for the entire Muslim world.

My company, MAIN, was charged with developing integrated electrical systems that would enable Suharto and his cronies to industrialize and become even richer, and would also ensure long-term American dominance. My job was to create the economic studies necessary to obtain financing from the World Bank, Asian Development Bank, and U.S. Agency for International Development (USAID).

Soon after my arrival in Jakarta, the MAIN team met at the elegant restaurant on the top floor of the Hotel Intercontinental Indonesia. Charlie Illingworth, our project manager, summarized our mission: "We are here to accomplish nothing short of saving this country from the clutches of communism." He then added, "We all know how dependent our own country is on oil. Indonesia can be a powerful ally to us in that regard. So, as you develop this master plan, please do everything you can to make sure that the oil industry and all the others that serve it—ports, pipelines, construction companies—get whatever they are likely to need in the way of electricity for the entire duration of this twenty-five-year plan."

Most government offices in Jakarta in those days opened early, around seven A.M., and shut their doors at about two P.M. Their employees broke for coffee, tea, and snacks; however, lunch was postponed until the closing hour. I made a habit of rushing back to the hotel, changing into my bathing suit, heading for the pool, and ordering a tuna fish sandwich and cold Bintang Baru, a local beer. Although I dragged along a briefcase stuffed with official papers I had collected during my meetings, it was a subterfuge; I was there to work on my tan and ogle the beautiful young bikini-clad women, mostly American wives of oil workers who spent their weekdays in remote locations or executives with offices in Jakarta.

It did not take long for me to become enamored with a woman who appeared to be about my age and of mixed Asian-American heritage. In addition to her stunning physique, she seemed unusually friendly. In fact, sometimes the way she stood, stretched, smiled at me while ordering food in English, and dove into the pool appeared flirtatious. I found myself quickly turning away. I knew I must be blushing. I cursed my puritanical parents.

Every day, around four o'clock, approximately an hour and a half after my arrival, she was joined by a man who, I was certain, was Japanese. He arrived dressed in a business suit, which was unusual in a country where formal attire generally consisted of slacks and a well-pressed shirt, often made from local batik cloth. They chatted for a few moments and then departed together. Although I searched for them in the hotel bars and restaurants, I never saw them together or alone anywhere except at the pool.

One afternoon, as I rode the elevator to the ground floor, I steeled myself. I would approach her, talk with her. I told myself there was nothing to lose, I knew she was married to the Japanese man and I just wanted to speak with someone in English. How could she possibly object? Once I made that commitment, I felt jubilant.

I strolled toward the pool with a buoyant sense of anticipation, humming a favorite song. But, as soon as I arrived, I stopped in my tracks, dismayed and confused. She was not in her usual place. I searched frantically around, but there was no sign of her anywhere. I dropped my briefcase next to a lounge chair and rushed into the surrounding gardens. I had never explored them before and now found that they were vast, bursting with orchids of every conceivable color, a profusion of birds-of-paradise, and bromeliads that dwarfed those I had seen in the Amazon; but all I could think about was my missed opportunity to admire them with her. Palms and exotic bushes formed little nooks and hideaways. I thought I spied her lying on a towel in the grass on the other side of a hedge. I raced around it—and managed to wake up a woman. She clutched her loose bikini top to her breasts, sat up, glared at me menacingly, her eyes accusing me of voyeurism, and shouted in a language I did not understand. I apologized as best I could and returned to the spot where I had left my briefcase.

When the waiter approached to take my order, I pointed at the vacant chair where she usually sat. He bowed, smiled, and picked up my briefcase to move it there for me.

"No, no, *tidak*," I said, still pointing. "The woman. Where is she?" I figured that it was part of a pool waiter's job to know the habits of regular clients. I suspected the Japanese executive was a good tipper.

"No, no," he repeated. "*Tidak*."

"Do you know where she went?" I threw my hands out at my sides and shrugged in what I thought was a universal gesture.

He mimicked my movements, smiled idiotically, and parroted back my words, "Where she went."

"Yes. Where?"

"Yes," he repeated. "Where?" He shrugged again, his expression aping *Alice in Wonderland*'s Cheshire Cat. Then he snapped his fingers. "Yes." He laughed.

I held my breath, relieved that my theory about pool waiters was about to be confirmed.

"Tunafich sanich and Bintang Baru," he stated.

Deflated, I only managed to nod. He trotted off.

Four o'clock came and went. There was no sign of either her or the man who had always joined her. I trudged off to my room, showered, dressed, and headed out. I had to get away from this hotel. I would immerse myself in the local scene.

Pirating Lepers

It was a typical Jakarta evening, hot and sticky. Heavy clouds hung over the city, threatening rain. I had never left the hotel before, except in my private chauffered jeep. As soon as I stepped off the curb of the hotel's sweeping driveway, I was nearly run down by a three-wheeled bicycle cab, known as a *becak*. I had passed hundreds while being driven to various meetings and had always found the rainbow-colored murals painted on the boxlike sides of the high seats picturesque, quaint reminders that Indonesia was a land of artists. Now I saw another aspect; these drivers were impoverished men in rags desperately competing for customers. They rushed at me ringing bells and shouting to get my attention. In an attempt to avoid being run over I nearly stepped into a gutter that was black as tar, littered with garbage, and reeking of urine.

The gutter drained down a steep incline to one of the many canals built by the Dutch during the colonial era. Now stagnant, its surface was covered with a green and putrid-looking scum; the stench that arose from it was nearly intolerable. It seemed preposterous that the inventive people who had turned the sea into farmland had attempted to recreate Amsterdam amid this tropical heat. The canal, like the gutter that fed it, overflowed with debris. I could even distinguish the two by their distinctive stenches. The gutter had an immediacy about its odor, rotting fruit and urine, while the canal carried a darker, longer-term pungency, the mixture of human excrement and decay.

I continued along, dodging the bicycle cabs that hugged the sides of the road. Beyond them, in the mainstream of the thoroughfare, was a frenzy of automobile and motorbike traffic; the sound of honking horns, backfiring engines, and muffler-deprived cars was overwhelming, as was the acrid stench of oil on hot pavement and gas fumes in the humid air. The weight of all this began to impact me physically.

I stopped for a moment, feeling assaulted and defeated. I was tempted to give up and return to the serenity of my hotel. Then I reminded myself that I had endured the Amazon jungle and had lived in mud shacks with peasants in the Andes who survived on a daily ration of a potato and a handful of legumes and, when asked to name their children, would include the dead as well as the living, the former often outnumbering the latter. I thought about the other members of my team and about all the traveling Americans who intentionally avoid seeing the countries they visit the way the majority of the people living there see them. I was suddenly struck by the realization that my experiences as a Peace Corps volunteer—the bonds I had forged with some of those people; the way they had opened their lives to me; shared their meager provisions so self-lessly; welcomed, warmed, nurtured, and even loved me—had profoundly impacted me. Standing alone in the descending Jakarta night, I had to wonder whether I was really cut out to be a pirate. How could I rape and pillage the *becak* drivers, the young men and women who served me at the hotel and in the offices I frequented, the peasants toiling in their rice paddies, the fishermen, seamstresses, shopkeepers, and carpenters? It was one thing to be a Robin Hood stealing from the rich or a pirate attacking Spanish galleons laden with the king's gold, and quite another to loot the poor. Yet that was exactly what I was being called upon to do; I would rob from the poor and give to the rich—and in the process receive my commission. How could I do it? How could Charlie Illingworth and everyone else with related jobs live with themselves?

In that moment I had to accept my personal responsibility, had to acknowledge the possibility that my years in Ecuador had given me a perspective unlike that of the others who did my type of work or the citizens whose taxes supported us. I had been blessed—or cursed—with insights shared by few Americans. Everyone found ways to rationalize. Charlie fought the Communists. Others were simply profiteering. "A dog-eat-dog world," they said. "My family comes first." Some wrote off other races or classes as inherently inferior or lazy, deserving whatever misfortunes befell them. A few, I supposed, actually believed that investing fortunes into electrical grids would solve the world's problems. But me: What was my justification? I was a young man who suddenly felt very old.

I stared down at that canal. I wished I had a copy of Tom Paine's *Common Sense* so I could hurl it into those rank waters.

My eyes were drawn to something I had not spotted before. A large and battered cardboard box slumped, like a collapsed beggar's hat, near the edge of the stagnant water. As I stared, it shuddered, reminding me of a fatally injured animal. Figuring I was delusional, that the heat, fumes, and noise had gotten the better of me, I decided to resume walking; but before I turned, I caught a glimpse of an arm protruding from around the side of the box—or rather, what appeared to have once been an arm, now reduced to a bloody stump.

The shaking intensified. The bloody stump moved along the edge of the box to a corner at the top. It shot straight up. A nest of black hair followed it, appearing like Medusa's snakes above the box, knotted and mangled with mud. The head shook itself and a body began to emerge, up until now hidden by the box, a body that sent waves of revulsion through me. Bent and emaciated, the body of what I took to be a woman crept along the ground to the edge of the canal. It struck me that I was seeing something I had heard about all my life but never encountered before. This woman, if that in fact was her gender, was a leper, a human being whose flesh was decaying right before my eyes.

At the canal's edge, the body sat down, or, more accurately, collapsed into a pile of rags. The arm I had not seen before reached out and dipped a tattered cloth into the fetid canal water, shook it slowly, and wrapped it around the bloody stump, which had several open wounds where fingers should have been.

I heard a groan, and realized that the sound came from me. My legs wobbled. I had an urge to race back to the hotel, but I forced myself to remain at that spot. I had to bear witness to this person's agony. I knew in my heart that any other action was futile. This woman's struggle was probably repeated several times a day by her alone. I wondered how many other abandoned souls were performing such doomed rituals here in Jakarta, throughout Indonesia, in India and Africa.

A movement caught my eye, another twitching of the cardboard walls. The leper turned slowly to stare at the box. Her face was a blur of red pustules; it lacked lips. I followed the sunken eyes.

A baby's head came into view beside the box. I wanted not to watch but was fascinated, like a man witnessing a murder he is powerless to stop. The baby crawled toward the woman. It sat down beside the leper and began to cry. I could not hear the sound, either because the voice was too weak or the traffic too loud, but I could see the open mouth and the spasms of the little body.

The leper suddenly looked up and spied me watching her. Our eyes met. She spit onto the ground, rose to her feet, shook her bloody stump at me, caught the baby up in her arms and, scurrying faster than I imagined possible, disappeared back inside the box.

As I stared at the spot where the woman had been, something bumped my back. Instinctively, I whirled and reached for the wallet in my hip pocket. I was relieved to find it was still there and relieved also by the distraction. Two attractive young women sauntered by. They giggled and smiled at me. One wore tight jeans, the other a revealing miniskirt. Spiked heals and halter tops. They stopped. "No pickee pockets," the one in the mini said. "We lohvas." She crooked her finger. "Come. Lohve us."

I shook my head.

"Oh, he like boys," she said. They turned away.

Up ahead of them, a pedestrian bridge crossed over the frantic traffic. They strolled toward it, two tigresses on the prowl, flaunting the sexuality of their swaying hips. The one in the mini turned, grinned, and waved at me. Then they headed up the steps of the bridge.

I glanced at the cardboard box. It did not move. A little breeze came up, sending ripples across the canal. I was half tempted to clamber down and hand that woman all the cash in my wallet, but then I spotted her tattered cloth lying on the ground where she apparently had dropped it in her haste to get away from me. I thought it best to allow her the dignity of her privacy. I hurried toward the pedestrian bridge, having no idea where it might take me.

The sun sets quickly and brilliantly along the equator. But on this day the heavy clouds created a deception, letting the light linger until suddenly, by the time I reached the bridge, it was nearly dark. On the other side, a neon sign flashed RESTAURANT in English. I climbed the stairs.

A tall woman leaned against the railing. In the failing light, it was difficult to be certain, but she looked beautiful. When I came abreast of her, she said in a shockingly husky voice, "I yur goodtime man. We fuki fuki." She pointed at her Adam's apple, made it bob, then her ass, and gave me a smile. Now I saw the layers of makeup. I hurried on.

Several street lights suddenly flickered to life at intervals along the bridge. They sputtered irregularly and cast an eerie yellow glow that gave the place a hazy, almost swampy look. I stopped beside one of them, thinking that my job of forecasting electricity demand must involve researching such things. The cement pillar was cracked, flaking, and dappled with mold. I avoided touching it.

I walked on, staring down at my feet and the pock-marked floor of the bridge. Rusty bits of rebar protruded from the concrete, like angry maggots in the swampy yellow light. I tried to think about the bridge, its age, the men who had built it, and yet I was distracted. An image of that beautiful woman at the hotel pool had crept into my mind. In a way it was a welcome relief from the reality surrounding me; but it also haunted me. I could not erase her from my mind. The idea that I had fallen in love and been abandoned swept through me; I assured myself that this was absolute foolishness.

I glanced up in time to see that I had nearly reached the steps at the other end of the bridge. The RESTAURANT sign was immediately in front of me, attached to the roof of a low complex of buildings on a street set back from the main highway. Below, in smaller letters, it read: FINE CHINESE MEALS. A black sedan, similar to ones at the U.S. embassy, slowly approached the restaurant. The lone vehicle seemed out of place amid the city hustle.

3

Geishas

I descended the steps. The sedan stopped in front of the doorway. It idled there for a moment and then inched forward, its occupant apparently not liking what he saw or not finding the person he sought. I tried to peer through the car's windows, but found only the reflection of the restaurant's neon sign. Suddenly, the driver gunned the engine and sped away.

When I reached the restaurant, its interior was obscured by thin curtains. I pressed my face against the glass. It was dark inside, except for small globes of flickering light that I took for candles. I stepped to the door.

It opened into a darkened room with a lantern on each of a dozen or so tables. A quick survey of the ones where guests were seated suggested cultural diversity: There were Asians and Europeans or Americans.

A Chinese lady bowed to me. "Welcome," she said. "Good evening. Dinner for one?" Her accent suggested she had studied with a British teacher. She led me into the room.

I froze, disbelieving what I saw.

The woman from the pool, *my* lady, the person I had tried so hard to locate, sat at a table with another Asian woman, staring back at me. Then she smiled and beckoned. The hostess, observing her, led me to her table. "Friends?"

"Yes." The woman from the pool did not hesitate. "Will you join us please?"

The hostess pulled out an empty chair, bowed again, and walked away.

I was reeling with confusion. "Where's your husband?" I asked.

The two women exchanged glances and broke into laughter. "I'm not married," she said at last.

"But the man at the pool."

"A business associate." Stifling a giggle, she indicated the chair. "Please have a seat. We just ordered. More than enough for all of us—at least to begin. Or are you determined to dine alone?" Her English was close to perfect, with just the hint of an accent.

I sat down. One part of me could not believe my good fortune. Another felt apprehensive, as though I were involving myself in something illicit. A waiter came over and set a small cup in front of me.

The lady from the pool pointed at a little porcelain pot. "Sake? We have been drinking lots. This is our night to let go. Very good sake here." She filled my cup. "Cheers." Our three cups clinked. "Oh yes," she said, wiping her lips with a white linen napkin. "How rude. I'm Nancy and this is Mary."

"John." I shook hands with each.

"I've observed you at the pool, John. I waited for you to come say hello. You seem very lonely and nice, but I think you're terribly shy. Or perhaps . . ." She leaned toward me, so close I could smell the liquor on her breath. "You're madly in love with a wife."

It was my turn to laugh. "Getting divorced."

"In luck," Mary said. "Here's to broken marriages." She raised her glass. She spoke with a similar accent, a bit heavier than Nancy's.

The waiter arrived with several heaping plates of food. As we ate, we exchanged information about our backgrounds. Nancy and Mary shocked me when they described themselves as geishas. I admitted that I thought those days were long gone; they assured me that I was mistaken. "Oil," Mary said, "revived this ancient art. Different, yes, but it's alive and well today."

Their pregnant Taiwanese mothers were abandoned by their fathers, American army officers assigned to their country after World War II. The women turned their newborn daughters over to a Japanese businessman; he arranged for foster care and their schooling, which included extensive lessons in English as well as in U.S.

history and culture. When they reached maturity, they went to work for him.

"You've probably seen the women on the street out there." Nancy pointed toward the pedestrian bridge outside the curtained window. "That could be us. We're lucky." She went on to say that the Japanese businessman paid them well and seldom dictated how they should act or specified what they should do. "He asks for results. That's all. Up to us how we get them." She poured us each more sake.

"What sort of results?"

"How naïve," Mary said. "He must be new here."

I admitted that it was my first trip, my initial assignment, adding that I was eager to learn.

"We're happy to teach you," Nancy proclaimed. "You're a gem in our world. But we may ask for something in return. Not tonight, but sometime."

"At your service." I tried to appear nonchalant.

They sounded more like college professors than geishas as they explained that men in power have always been willing to spend fortunes and sacrifice the lives of others in order to amass resources and power. I was amazed at their frankness and attributed it at least in part to the sake, although everything they said made absolute sense. They talked about the importance of the spice trade in the time of the great European explorers and of the role gold had played for centuries.

"Today it's oil," Nancy continued. "The most precious resource ever. Everything depends on it. Spices and gold were luxuries without much real value. Good to taste, use as a preservative, for jewelry and artifacts. But oil . . . oil's life itself. Nothing in the modern world works without it. This is the biggest resource grab in history. The stakes are huge. Should we be surprised that men are willing to risk everything to control it? They'll cheat and steal. Build ships and missiles, and send thousands—hundreds of thousands—of young soldiers to die for oil."

"Is that what you learned in the history books?"

She gave me a smirk. "Of course not. That came from the school of hard knocks."

"Hard knocks!" Mary was beside herself with laughter. "I can't believe you said that, Nance. That's perfect. I got to remember it. Hard knocks." She shook her head.

But I was thinking about Charlie and the speech he had given that first night at the restaurant on top of the Hotel Intercontinental about how we had come to Indonesia to save it from Communists and secure oil for the United States. Then my thoughts turned to Claudine, the woman in Boston who had mentored me as an EHM. It occurred to me that she was part of the same tradition as these two Asian-American women. I had to wonder if she ever thought of herself as a geisha. My eyes went from the laughing Mary to Nancy, and in that moment I saw Claudine and realized how much I missed her. I wondered whether my infatuation with the woman across the table, my poolside obsession, had grown out of my loneliness and perhaps a subconscious connection I had made between her and Claudine.

I forced myself back to the present. Mary was wiping the laughter from her eyes with her napkin. I spoke to Nancy. "And you. What's your role?"

"We're like those soldiers, expendable but necessary. We serve the Emperor."

"Who is the Emperor?"

Nancy shot a look at Mary. "We never know. Whoever pays the highest price to our boss."

"The man at the pool?"

"He's my contact here, not the real boss. He takes me to my clients."

"In the Hotel Intercontinental?"

"Honeymoon suite." She giggled, but stopped herself. "Sorry. Mary and I always say that sometime we want a real honeymoon in that suite." She glanced away toward the curtained window.

I recalled the black sedan that had cruised by, wondering if its occupant had been looking for one of them. "Only there—your work, the Hotel Indonesia?"

"Of course not. Country clubs, cruise ships, Hong Kong, Hollywood, Las Vegas . . . you name it. If oil men and politicians like it, we've been there."

My eyes roamed from one to the other. They seemed so young—and so worldly. I was twenty-six; I knew from their stories that they were about five years my junior. "Who are your clients?"

Nancy lifted a finger to her lips. She glanced around the restaurant, like a doe I had seen in a New Hampshire field terrified by a dog barking in the distance. "Never," she said and her voice took on a solemn quality, "ask that question."

The Bugiman

I returned to Indonesia frequently during the next few years. The World Bank, its affiliates, and the Suharto government appreciated MAIN's willingness to provide reports necessary for securing huge loans that would benefit U.S. corporations and the Indonesian rulers. They did not care that these loans would leave the country deeply indebted. For the banks, that was part of the plan. As far as Suharto was concerned: By investing his mushrooming fortune overseas, he sheltered himself against the future of a bankrupt Indonesia.

Over the years, my assignments took me to idyllic villages in the mountains of Java, remote beaches along the coasts, and exotic islands. The language, Bahasa Indonesia, was invented by linguists after World War II to help unite the islands; its simplicity enabled me to learn the basics quickly. I enjoyed exploring areas seldom visited by foreigners, talking with the people, and trying to understand their culture. My Peace Corps training had taught me the value of departing from the paths traveled by most businessmen, diplomats, and tourists, of meeting farmers, fishermen, students, shop owners, and street urchins. Yet it also assured that I would continue to be haunted by the guilt I felt over the terrible impact men like me had on the majority of Indonesia's people.

When in Jakarta, I spent as much time as possible at the Hotel Intercontinental Indonesia's swimming pool. I was disappointed that I never again saw either Nancy or Mary. However, I frequently observed their counterparts at work around the pool. I became intimate with one of them, a young Thai woman, and discovered that the use of geishas was not restricted to the Japanese. We Americans had our own version, as did the Europeans and other Asians; however, it seemed a consensus among these women that the Japanese were the ideal employers, and that they had perfected this profession in a manner unequaled by other cultures—appropriate, I thought, given their long history

The Thai woman befriended me not to gain anything or because someone had hired her to compromise me—after all, I had already been bought. She did it either from the goodness in her heart, because she needed someone like me in her life, or perhaps due to the chemistry that passed between us. I was never entirely sure of her motives, only that she was a companion, erotic inspiration, and confidant. She also enlightened me about the ways of high-level international business and diplomacy. "Expect hidden cameras and tape recorders in the rooms of ladies who try to seduce you," she said, quickly adding with a smile, "not that you're unattractive, just that things aren't as they appear." She taught me that women like her played a pivotal role in shaping some of the world's most important deals.

A couple of years after my first assignment, I was sent for three months to Sulawesi, the remote island east of Borneo. Known affectionately as the "running drunken giraffe" because of its shape on maps, this island was singled out to serve as a model for rural development. Once an important part of the East India spice trade, it became a twentieth-century backwater. Now the Indonesian government was determined to make it a symbol of progress. We Americans saw it as a potential cash cow for mineral, forestry, and agricultural industries. Several mammoth corporations coveted its gold and copper potentials and its exotic trees; a large Texas ranch had bought thousands of acres of forests, cleared and sold them, and planned on shipping beef in football field–size barges to the lucrative Singapore and Hong Kong markets. Sulawesi was also viewed as a cornerstone of the government's transmigration program—a scheme similar to the colonization of the Amazon that had impacted the people I worked with during my Peace Corps years, aimed at moving the urban poor from cities in Java (which had the highest population density in the world) to underpopulated areas. Like its Latin American version, this program was supported by the international development agencies as a method for disbursing impoverished slum dwellers to unsettled rural regions and thereby mitigating against the likelihood of antigovernment rebellions. The policy continued despite the fact that experts soon discovered that, on both continents, such programs often turned disastrous. Local indigenous people were displaced, their lands and cultures destroyed, while newly transplanted urban populations struggled unsuccessfully to cultivate the fragile soil.

When I arrived in Sulawesi, I was given a government-owned house outside the old Portuguese city of Makasar (renamed Ujung Pandang in one of Suharto's nods at nationalism), complete with maid, gardener, chef, jeep, and driver. My job, as usual, was to travel to any region that appeared to have resources multinational corporations might exploit, meet with community leaders, collect all available information, and write a glowing report proving that huge loans to develop electric power and other infrastructure projects would turn this medieval economy into a modern success.

A town known as "Batsville," located near the budding Texas cattle ranch, had been identified as a possible location for a power plant. Early one morning, my driver drove us out of Ujung Pandang, up the spectacular coast, to the port city of Parepare. From there, we wound cautiously into the mountains of the remote interior, the road barely more than a dirt trail cut through jungle. I felt like I had returned to the Amazon.

When the jeep pulled into the village of Pinrang, the driver announced, "This is it. Batsville."

I glanced around; the name of the village had piqued my interest. I searched for the bats, but saw nothing unusual. The driver cruised slowly past a plaza that resembled many others in towns throughout Indonesia: It had a couple of benches and several trees with huge dark clusters hanging from their branches, like extra-large coconuts.

Then suddenly, one of those clusters opened up. My heart caught in my throat as I realized that a gigantic bat was stretching her wings.

The driver pulled to a stop. He led me to a spot beneath one of the bats. The amazing animal was moving above us, her wings sluggishly uncoiling, her body as large as a monkey. The eyes opened. The head turned and stared at us. I had heard rumors that these bats shorted out electric lines, indicating that their wing spans measured in excess of six feet; however, even in my wildest imagination I had never expected anything to compare with what I was seeing.

Later, I met with the mayor of Pinrang. I quizzed him about local resources and likely attitudes toward building a power plant and industries owned by foreigners in his area, but the bats dominated my thoughts. When I asked whether they caused problems, he replied, "No. They fly away every evening and eat fruit far out of town. They return mornings. Never touch our fruit." He raised his teacup. "Very much like your corporations," he said with a sly smile. "They fly off, feed on resources far away, defecate on lands people from the United States will never visit, and then return to you."

I heard this theme often. I had begun to understand that although most Americans have no idea that their lifestyles are built on exploitation, millions of people in other countries are aware of it. Even in the 1970s they viewed our military not as a defender of democracy but rather as an armed guard for exploitative corporations—and they were frightened and angry as a result.

Sulawesi was also the home of the infamous Bugi tribe. European spice traders centuries ago feared them as the fiercest, most bloodthirsty pirates in the world. When they returned home, the Europeans threatened disobedient children with the warning that if they did not change their ways "the Bugimen will get you."

During the 1970s the Bugis continued to live much as they had for hundreds of years. Their magnificent sailing ships, called *prahus*, formed the backbone of interisland commerce. The sailors who manned these black-sailed galleons wore long sarongs, brilliantly colored headscarves, and dazzling gold earrings; they carried vicious machetes thrust through sashes at their waists. They looked as though they still cherished their ancient reputation.

I became friends with an elder named Buli, a shipbuilder who practiced his art in the manner of his ancestors. One day, when he and I were lunching together, he observed that his people never saw themselves as pirates; they were merely defending their homeland against intruders. "Now," he said, handing me a slice of a luscious fruit, "we're at a loss. How can a handful of people in wooden sailing ships fight off America's submarines, airplanes, bombs, and missiles?"

Questions like that got to me. Eventually, they convinced me to change my ways.

5

A Corrupt and Brutal Country

Years after my conversation with the Buginese shipbuilder, I ended my EHM career. The decision to do so, as described in *Confessions*, was made while on a sailing vacation among Caribbean islands that once were strongholds for pirates who plundered Spain's Gold Fleet. Late one afternoon, sitting on the ruined walls of an ancient sugar plantation, contemplating the horrors experienced by the African slaves who constructed those buildings, I understood that I too was a slaver. Following years of emotional turmoil, I made up my mind to get out. I flew back to Boston and quit. But I did not expose the horrible facts behind this new empire. I succumbed to threats and bribes. I deferred. And, during the ensuing years, my past haunted me. I had to live with what I had done and what I knew. Then shortly after 9/11, standing at the edge of that horrible, smoldering pit that had once been the World Trade Center, I knew that at last I had to step forward. I had to confess.

After the publication of *Confessions of an Economic Hit Man* in 2004, as I began to field questions from radio interviewers, I realized that I understood little about the ways my actions as an EHM impacted the countries where I had worked. We had defeated the Soviet Union and emerged as the world's first truly global empire, unchallenged by any other superpower. We bragged about "progress" and "industrialization." We had created a new class of Third World elites, the lackeys of the corporatocracy. But what about the majority of the people in the places we had subjugated? I decided to update myself, beginning with the country where I had started my career.

I had kept abreast of general events in Indonesia, through the mainstream media; now I began to dig deeper, researching information that was available from nongovernmental organizations (NGOs) and academics, as well as from the United Nations, the World Bank, and the other organizations I once had served. My curiosity deepened as I became more familiar with the circumstances surrounding the 1997 Asian economic collapse, also known as the "IMF crisis." This debacle began in Asia, where it impacted hundreds of millions of people and resulted in thousands—possibly millions—of deaths from disease, starvation, and suicides, and then spread across the globe. For those willing to listen, it sent a strong message about the true intent of the IMF and the World Bank, a lesson in how not to manage an economy, unless the goal is to further enrich the corporatocracy at the expense of everyone else.

On first glance, the official statistics indicated that our work in the 1970s in Indonesia had produced an admirable economic record, at least until 1997. Those statistics bragged of low inflation, foreign exchange reserves totaling more than \$20 billion, a trade surplus of more than \$900 million, and a solid banking sector. Indonesia's economic growth (measured by GDP) averaged nearly 9 percent every year in the 1990s, until 1997—not as spectacular as the double-digit forecasts I had been paid to produce, but highly impressive nevertheless. Economists at the World Bank, IMF, consulting firms, and academic institutions used such statistics to argue that the development policies promoted by us EHMs had proven successful.

I soon ascertained, however, that the statistics did not address the extremely high price the Indonesian people had paid for what the economists referred to as an "economic miracle." The benefits were restricted to those at the top of the economic ladder. Rapid advances in national income were achieved through the abuse of cheap and plentiful labor, in sweatshops where workers endured long hours and suffered life-threatening conditions, and with policies granting foreign corporations licenses to destroy the environment and conduct activities that were outlawed in North America and the rest of the "First World." Although the minimum wage rose to around three dollars a day, it was often ignored. In 2002, an estimated 52 percent of Indonesia's population lived on less than two dollars a day, which from most perspectives is comparable to modern-day slavery. Even three dollars a day was not sufficient to provide basic amenities to many of the workers and their families.

It is no coincidence that Indonesia acquiesced to policies that so burdened her people. The horrendous debts incurred to amass fortunes for the country's elites left it no choice. According to the Global Development Finance report of the World Bank and IMF-IFS (IMF's International Financial Statistics), the country consistently averaged the highest foreign debt (as a percentage of gross domestic product, or GDP) of all Asian countries. During the critical 1990–96 period that ushered in the 1997 Asian collapse, this number hovered around or above 60 percent (compared to about 35 percent for Thailand, 15 percent for both China and Hong Kong, and 10 percent for Singapore and Taiwan). Its debt service plus short-term debt as a percentage of foreign reserves averaged close to a whopping 300 percent during the 1990–96 period (compared to about 120 percent for Thailand, 60 percent for China, and 25 percent for Hong Kong and Taiwan [this figure not available for Singapore]). It was clear that we had burdened this country with such staggering amounts of debt that it could not possibly repay them; Indonesians were forced to redeem themselves by satisfying the desires of our corporations. We EHMs had achieved our objective.[1]

Once again national economic yardsticks had proven highly deceptive. As is so often the case, in Indonesia the glowing foreign exchange, favorable trade balance, low inflation, and impressive GDP growth figures described the condition of a small, wealthy segment of the population. Everyone else lived outside the mainstream—measurable—economy; they carried a terrible burden.

Perhaps nowhere is the connection between poverty, corporate abuses, and the U.S. consumer more apparent than in Indonesian sweatshops (which are typical of those in many other countries).

Major international corporations, supported by World Bank and IMF policies that encourage privatization and tax relief for foreign companies, either own factories or contract out to ones where human beings are grossly underpaid and, if they protest, are beaten or killed. They suffer horrible lives so that merchandise can be sold at low prices in "First World" stores.

People approached me as I traveled around the United States on my book tour for *Confessions* to tell me that companies like Nike, Adidas, Ralph Lauren, Wal-Mart, and The Gap were benefiting from what amounted to slave labor. One intrepid couple offered a particularly disturbing account based on their own shocking personal experiences in Indonesia.

6

Sweatshops

In 2005 I was contacted by two filmmakers, Jim Keady and Leslie Kretzu. They requested an on-camera interview with me. Talking over the phone and through e-mails with them, I concluded that they were the antithesis of EHMs and represented a new wave of activists.

"In addition to interviewing you, we want you to know about Indonesia's sweatshops," Leslie told me when we finally got together. She briefly explained that in 2000 they had lived with Nike factory workers in Indonesia, "under the same terrible conditions, surviving on the same wages— or at least trying to."

I asked what had motivated them to do it.

"It seems so long ago," Leslie said. "I joined the Jesuit Volunteer Corps. They warned me that I'd never be the same. Their motto is 'JVC: Ruined for life.' I saw things I couldn't believe: poverty and suffering. I guess I was ruined for life. Then I worked with Mother Teresa's folks in India. I wanted to help her 'poorest of the poor.' Once you've lived with people like that you can never be the same, never return to your old ways, never forget. You simply have to do something."

I looked at Jim.

"I was kidnapped by God," he said, laughing. "Sounds funny, but I'm absolutely serious. When I was in high school I thought I would go to Wall Street, make millions, and retire by thirty-five. Then I took a trip around the world in 1993. I was twenty-one. I visited developing countries for the first time: Indonesia, Laos, Vietnam, Burma, Nepal, to name a few. I saw real poverty. It contextualized the sixteen years of Catholic school teachings I had received, including a B.S.

from Saint Joseph's University. I now understood who Jesus was fighting for. It was the beginning of my commitment to fight for the same things. Not just Jesus, of course, but also the Prophet Muhammad, the prophets in the Jewish tradition, the Buddha, and every other revered spiritual figure. In fact all of the world's major religions have social justice at their core."

I asked them to summarize their story in writing.

We started paying attention to Nike's labor practices back in 1998 when Jim was an assistant soccer coach at St. John's University in New York City. He was studying for a Masters degree in Theology while coaching, and decided for a paper topic to examine Nike's labor practices in light of Catholic Social Teaching. As he started his research, the Athletic Department at St. John's University began to negotiate a $3.5 million dollar endorsement deal with Nike that would require all coaches and athletes to wear and promote Nike products. He first said privately, then publicly, that as a matter of conscience, he did not want to be a walking advertisement for a company with alleged sweatshop labor practices. At one of the largest Catholic universities in the country he was given an ultimatum: Wear Nike and stop questioning the deal, or resign. In June 1998, he was forced to resign.

Jim wanted to be 100% sure of his position, so he asked Nike if he could work in one of their factories for a month to get a sense of the conditions. Nike said that one month wouldn't be long enough, that he didn't speak any Southeast Asian languages, and that he would displace a worker. Jim wrote back that if one month wasn't long enough, he'd go for 6 months or a year—however long it would take to get a sense of the working conditions and determine whether or not these were sweatshop jobs. He pointed out that since he spoke Spanish, Nike could send him to a factory in Central America. And for the worker he displaced, Jim found a nonprofit in Oregon (where Nike headquarters are based) that agreed to fly the worker to the US and give him or her a room, board, and living stipend, essentially a vacation for the duration of the time Jim took over the job. Nike wrote back saying that they weren't interested in his offer.

Because Jim could not work in a Nike factory, we decided to do the only thing we could think of as an alternative: to live with workers in their village and economically restrict ourselves to the wages that they are paid. So in 2000, we went to Tangerang, Indonesia, outside Jakarta, to live with Nike factory workers on their basic wage—$1.25/day.

In one month, Leslie lost 15 pounds and Jim lost 25 pounds. Like Nike's workers, we lived in a small 9×9 cement box, with no furniture and no air conditioning—in this steaming tropical city. We slept on thin mats on an uneven cement floor covered in shelf paper, which had a constant layer of ash and grit from the burning garbage, factory pollution, and car exhaust fumes. The toilets drained into open sewers on both sides of every street. Because of the sewers, the village was infested with fist-sized cockroaches and the biggest rats we'd ever seen.

Some people say to us, "You can live like a king on $1.25 a day in a place like Indonesia." It's a statement filled with apathy and misinformation. Most who make such claims have never even been to Indonesia. For $1.25 we were able to buy 2 small meals of rice and vegetables and a couple of bananas. If we wanted soap or toothpaste, we had to eat less food. One day Jim knocked over the kerosene for our small portable stove while cleaning, and we had to use our laundry soap to clean up the mess. It was a disaster—devastating financially, and therefore emotionally as well.

Try on these shoes. You are a 20-something adult working 8am to 8pm, Monday through Saturday and sometimes Sunday. That doesn't include travel time or preparing yourself for work. You don't have the money to celebrate a friend's birthday. You can't afford a radio or even think about a television. You haven't bought yourself something new to wear in over 2 years. When you get home at the end of the day, you have to spend 30–45 minutes doing your laundry by hand. You don't have many clothes, and whatever you wear is visibly dirty at the end of the day. If you're a woman, when you menstruate you still get only the allotted two bathroom breaks per day allowed to everyone; so you have to tie a scarf around your waist or wear a long shirt to cover the blood stains on your pants.

You're exhausted. You can feel the tired in your bones. You're afraid that if you speak up, you'll lose your job. And the multinational company you work for is telling the world that they've made serious changes, and consumers need not worry. You're 100% happy.

Unfortunately, it wasn't just Nike workers who lived in these conditions and on these wages. We spoke to people producing for Adidas, Reebok, The Gap, Old Navy, Tommy Hilfiger, Polo/Ralph Lauren, Lotto, Fila, and Levi's. All earned the same poverty wages, lived in the same type of slums, and had the same requests of their corporate buyers: give us higher wages and the freedom to organize independent unions.

Nike workers were living degraded, unhealthy lives—ones most people from the United States cannot imagine. But wealthy Indonesians, along with foreigners, enjoyed the good life. When I was an EHM, there was one hotel in Jakarta that was the place where people like me stayed: the Intercontinental Indonesia. Today, the vast selection includes a Four Seasons, Marriott, Hyatt, Hilton, Crowne Plaza, Sheraton, Mandarin, Le Meridien, Millennium, Ritz-Carlton, and a number of others. These are the homes-away-from-home for U.S. corporate executives, where they wine and dine their Indonesian underlings and clients. From their rooms, high above the city, they can look out toward Tangerang and the other "suburbs" where the city's workers live. They may try to deny culpability by pointing out that their companies do not own the factories, but they must feel the terrible guilt that comes from the deeper understanding that they are responsible.

"Nike squeezes the factory owners mercilessly," Jim said. "Nike's people know the cost of producing every shoelace and sole—to the penny. They push and push, forcing the owners to keep the costs at a bare minimum. In the end, the factory owner—often Chinese—is compelled to accept a very small profit."

"The owners are a lot better off than the workers," Leslie said, sighing. "But they too are exploited. Nike calls the shots. And pockets the dough."

"We zero in on Nike," Jim explained, "because it's the industry leader—it has a much greater market share than all its competitors. It sets the pace. If we can force Nike to do better, everyone else will follow."

Another aspect of "progress" in Indonesia is experienced by the corporate executives every time they step out of one of their luxury hotels. The *becaks* are gone. Those bicycle cabs festooned with fanciful murals were banned from Jakarta's main streets in 1994. President Suharto claimed they symbolized a backward country. Unfortunately, his decision relegated tens of thousands of drivers to the ranks of the unemployed. The visitor will instead be assaulted by Bajajs, small motorized three-wheeled scooter "taxis" enclosed in orange metal shells. Developed originally for India by Vespa, the Bajaj, according to Suharto, represented modernization. It is noisy, polluting, hot, and dangerous. Unlike the *becaks*, Bajajs are all identical, the brilliant rainbow-colored paintings replaced by ubiquitous orange. An estimated twenty-thousand now clog the capital's streets. Most *becak* drivers never received the training necessary to operate a Bajaj; many also work in sweatshops.

One U.S. administration after another supported Suharto's dictatorship. However, the Jakarta government came under harsh criticism from NGOs. Watchdog organizations condemned its serious violations of international and local laws, its human rights abuses, and its willingness to sacrifice democratic principles in order to satisfy multinational corporations and members of the president's inner circle. *The New York Times* reported that "Indonesia regularly ranks among the world's most corrupt countries in international surveys."[2]

"I can't believe how bad things got," Neil, a former CIA operative, told me. He attended one of my book signings, lingered afterward, and offered to buy me a beer. We spent several hours talking into the night. We met again several months later when I visited my in-laws near San Francisco. He had joined the CIA because his Chinese parents raised him to hate Mao. "I was idealistic when I was stationed in Jakarta. It was '81. I believed we had to keep the Commies out of

Indonesia." He became disillusioned during the U.S. invasion of Panama in 1989, feeling that it would turn people around the world against the United States. He retired from government work shortly afterward and went into "private practice." Eventually, in 2005, he returned to Indonesia to head up a security team guarding tsunami reconstruction efforts against freedom fighters in Aceh province. "My God, this last trip was an eye-opener! Jakarta looks like a big modern city—sparkling skyscrapers, luxury hotels, but beneath the surface . . . things are worse than ever. Corruption's rampant. And we do the corrupting."

When I asked why, after quitting the CIA, he continued in a similar profession, he answered, "It's all I know, a living." Then, the second reason that, like the first, I hear often from jackals. "Besides, there's no substitute for the high you get. Skydivers and motorcycle racers do it for the rush, but that's nothing compared to facing a man who wants to kill you."

Statements like that send chills along my spine. I think about my dad and other World War II heroes. How would they feel to know that our corporations and government encourage men to become addicted to killing for killing's sake? In writing *Confessions*, I wrestled with the horrible guilt of what I had done. Now I was discovering that the consequences were more tragic than even I had imagined.

7

United States–Supported Slaughter

Some of the worst Indonesian human rights and environmental violations began in East Timor about the time I was living in Ujung Pandang. Like Sulawesi, East Timor was a remote island that was considered to be rich in oil and gas deposits, in addition to gold and manganese. Unlike Sulawesi, which was part of Indonesia, East Timor had been governed by the Portuguese for four centuries. While 90 percent of Indonesians were Muslims, East Timor was predominantly Roman Catholic.

East Timor declared itself independent from Portugal on November 28, 1975. Nine days later Indonesia invaded. The brutal occupation forces slaughtered an estimated 200,000 people, one third of the population of East Timor.[3]

Documents released by the National Security Archive establish that the U.S. government not only supplied the weapons used in the massacre but also explicitly approved the invasion. According to these records, President Gerald Ford and Secretary of State Henry Kissinger met with Suharto on December 6, 1975, and agreed with his planned attack, which was launched the next day. The documents also reveal that the Carter administration blocked declassification of this information in 1977.

Joao Carrascalao, brother of the former governor of East Timor and a political leader now in exile, was interviewed by Amy Goodman on *Democracy Now!* thirty-five years to the day after the invasion. He stated: "I arrived at Jakarta one hour before President Ford and Henry Kissinger landed in Jakarta. And on the same night, I was informed by Colonel Suyanto—he was a top officer in the Jakarta administration—that America had given the green light for Indonesia to invade Timor."

Brad Simpson, assistant professor of history at the University of Maryland and research assistant to the National Security Archive, told Amy: "These documents lay out a 25-year pattern of deceit by successive U.S. administrations. Keeping the details of Indonesia's planned invasion of East Timor from the American public and from the international community, systematically suppressing or discounting credible reports of massacres taking place in East Timor through the mid-1980s, and working to circumvent possible congressional bans on military systems to keep the pipeline of weapons flowing."[4]

Twenty years after the invasion, two of Indonesia's most vocal critics were elevated to international status. East Timorese activists Bishop Carlos Filipe Ximenes Belo and José Ramos-Horta received the Nobel Peace Prize in 1996. The award sent shock waves through Jakarta, Washington, and into the corridors of Wall Street.

The East Timor massacre is just one of many police-state policies carried out under Suharto. Dispatching the military to these independence-minded regions was justified as necessary to halt communism during the 1970s. The idea that most rebellions were driven by a desperate desire to shake off the yoke of Suharto's repressive regime and that the rebels turned to countries like China only as a last resort—for military and medical assistance—was ignored by the mainstream U.S. press. Also ignored by the media was the fact that bolstering Suharto served the corporatocracy's interests. Suharto's determination to control the entire archipelago—even regions that did not possess coveted resources—was taken very seriously by both Washington and Wall Street. The corporatocracy understood that it had to support the dictator's grandiose vision of a united Indonesia if it wanted to enjoy a free reign over areas that possessed the resources it craved.

On the northern tip of Sumatra, in oil- and gas-rich Aceh province, more than ten thousand people have been killed by the military since the time I lived in Indonesia. Thousands more died in clashes in the Molucca Islands, West Kalimantan (Borneo), and Irian Jaya (New Guinea). In case after case the true objective of the armed forces was to secure resources coveted by multinational corporations that, in essence, funded Suharto's government. Although oil- and other mineral-extracting companies took the lead, they were joined by a wide variety of corporations that benefited from Indonesia's cheap labor, natural resources, and markets for development projects and consumer goods. Indonesia is a prime example of an economy built around investment by the international banking and commercial communities. Backed by the promise of paying off loans through its resources, it went deep into debt to finance infrastructure projects that in turn generated demand for hotels, restaurants, shopping malls, and the construction, service, banking, and transportation activities that accompany these. Wealthy Indonesians and foreigners gained, while the majority of Indonesians suffered. Resistance movements were beaten back by the armed forces.

Like the people, Indonesia's environment suffered severely. Mines, pulp and paper factories, and other resource-exploiting industries denuded enormous areas of one of the world's largest rainforests. Rivers were clogged with toxic wastes. The air around industrial sites and cities was laden with pollution. In 1997, Southeast Asia made world headlines when it was covered in a haze of noxious smoke generated by out-of-control forest fires in Indonesia—the consequence of EHM-induced corruption.

Other victims of the "economic miracle" are the Bugis, Dyaks, Melanesias, and other indigenous cultures; their lands have been stolen and their lives and traditions destroyed. This modern genocide cannot be measured solely in terms of human suffering; it is an attack on the soul of humanity, and especially discouraging in light of earlier genocides, including ones conducted in the United States against our indigenous people. While those are condemned today, the model is repeated—and financed by the U.S. government and our corporations.

When the growing economic crisis began to severely impact his country, Suharto bought into the IMF Structural Adjustment Package (SAP). The IMF recommended that Suharto drop fuel and food subsidies and many other social services to decrease spending. Blatantly imbalanced in favor of the rich, these policies resulted in increased starvation, disease, and antagonism.

Masses of Indonesians finally took to the streets. Even the wealthy, fearing increased mayhem, demanded change. Suharto was forced to resign in May 1998, ending his thirty-two years of dictatorial rule. In September 1999, the Clinton administration severed all military ties with the Indonesian military.

However, these events by no means marked the end for the corporatocracy. On the contrary, they ultimately strengthened its position. Indonesians in power took credit for ousting the dictator and portrayed themselves as friends of the people. The U.S. government and multinational corporations hailed Suharto's downfall and supported the new regime. Then on December 26, 2004, a tragedy occurred that would provide new opportunities for the corporatocracy to entrench itself. The day after Christmas, the tsunami struck.

Around a quarter million people would ultimately die from the huge waves. However, the businesses involved in the reconstruction—many of them U.S. firms—saw the devastation as a profit-making occasion. Earthquakes, hurricanes, and tsunamis kill hundreds of thousands of people and destroy property, yet they boost GDP. The death and destruction does not make it into the economic statistics books; yet the billions of dollars spent on reconstruction do, creating a falsely positive impression.

Most U.S. citizens are not aware that national disasters are like wars: They are highly profitable for big business. A great deal of the money for rebuilding after disasters is earmarked for U.S. engineering firms and for multinational corporations that own hotel, restaurant, and retail chains, communications and transportation networks, banks, insurance companies, and other corporatocracy industries. Rather than helping subsistence farmers, fishermen, mom-and-pop restaurants, bed-and-breakfasts, and local entrepreneurs, "disaster relief" programs provide one more vehicle for channeling money to the empire builders.

8

Tsunami Profiteering

December 26, 2004, was a black day. Not only for the immediate victims of the terrible tsunami, but also for all of us who believe in compassion, charity, and goodwill to our fellow inhabitants of this planet. The tragic story behind the shameless exploitation began several months before that natural disaster struck.

Indonesia selected another military man as president in September 2004. Gen. Susilo Bambang Yudhoyono, according to *The New York Times*, "moved swiftly up the ranks during the authoritarian rule of Gen. Suharto . . ."[5]

He had been chosen for military training at Fort Benning, Georgia, in 1976, and completed two tours in the United States under the International Military Education and Training Program. After the tsunami, he became the perfect leader to shatter the independence movement in Aceh province.

Like many of the local movements throughout the archipelago, the one in Aceh was driven by a desire to gain independence from a government that was viewed as economically exploitative and brutally repressive. While their environment and culture suffered at the hands of foreign corporations, the people of Aceh received few benefits. One of Indonesia's largest resource projects, a liquefied natural gas (LNG) facility, is located in Aceh, yet only a tiny percentage of the LNG profits are directed to local schools, hospitals, and other investments that would help those most adversely impacted by the venture.

"Resource-rich Aceh has been yearning for independence from Indonesia for five decades," according to Melissa Rossi, an award-winning journalist who has written for *Newsweek*, *Newsday* (New

York), *Esquire, George,* MSNBC, and *The New York Observer,* and who occasionally sends me personal e-mails from global hot spots. "Oil wells line the coasts, which explains why the Indonesian government is clamped onto Aceh like a leech."[6] Although few records were released to the public, an estimated ten to fifteen thousand people were killed during thirty years of fighting in the province before the tsunami swept out of the ocean and across the land.[7]

Secret talks between the government and the Free Aceh Movement (GAM, in Indonesian, for Gerakan Aceh Merdeka[8]) began in 2004. GAM appeared to have gained a bargaining position that would allow the people of Aceh to share some of the profits generated from oil, gas, and other local resources; a degree of local self-rule; and other rights demanded for decades. However, the tsunami changed all that.

Because GAM was a local organization, centered in the area destroyed by the giant waves, it was seriously impaired by the chaotic aftermath. Some of its key people died or suffered the loss of family members. Its communications and transportation systems were devastated. It redirected its activities away from the resistance and bargaining processes and into caring for tsunami victims and managing recovery efforts.

The government, on the other hand, moved quickly to take advantage of the pandemonium. Fresh troops were flown in from Java and other unaffected areas of Indonesia; within months they would be bolstered by U.S. military personnel and mercenaries, like Neil, the ex–CIA operative who headed up a team that guarded U.S. contractors. Although the armed forces took command under the pretext of relieving disaster victims, their unspoken goals included quashing GAM.

The Bush administration wasted no time. In the month after the tsunami, January 2005, Washington reversed the 1999 policy implemented by Clinton that had severed ties with Indonesia's repressive military. The White House dispatched $1 million worth of military equipment to Jakarta. *The New York Times* reported on

February 7, 2005: "Washington is seizing on an opportunity that came after the tsunami . . . Secretary of State Condoleezza Rice has moved to strengthen American training of Indonesian officers considerably . . . In Aceh, the Indonesian Army, which has been fighting a separatist rebellion for 30 years, has been on full display since the tsunami . . . The army's uppermost concern appears to be to keep a stranglehold on the armed forces of the Free Aceh Movement."[9] In November 2005, Washington lifted the arms embargo and resumed full relations with the Indonesian military.[10]

Exhausted by their efforts to recover from the disaster and help local communities rebuild, and faced with overwhelming pressure from the Indonesian army and its U.S. supporters, GAM signed a very one-sided peace treaty with the government. Once again, the corporatocracy was—and is—the big winner. The tsunami virtually assured that the exploitation of Aceh will continue unabated.

A cogent example of the way natural disasters are exploited by the corporatocracy is offered by Aceh's Leuser Ecosystem. For three decades, local resistance had kept lumber and oil companies out of one of the world's richest forests. Now that GAM has been crushed, the region is reopened to exploitation.

Mike Griffiths, a former oil company executive, left his lucrative job and devoted himself to ecological conservation in the mid-1980s. He helped found the Leuser International Foundation in 1994. He guided NPR's *Radio Expeditions* program to Aceh in 2006. *Radio Expeditions'* host, Michael Sullivan, reported, "With peace, the pressure on the forest is likely to increase, and the biggest threat—even more than logging of valuable tropical hardwoods and oil palm plantations—is roads." The radio program went on to explain that immediately following the tsunami, U.S. engineering and construction companies lobbied the World Bank and other "aid" agencies for money to construct these roads, which will primarily serve the lumber and oil industries. Mike Griffiths told NPR: "If you loose the Leuser Ecosystem, you don't only lose the last real chance for the tiger, the orangutan, for the elephant and for the rhino; you lose the basic foundations for the welfare for four million people—that is how many rely on this place for water, flood protection and erosion protection."[11]

The relationship between Indonesian ruling elites, the U.S. government, and international corporations is indicative of methods employed by the corporatocracy around the world during the post–World War II era. Empire building has been conducted largely in secret. Since democracy assumes an informed electorate, these methods pose a direct threat to America's most coveted ideal. They also serve as a disturbing commentary on the results of my work and that of so many "development experts."

The insidious nature of our work was highlighted for me personally by three separate incidents. They were exposed after the 2004 tsunami, although the roots of each reached back into my earlier career.

9

Fruits of Corruption

In *Confessions of an Economic Hit Man* I describe my connection in the late 1980s and 1990s with Stone and Webster Engineering Company (SWEC), at that time one of the nation's largest and most respected consulting and construction firms, and the fact that I was paid about a half million dollars by SWEC with the understanding that I would desist from writing a book about my EHM life. Occasionally, the company asked me to actually perform a service for them.

One day in 1995, a high-level SWEC executive called to request a meeting with me. Over lunch, he discussed a project to construct a chemicals processing complex in Indonesia. It would be, he assured me, one of the largest projects in the company's one-hundred-year history, worth about $1 billion. "I'm determined to land this one," he said and then, lowering his voice, admitted, "but I can't do it until I figure a way to pay one of Suharto's family members $150 million."

"A bribe," I responded.

He nodded. "You've spent a lot of time in Indonesia. Fill me in on how to make this happen."

I told him that I knew of four ways to pay the man a "legal bribe." SWEC could arrange to lease bulldozers, cranes, trucks, and other heavy equipment from companies owned by him and his friends and pay excessive fees; they could subcontract portions of the project to similarly owned companies at inflated prices; they could use that same model to contract for food, housing, cars, fuel, and other such items; and they could offer to arrange for the sons and daughters of the Indonesian's cronies to attend prestigious U.S. colleges, cover all their expenses, and pay them consultant or intern salaries while they were in the United States. Although I acknowledged that arranging for such a large sum would probably require all four approaches and would take several years, I assured him that I had seen all of these schemes used very successfully and was unaware of any legal actions ever taken against a U.S. company or its executives as a result. I also suggested that he explore the idea of retaining geishas to help seal the deal.

"The geishas," he informed me with a conspiratorial grin, "are already hard at work." As to the rest, he expressed concern that Suharto's man wanted "cash up front."

I had to admit that I knew no way to make such amounts of cash available "up front." At least not legally.

He thanked me. I heard nothing further from him on this issue.

A decade later, on March 15, 2006, *The Boston Globe* carried the following banner headline across the front page of its Business section: THE 'BRIBE MEMO' AND COLLAPSE OF STONE & WEBSTER. The article told the tragic story of how the company's glorious history, which began in 1889, came crashing to an end when it filed for bankruptcy in 2000 and ended up owned by the Shaw Group. According to the *Globe*, "well over 1,000 employees were fired, their savings in Stone & Webster stock lost." *Globe* reporter Steve Bailey concluded that the downfall could be traced to "The critical memo (that) lays out in detail a previously unreported secret attempt by the company to pay an illegal $147 million kickback to a relative of Indonesian President Suharto to secure the largest contract in Stone & Webster history."[12]

The second incident started with an e-mail I received from the son of an Indonesian government official whom I had worked with during the 1970s, requesting a meeting with me.

Emil (not his real name) joined me at a quiet Thai restaurant on New York's Upper West Side. He told me that he had been deeply moved by *Confessions of an Economic Hit Man*. His father had introduced him to me in Jakarta when he was about ten years old. He remembered hearing my name often. He knew, he said, that his father was one of those corrupt officials I described in my book. Then, looking me squarely in the eye, he admitted that he had followed in his father's footsteps. "I want to come clean," he told me. "I want to confess, like you." He smiled softly. "But I have a family and a great deal to lose. I'm sure you understand what I mean."

I assured him that I would never divulge his name or in any way expose his identity.

Emil's story was a revealing one. He pointed out that the Indonesian military has a long history of collecting money from the private sector in order to finance its activities. He tried to make light of this, shrugging it off with a laugh, observing that such activities were common in Third World countries. Then he grew serious. "Since the fall of Suharto in 1998, things have gotten even worse. Suharto was truly a military dictator who was determined to keep the armed forces under his control. Once his reign ended, many Indonesians tried desperately to change the law so that civilians would have more power over the military. They thought that by reducing the military budget, they could accomplish their objectives. The generals knew where to go for help: foreign mining and energy companies."

I told Emil that his words reminded me of similar situations in Colombia, Nigeria, Nicaragua, and so many other countries where private militias are used to supplement national armies.

"Yes," he agreed. "We've got many mercenaries in Indonesia. But what I'm talking about is worse. In the last few years, our army's been bought out by foreign corporations. The implications are frightening because, you see, these corporations now own our armed forces as well as our resources."

When I asked him why he was divulging this information, he turned away and looked outside the window of the restaurant at the passing traffic. Finally, his eyes returned to meet mine. "I'm a collaborator. I've taken my father's corruption a step further. I'm one of the people who make the arrangements, collect the money from companies, and pass it on to the military. I'm ashamed. The least I can do is talk to you and hope you let the world know about what's going on."

Weeks after my meeting with Emil, an article caught my eye as I scanned *The New York Times* Web site. It detailed the activities of a New Orleans–based company, Freeport-McMoRan Copper and Gold, that made "payments of $20 million to military commanders and units in the area (Papua) in the last seven years in exchange for protection of its facilities in the remote province." The article went on to assert that, "Only one-third of the financing for Indonesia's armed forces comes from the state budget, while the rest is collected from nontransparent sources such as 'protection payments,' allowing the military brass to operate independently of the government's financial controls."[13]

That article led me to two others that had appeared on *The Times* Web site in September 2004. They described recent events in my old stomping ground, Sulawesi, documenting allegations that the world's largest gold-producing company, Newmont Mining Corp., based in Denver, was illegally dumping arsenic and mercury into the ocean at Buyat Bay. As I read these articles, I realized my work—the electrical systems, roads, ports, and other infrastructure that we EHMs financed and built back in the 1970s—had created the conditions that enabled Newmont to conduct its mining activities and poison the ocean. As my project manager, Charlie Illingworth, pointed out on my first trip, we were dispatched to Indonesia to make sure the oil companies got everything they needed; it did not take long for me to understand that our mission was not limited to oil companies. Sulawesi was a prime example of how "aid" money benefits the multinationals.

The *Times* article pointed out that "the fight with Newmont has fueled a growing popular impression that mining and energy companies hold a tight grip over Indonesia's weak regulatory system. Many blame the corruption, cronyism and unevolved legal structure inherited from General Suharto, the dictator whose rule ended in 1998 and who, for a price, eagerly opened the doors to foreign investors."[4]

As I stared at those articles, the allegations by the mayor of "Batsville" and the Bugi shipbuilder superimposed themselves over my computer screen, like biblical prophets come back to haunt me. The United States had indeed sent its bats off to exploit and pollute foreign lands. Sailors on ancient wooden galleons, armed with machetes, had little chance of defending their homeland against the might of the Pentagon.

Or against the more subtle armies of corporate henchmen.

10

Attacked and Beaten in Indonesia

During my talks, audience members sometimes refer to news reports that Nike and similar companies are improving. I, like most people I meet, want to believe this. We hope that Nike founder Phil Knight and other executives in leadership positions act responsibly. I contacted Leslie and Jim, the couple who had tried to live like Nike factory workers in Indonesia and were now producing a documentary movie about sweatshops. Their e-mailed reply was not reassuring:

Since our trip in 2000, we have returned twice and have kept in contact with workers and labor organizers. Marginal changes at best have been made, but the real issues of wages and the rights to form independent unions are no better for workers now than they were in 2000, despite Nike's attempts to make the public think otherwise.

The government minimum wage has risen in Indonesia, but the price of food, water, cooking oil, clothing, housing and other basic necessities has risen at the same rate. Workers are still forced to make decisions like "eat or let my child eat." The last time we were in Indonesia, a Nike factory worker whom we have interviewed since 2000 and who has worked in a Nike factory for 8 years came to greet us. She gave us a solemn hug, a strained half-smile and said forcefully "nothing's changed."

What has changed is the price of oil, and therefore the cost of transportation to and from the factories. It now costs workers up to 30% of their already inadequate salary just to get to and from work. Where does the money come from for increased transportation costs? The women and men working 6–7 days a week for multi-billion dollar corporations are sometimes forced to eat rice with salt for their two meals per day.

In the late 1990's, Nike responded to criticism about sweatshop conditions saying that critics didn't know what they were talking about and that the subcontracted factories were owned by someone else—therefore Nike did not have the power to make changes. In 2000, Nike's response was "right issue . . . wrong company." By 2002, Nike executives were following us around the US at the colleges and high schools where we gave lectures on this subject. They would send a packet prior to our visit denouncing what we were going to say, then follow up with an editorial in the student newspaper claiming we didn't have all of the facts. And now, Nike's strategy seems to involve attending social responsibility conferences and admitting that there are some problems but that the answers lie in all stakeholders working together (on Nike's terms).

Meanwhile, the same problems uncovered in the 1990's from starvation wages to bathroom breaks limited to twice a day to verbal, physical and sexual abuse to threats and physical violence toward union organizers continue to occur in Nike's factories around the globe.

If Nike were to double all of their workers' wages in Indonesia (roughly 1/6 of their workforce), it would cost them approximately 7% of their $1.63 billion advertising budget. If Nike redirected a portion of their advertising budget to paying the factory more money per good, we could see most of these sweatshop labor conditions vanish.

Leslie and Jim may be the antithesis of EHMs but they are not beyond the reach of the jackals. They told of a dark night when they; their cameraman, Joel; and their Indonesian driver and translator were chased down by a group of armed thugs.

"They surrounded our car on motorcycles," Jim said. "Our driver raced to a nearby Army checkpoint, but the soldier there waved us through."

"He was frantic to get rid of us," Leslie added. "He wasn't about to cross those guys, the equivalent of an Indonesian mafia.

"Our driver was forced to pull over. We were hustled out at gunpoint and pushed around. I thought sure," Leslie said with a visible shudder, "that we were goners, would be listed among the 'disappeared.'"

They survived but their driver was severely beaten. "A warning," Joel muttered.

"Did you get the message?" I asked.

"We'll be more careful in the future," Jim responded. "Watch where we go. At what hour. But we will go back. We will complete this documentary. And show it to the world."

Reading articles about SWEC, Freeport-McMoRan, and Newmont, and hearing from Jim, Leslie, and Joel about their experiences forced me to come face-to-face, once again, with the legacy of my own actions—and those of everyone who purchases sweatshop-made goods and products derived from exploitative industries. Indonesia's story is one that has been repeated over and over; it is the secret history of the American empire.

Unfortunately, that empire has established itself as a new standard, a model that, despite its obvious failures, is being emulated. A 2004 trip to Tibet taught me that China has its own brand of EHMs and jackals. Ultimately theirs may prove more effective—and destructive—than ours.

11

Don't Become a Buddhist

Tibet is famous as the homeland of the Dalai Lama, the spiritual leader who represents, perhaps more than any other living person, a commitment to nonviolence. However, Tibet has not always enjoyed such a reputation. Between 609 and 649 A.D., the Tibetan King Songtsen Gampo formed alliances among warring chieftains intent on conquering neighboring fiefdoms. As a result, the king was able to forge a vast empire. Later the region was invaded by Genghis Khan. It became part of an empire that has gone down in history as the epitome of brutality.

In June 2004 I led a group of thirty-four people to Tibet.

Driving through the countryside toward our first stop, the city of Tsedang, it became obvious that one of our female guides knew little about Tibet and barely spoke its language—in fact, it appeared that "Suzie's" awkward English was better than her Tibetan. Word quickly spread that she was a Chinese spy and we should be careful of what we said. Our Nepalese guide quietly confirmed this to several of us and asked us to spread the word. One time, when Suzie got off the bus at a rest stop, he told us that we should always assume that we were being listened to by someone.

"Even in the monasteries and temples?" a woman asked.

"Especially in those places," he replied.

Tsedang sits on a Tibetan plateau. Overshadowed by snow-capped Himalayan peaks, it is one of this land's most ancient centers of civilization. We checked into a sterile Chinese hotel. I deposited my bags in my room and headed out. I felt the need to get away from the group for a spell, adjust to the altitude, walk off my jet lag, and experience Tibet. However, as I wandered around in the late afternoon,

I was appalled to discover that had I been deposited on Tsedang's streets by a magic carpet. I would never have guessed that I had arrived in old Tibet; instead, I would have thought I had landed in a Chinese military base.

Uniformed soldiers hustled along the newly cemented sidewalks. Open-air markets and small shops sold Chinese produce. Sidewalk vendors hawked garishly colored plastic utensils, pails, and toys. While a few ancient buildings remained, many had been replaced by military gray concrete structures. The Tibetan people stood out in their traditional clothes. Like museum oddities in fifteenth-century fur hats, boots, and coats, they were apparent strangers in their own land. The soldiers regarded them with distain, as they might treat deranged beggars. Tension rippled through the thin Himalayan air.

As I walked on, I was burdened by a fatigue that grew more severe with each step. At first I blamed it solely on the altitude, similar to the Andes and Kashmir. Fatigue soon turned to dizziness. I felt nauseated. I made my way to a cement bench and sat down. The slogan "Free Tibet" rang in my ears and I realized that I was suffering emotionally as well as physiologically. I forced myself to focus on my surroundings. People scurried past. The many Chinese and the few Tibetans appeared not to notice me. I felt visible and vulnerable; yet apparently no one saw me sitting there. I too could have been a deranged beggar.

When I began to recover, I remembered the photo of the Dalai Lama I carried in my pocket. I reached for it cautiously, aware that merely possessing it could land me in prison; photos of this man are illegal in modern Tibet, despite the fact that millions there still consider him their leader. I had smuggled it past the Chinese security guards at the airport partly out of defiance, partly because I thought I might gift it to one of his followers, but mostly to honor the time I had spent with His Holiness nearly five years earlier.

The organizer of this trip, Sheena Singh, had also arranged that 1999 trip. We had journeyed into the Indian protectorate of Ladakh in the Kashmir region between Pakistan and India, which today is populated by thousands of Tibetan refugees who are determined to carry on the traditions forbidden by the Chinese in their homeland. As fate would have it, the Dalai Lama was in Ladakh that same week. Sheena knew of his interest in indigenous cultures; she sent one of my books on the subject to him, along with a note requesting a private audience for our group. A day later, several of his staff arrived at our hotel with a gracious reply explaining that his calendar was full; they presented us with a box of his autographed books.

On our last morning in Tibet, as we waited to board our flight to northern India, we were surprised to see the Dalai Lama and his entourage sweep into the tiny airport. Sheena immediately approached his secretary. The boarding process began. Before I realized what had happened, I found myself being hustled up the steps of the plane, prepped by our Indian guide that protocol dictated kissing one of the Dalai Lama's shoes, and led to the front row of the Boeing 737. The Dalai Lama smiled up at me and patted the seat beside him. The idea of kissing a shoe seemed rather odd, but having learned long ago the importance of respecting local traditions, I awkwardly started to lean over the seat toward his foot.

The Dalai Lama gave a little laugh and, placing a hand beneath my chin, gently lifted my head. "Not necessary," he said in that softly chuckling voice that the world has come to love. He patted the seat again. "Please sit." He tapped the edge of a book he was holding on his lap. "Wonderful," he said, turning the front cover of my book toward me. "I'd like to learn more."

We talked extensively about indigenous people and their commitment to balance. I told him that the reason the Shuar of the Amazon became headhunters and went to war was, according to their own mythology, because they had allowed their populations to grow out of control and that the resulting imbalances threatened to destroy many life-forms; consequently, a god ordered them to take responsibility even if that required "weeding your own garden" (killing other men).

This story seemed to strike a chord with the Dalai Lama. He observed that while he did not condone violence, peace arrives only when humans show true compassion for all sentient beings and when we take individual and collective responsibility for good stewardship of the planet. He pointed out that economic development usually destroys other life-forms and creates disequilibrium, making the rich richer and the poor poorer. We discussed at length the importance of taking actions to make this a compassionate world, not simply talking about it or praying for it.

After that flight, the Dalai Lama invited our group to his home in Dharmasala, India. Following a cordial greeting, he said something that seemed most unusual, given his position as the leader of a spiritual movement. "Don't become a Buddhist. The world doesn't need more Buddhists. Do practice compassion. The world needs more compassion."

Those words echoed in my mind as I sat on the bench in Tsedang, cupping that photo in my hands. I could not imagine hearing such advice from the Pope. Nor from China's head of state. Nor from the president of the United States. It was a direct refutation of proselytizing and of all forms of imperialism. Staring at the Dalai Lama's photo, contemplating his insistence that his people not enter a cycle of violence that would taint future generations, I felt my own inadequacy. I was furious at China. Here in this city that epitomized the brutality of colonial empires I felt the inappropriateness of my own anger.

I made a vow then and there that I would devote the rest of my life to turning things around. I would write and speak out about the dangers of a world based on exploitation, fear, and violence. I would search for real solutions and try to inspire people to take concrete actions. At the same time, I understood that I had to work on my own attitudes. I realized that it was not enough to exchange one empire for another, to fight fear with more fear. We had to break that cycle.

12

Biological Imperatives

We explored Tibet in a convoy of eight Toyota Land Cruisers. As we passed peasants trudging under heavy loads, I could not help thinking that we must convey the impression of feeling superior, that we are The Chosen People. When we stopped for a "restroom break" high in a mountain pass, I wandered over to a cluster of our people and joked that we must appear to the locals like a caravan of royalty.

"Are you kidding?" one of the men scoffed. "This is a trip from hell. We got cars, sure, but my driver can't even shift properly, grinds gears all the time. The Cruiser ahead of us leaks oil. That one"—he pointed at a cloud of dust on the road behind us—"can't keep pace with the rest. I don't think royalty would tolerate this!"

It was true that, by American standards, the trip was rough. We struggled over ancient silk roads that at times were no more than potholed riverbeds. The thin Himalayan air took a toll on both vehicles and people. At one stop, we were inundated by clouds of biting insects. On the other hand, the scenery was spectacular beyond imagination and we usually enjoyed clean beds and decent food. We talked with nomads who defied Chinese edicts not to speak to foreigners. Our guides dutifully showed us the home of the Panchen Lama, who at six years old had been handpicked by the Chinese to replace the boy previously chosen by the Dalai Lama, who had disappeared. Since the Panchen Lama must confirm the next Dalai Lama, Buddhist monks and civilians alike took to the streets in protest; untold numbers were imprisoned, expelled, and executed. As we continued along, we paid our respects at numerous monasteries that had been destroyed during the Cultural Revolution.

Traveling around Tibet, time and again we witnessed Chinese oppression. It had a profound impact, serving as a constant reminder that Tibet was an occupied land, its people enslaved, its natural wealth exploited. We discussed the idea that the United States behaves in similar fashion in countries with resources our corporations covet. Several of the participants had traveled to the Amazon with me. They had witnessed the terrible destruction of cultures and rainforests at the hands of our corporations. They had heard the voices of indigenous people determined to die fighting if necessary to protect their offspring against our encroaching materialism. They had seen U.S. soldiers wandering the streets of Amazonian towns, in a fashion similar to that of the Chinese in Tibet. Members of our group often compared the Chinese presence with that of the United States government and our oil, lumber, beef, pharmaceutical, and consumer-goods companies throughout the Amazon, Middle East, Africa, and Asia, and in the wars of occupation in Afghanistan and Iraq.

On our way back to Lhasa and knowing that we would depart for Nepal the following morning, we drove across the spectacular Karo La and Khamba La passes. At seventeen thousand feet, our caravan stopped to view a glacier. One of our guides explained that the ice had reached almost to the road two decades earlier, but changes in climate had caused it to recede by a quarter mile or more. Sheep and yaks grazed beside our vehicles. Between them and the glacier were several black tents. Roughly shoulder height and perhaps twelve by fifteen feet, they were firmly anchored to the ground by heavy straps that traversed their ridge poles. Smoke poured through their roofs. Behind the tents, red, blue, yellow, green, and white prayer flags, suspended from a series of tall poles interconnected by a web of twine, fluttered in the chill breeze that swept down off the glacier.

As we stepped out of the Cruisers, Tibetans emerged from the tents. The men wore woolen slacks, heavy jackets, and caps, the women long dresses festooned with brightly colored aprons. Our guides explained that they were nomads who live much as their forefathers did before the time of Christ. Through our interpreters, the nomads told us that Yetis ("Abominable Snowmen") lived on the glacier. They assured us that until recently they had seen them several times a year, but over the last ten years, with the glacier receding, the Yetis had vanished.

As we talked about the devastating impact of global warming on the earth's glaciers, someone noticed that the nomads had set up a little stand, and that one of our women, famous for her ability to hone in on a bargain, was hustling from it toward us. She informed the group that the nomads were selling crystals they had found on the ground vacated by the glacier. The majority of our people rushed to the vendor's stand as the word quickly circulated that this would be the last opportunity to buy directly from the people—as opposed to Lhasa stores.

When I asked a guide about the authenticity of the crystals, he muttered that he did not want to interfere with the nomads' income; then, shaking his head, he added that he had heard about a factory in China that produced such things.

I and a couple others stood watching as our group bargained with the Tibetans.

"So much for global warning," one of my companions observed.

"There's that magnificent glacier," the other said. "Here are these tents, the people, yaks . . . and our group gets seduced by crystals that are probably nothing more than glass."

Asking a translator to accompany me, I approached an old man and woman and a young girl who were sitting nearby. The old woman was holding a long rope that was attached to a yak. The animal's shaggy back was covered with a beautiful blanket decorated with brown and tan triangles; thrown across it was a small saddle that I took to be the little girl's. The three of them smiled warmly at me. The old woman stood and brought the yak to my side offering to let me pat it. Then she sat back down and invited me and the translator to join them.

After introductions, I asked how they felt about the Chinese. They glanced at each other. The girl hid her face and peered through spread fingers, first frowning at me and then giggling. The old man spoke up.

"You know," he said with a toothless grin, "we are accustomed to rulers from other lands. Our stories go back long before my grandparents' grandparents, of kings who invaded us. We have a name for their soldiers: *Nomad Killers*." He patted the girl on the shoulder. "Why should things be different in her time?"

"The problems began," the old lady continued, "when men took over."

I asked what she meant.

"Look at today. Everything is run by men. I once lived in the city and tried Buddhism, but I saw that all the important jobs there, just like the government, were held by men."

"I have to agree," the old man said. "In past times the women kept us men under control." He grinned. "We can get pretty wild, hunting and cutting forests, that sort of thing. The women used to say when we had done enough."

This talk reminded me of the Shuar of the Amazon. They believe that men and women are equal, yet have different roles. Men kill animals for food, cut trees for firewood, and fight other men. Women raise children, grow crops, tend the household fires, and have the very important job of telling men when it is time to stop. The Shuar explain that men hunt animals and cut trees even when there is enough meat and wood, unless women rein them in. When members of the Shuar visited the United States they were shocked by the way nature had been destroyed and paved over with highways, cities, and shopping malls. "What happened to the women?" they asked. "Why haven't they stopped the men? Why do your women always want to buy more things?"

It was amazing to find similar sentiments among tribes deep in the Amazon and nomads at the top of the Himalayas. On the drive back to Lhasa I kept thinking that perhaps those two groups represented true human values and that to change the world all we had to do was bring the male and female into balance. Given the corporatocracy's maleness and its interests in promoting mass consumption, the "all we had to do" was a pretty big "all"; nevertheless, defining it made the task seem less daunting. The important fact was that the corporatocracy's structure was based on masculine hierarchies and its power revolved around our willingness to accept as "normal" an extreme form of materialism. I also realized that we had to get both genders off the shopping addiction. How indicative that the U.S. president, after 9/11, urged citizens to go shopping to reduce stress, bolster the economy, and defy terrorists! Even here in Tibet, yak herders who were far removed from the world of shopping malls had received the message; despite their own nonconsumptive lives, they were selling to us.

I recalled Dr. Judith Hand's book, *Women, Power, and the Biology of Peace*. In it, she points out that warfare historically provided a vehicle for men to perform their biological imperative of spreading sperm, while social stability is preferred by women, who are charged with bearing, nurturing, and raising children. She contends that in order to realize more peaceful societies women must play larger roles in the decision-making process. What I had just heard from the nomads seemed to confirm Dr. Hand's conclusions. It occurred to me that since women are often the primary shoppers in modern families, it is essential to help them understand that today's global strife is driven by the corporatocracy and that to promote peace they need to change their attitudes toward materialism. They also need to demand that the companies whose products they purchase treat their employees—regardless of where they live—equitably.

In the city where the Dalai Lama grew up, I would learn a very different lesson.

13

Dictatorships of Finance

Lhasa was the most Tibetan of all the cities we visited. The Potala Palace where the Dalai Lama was raised, the ancient winding alleys, multiroofed Buddhist temples, gigantic cone-shaped stupas, and festive shrines inspired a sense of tranquility that I had felt five years earlier in Ladekh and in the rural areas of Tibet, but that was lacking in Tsedang and the other cities. Nevertheless, the Chinese were ever-present. Soldiers swaggered down the streets, Chinese characters filled banners and billboards, and the plastic products that exemplify modern industrial societies were prevalent.

We checked into the most wonderful hotel, one designed, built, owned, and operated by Tibetans. I plunked down on my bed, stacked with colorful pillows, and reviewed notes I had filed on the tiny pocket PC I carry with me. I wanted to update my thoughts about materialism, commercialism, and the role of international business in the 1997 economic disaster that brought so much suffering to Asia. I had already delved into the way this crisis impacted Indonesia. But being in Tibet, seeing and feeling China's exploitation of this country, placed the tragedy of 1997 in a new perspective.

What became known as the "IMF crisis" hit South Korea, Thailand, and Indonesia particularly hard, but it also had devastating repercussions for many people—especially the poor—in Laos and the Philippines. Every one of those countries had bought into the IMF and World Bank ideology.

In the soul-searching and finger-pointing that followed the crisis, the IMF was criticized for what many economists referred to as "fast track capitalism"—the elimination of restrictions on capital flows, the encouragement of privatization, the maintenance of high interest rates as a means for enticing foreign investors and bank capital into securities markets, and the attempt to hedge against currency risk by pegging national currencies to the dollar, which also served the unspoken objective of strengthening the dollar. At the same time, prices for goods and services constantly increased due to inflation and those high rates of interest imposed by the IMF. It was an untenable situation. As one country after another fell into economic collapse, local businesses and national governments were unable to pay off loans they had accumulated in U.S. dollars; they discovered that their earned income, which was constantly diminishing and was paid in local currencies, had devalued. The IMF had manipulated those countries and their businesses into paying what amounted to a stiff tax; the owners of the big international corporations were the beneficiaries.

When the situation continued to deteriorate, the IMF came up with a "rescue plan." It offered new loans so the nations could avoid defaulting. However, the deal was conditional upon each country accepting a Structural Adjustment Package (SAP) similar to the earlier one forced on Indonesia. In essence, each country was required to allow local banks and financial institutions to fail, drastically reduce government spending, cut food and fuel subsidies and other services for the poor, and raise interest rates still higher. In many cases they were also told to privatize and sell more of their national assets to multinational corporations. As a direct result, an untold number of people, especially children, died of malnutrition, starvation, and disease. Many more suffered long-term consequences from lack of health care, education, housing, and other social services.

The collapse that began in Asia mushroomed to global proportions, triggering recessions in Europe, South America, and the United States. It was a lesson in how not to conduct economic policy, if the goal was to help local people and economies. It sent a strong message about the IMF and the World Bank.

Analyses confirmed that the countries that had refused to yield to the IMF demands did best. China was a prime example. Although implementing policies to encourage international investors, Beijing took a very different course from that advocated by the IMF. Foreign investments were channeled into factories rather than securities, thus insulating the country against future capital flight and also providing employment and other spin-off benefits. India, Taiwan, and Singapore defied the IMF; their economies remained robust. Malaysia acquiesced, endured a recession, then turned its back on SAPs and rebounded.

One of the strongest critics of the IMF was the winner of the Nobel Prize in Economics and—ironically—also the former chief economist of the World Bank, Joseph Stiglitz.

I had carried Stiglitz's book, *Globalization and Its Discontents*, with me to Tibet. Late in the afternoon, I took a walk by myself through the winding streets of Lhasa. I arrived at an area that bustled with pedestrians. Farther along, I came to a small park and sat down on an old wooden bench to bask in the fading sunshine.

Flipping through Stiglitz's book, I once again marveled at how closely his critiques resembled my own in *Confessions*. He wrote from an academic perspective while mine was a personal narrative; yet many of our conclusions were identical. For example, while I described how I had created falsely optimistic economic forecasts for developing countries, he wrote:

> To make its (the IMF's) programs *seem* to work, to make the numbers "add up," economic forecasts have to be adjusted. Many users of these numbers do not realize that they are not like ordinary forecasts; in these instances GDP forecasts are not based on a sophisticated statistical model, or even on the best estimates of those who know the economy well, but are merely the numbers that have been *negotiated* as part of an IMF program.[15]

I laid the open book across one knee and watched a cluster of soldiers stroll past. Stiglitz sometimes referred to the "old dictatorships of national elites." His comments got me to thinking that the Chinese occupation of Tibet was a whole lot more honest than the usurpation of power by what Stiglitz defined as the "new dictatorships of international finance." The Chinese, like the Romans, Spanish, and British before them, had openly conquered Tibet. Nothing subtle about it. Traditional empires might frame their actions in noble terms—advancing civilization, stimulating economic growth, lighting the way for progress—but there was no question that they were colonizers intent on colonizing. The corporatocracy, on the other hand, by using tools like the IMF and the World Bank, backed up by the CIA and jackals when necessary, was practicing a new form of conquest, imperialism-through-subterfuge. When you conquered with armies, everyone knew you were conquering. When you conquered with EHMs, you could do it secretly. This raised a question I was beginning to ask myself frequently about the toll such a concealment took on a democracy that presupposes an informed electorate. If voters were ignorant of their leaders' most important tools, could a nation claim to be a democracy?

14

The Quiet Giant

On June 22, 2004, we flew out of Tibet, heading toward our next stop, Nepal. I had to admit to a sense of relief. In an odd sort of way, I felt that I was leaving one of those funny mirrors that make you look very fat or very skinny. Chinese Tibet was a distorted image of so much of the world where I had served as an EHM—distorted, but nevertheless a reflection.

It was a crystal clear day. The pilot banked so close to Mount Everest that I spied a funnel of snow swirling, like a white twister, between two massive glacial ridges. It struck me as a fitting symbol for our destination. The world's only Hindu kingdom, a country dwarfed by two giants, India and China—both of which coveted Nepal's water and its hydroelectric potentials—this was a land spinning in turmoil. Maoist rebels launched a campaign to establish a "People's Republic of Nepal" in 1996. The king responded by declaring war on the Communists. Crown Prince Dipendra shot and killed his father, King Birendra, and other members of the royal family in June 2001. Although he also shot himself, rumors abounded that he was a Chinese agent. Civil strife erupted and the new king, Gyanendra, declared martial law, dissolved the government, and deployed the military in another round of attacks against the Maoists. By the time we arrived, an estimated 10,000 people had died in the war and 100,000 to 150,000 had been made homeless.

For our group, this would be a short visit, a sort of transition back into the developed world. As our bus rushed through the streets of Kathmandu, Sheena announced that she was gifting us this last night with reservations at the Dwarika's Hotel, a luxurious, top-of-the-line, world-class hotel. The bus exploded with cheers.

Dwarika's did not disappoint. Straight out of Kipling, it was elegant and picturesque; it was also a relic of colonial empires that reminded me of places where I had stayed during my EHM days.

Most of our group embarked on a final shopping trip to a nearby market our guides considered safe. I remained at the hotel. I needed time to make this transition and to reflect on the experiences of Tibet. I sat in my room and typed out a few notes. Then I went downstairs and wandered through the lush gardens. They had an uncanny resemblance to the ones in the Hotel Intercontinental Indonesia. I could not help reminiscing about the geisha I had mistaken for an oil executive's wife. I sat down on a wrought-iron settee and recalled that night when, disconsolate at her absence, I walked across the Jakarta footbridge and ended up in a restaurant with those two women. They said something that impressed me profoundly. It had stuck with me all these years:

> This is the biggest resource grab in history. The stakes are huge. Should we be surprised that men are willing to risk everything to control it? They'll cheat and steal. Build ships and missiles, and send thousands—hundreds of thousands—of young soldiers to die for oil.

Here we were, a quarter of a century later, the Vietnam War was long over, and we now were fighting a new one in Iraq. Men and women were dying for the same reason—the biggest resource grab in history. The Emperor—the corporatocracy—was richer than ever. And most Americans had no clue.

Asia, it seemed to me, was emblematic of this new approach to empire building. The old methods had not brought the expected outcomes in Vietnam, but the new methods had worked in Indonesia and so many other countries. Yet even when policies appeared to fail, business leaders were rewarded handsomely; the Asian "IMF crisis" caused destitution and death, but in the end the corporatocracy emerged victorious, controlling the Indonesian government and most of the others that had been burned by IMF and World Bank policies. Although Vietnam was a military failure, American corporations profited from weapons sales, expanded markets, and labor pools; they surfaced with innovative models for sweatshop production and outsourcing. The corporatocracy even found ways to take advantage of natural disasters.

My thoughts kept returning to China, the quiet giant lurking in the background. Tibet highlighted the fact that although China had employed the military approach, it had also observed the new techniques of empire building closely; its EHMs and jackals had learned from our mistakes.

Historically, China has eschewed the route taken by classical colonial powers. It has not sent its armies to distant countries, but has focused instead on regions it considered as part of its territory, including Tibet and Taiwan. In this regard, China is imitating the United States.

When Thomas Jefferson commissioned Lewis and Clark to explore the lands west of the Mississippi, he sent a message that the entire continent was subject to our jurisdiction—our equivalent of Tibet and Taiwan. The Louisiana Purchase, annexation of Texas, and acquisition of Alaska were justified in this context. The idea of Manifest Destiny was later interpreted as reaching beyond North America. It was applied to islands in the Caribbean and Pacific and also as an excuse for invading Mexico, Cuba, and Panama and then later for interfering in the politics of other Latin American nations. Washington tried to avoid overt actions that were outright violations of the founders' principles; nevertheless, one administration after another bought into the secret methods of empire building; each learned from the successes and mistakes of its predecessors. Now, it seemed, China was outsmarting Washington.

Long after I returned from that trip to Tibet and Nepal, I discovered that I was not alone in making this comparison. On September 18, 2006, the day before an important World Bank meeting in Singapore,

The New York Times published an article that carried the headline "China Competes with West in Aid to Its Neighbors." *Times* reporter Jane Perlez asserted that China, which is one of the World Bank's biggest customers, "is quietly shaking up the aid business in Asia, competing with the bank at its own game." Using Cambodia, Laos, Myanmar, and the Philippines as examples, the article stated that "China's loans are often more attractive than the complicated loans from the West." Perlez listed a number of reasons for this, including the fact that Beijing does not attach environmental and social standards or penalties for corruption as conditions to its loans. Significantly, the article zeroed in on the policy that more than any other has allowed EHMs to take jurisdiction over so many countries; Chinese requirements, Ms. Perlez observed, "rarely include the extra freight of expensive consultants, provisions that are common to World Bank projects."[16]

Of the four regions discussed in this book, Asia's challenges seem less threatening—and more manageable—to most Americans. Our psyches are ingrained with images from the Korean and Vietnam Wars; while these did not result in military victories, they ended in ways that allowed our lives to go on as usual, and they provided a tremendous impetus to the U.S. economy. Our respect for Japanese engineering and ingenuity encourages us to purchase cars, TVs, and computers from them. Our stores overflow with merchandise produced in many Asian nations. When we dial an 800 number we are likely to talk with someone in Asia. Even the military threats—primarily from China and North Korea—seem old-fashioned in a manner that is oddly comforting because it recalls the Cold War, which we won. We may fear atomic weapons but, unlike suicide bombers, we have dealt successfully with nuclear pressures for more than half a century. Perhaps most important of all, Asians have accepted our capitalistic model, one that advocates top-down control, collusion between big business and government, rampant materialism, and the belief that nature's abundance exists to be exploited by the relatively few.

Latin America is different. Just when we thought we had tamed it, ridding ourselves of the Allendes, the Noriegas, and the Sandinistas, when we anticipated the end of Castro, we discover that a quiet revolution is sweeping the region. And it is aimed at us. The Latins are defying the American Empire. In the process, they are exposing our secret history.

As I pondered the lessons offered by these two regions—Asia and Latin America—I was haunted by the words of the old Tibetan man I met beside the glacier; in describing the invaders of his land as "nomad killers" he had echoed a Guatemalan industrialist. These two people lived on opposite sides of the globe; one was impoverished, the other wealthy; one exploited and the other the exploiter, and yet they understood something vital about the world their children were inheriting. The Guatemalan had bragged that the bodyguards who protected him—and me—were "Maya killers."

Part 2: Latin America

15

Hired Guns in Guatemala

The elevator door opened. Three men stood inside. Unlike Pepe and me, they were not wearing business suits. They were dressed casually in slacks and sweaters. One wore a leather jacket. What got my attention, though, were the guns. All three carried AK-47s.

"An unfortunate necessity in Guatemala these days," Pepe explained. He ushered me toward the waiting elevator. "At least for those of us who are friends of the United States, friends of democracy. We need our Maya killers."

I had flown from Miami to Guatemala City the day before and checked into the city's most luxurious hotel. It was one of those few occasions when Stone and Webster Engineering Corporation (SWEC) asked me to do something for them, other than refraining from writing about EHM. Pepe Jaramillo (not his real name) had signed a contract with SWEC agreeing to help the company develop privately owned power plants in his country. He was one of the most powerful members of a small group of rich elites who have controlled the country since the time of the Spanish conquest. Pepe's family owned industrial parks, office buildings, housing complexes, and huge agricultural estates that exported to the United States. The important thing from SWEC's perspective was that he had the political clout necessary to get things done in Guatemala.

I had first visited Guatemala as an EHM in the mid-1970s. My job was to convince the government to accept a loan for improving its electric sector. Then, in the late 1980s, I was invited to join the board of directors of a nonprofit organization that helped Mayan communities organize microcredit banks and other grassroots endeavors aimed at pulling themselves out of poverty. Over the years, I had become very familiar with the tragic violence that had torn this country apart during the latter half of the twentieth century.

Guatemala had been the heart of the Mayan civilization that flourished for roughly a thousand years. That civilization already had entered a period of collapse that many anthropologists attribute to its failure to cope with the environmental damage caused by the growth of its spectacular urban centers, when the conquistadors invaded in 1524. Soon Guatemala became the seat of the Spanish military authority in Central America, a position that lasted until the nineteenth century and resulted in frequent clashes between Mayan and Spanish populations.

By the end of the 1800s, a Boston-based company, United Fruit, had beaten the Spanish at their own game and established itself as one of the most powerful forces in Central America. It ruled supreme and essentially unchallenged until the early 1950s when Jacobo Arbenz ran for president on a platform that echoed the ideals of the American Revolution. He declared that Guatemalans ought to benefit from the resources offered by their land; foreign corporations would no longer be permitted to exploit the country and her people. His election was hailed as a model of the democratic process throughout the hemisphere. At the time, less than 3 percent of Guatemalans owned 70 percent of the land. As president, Arbenz implemented a comprehensive land reform program that posed a direct threat to United Fruit's Guatemalan operations. The company feared that if Arbenz succeeded he would set an example others might follow throughout the hemisphere, and perhaps the world.

United Fruit launched a major public relations campaign in the United States; it convinced the American public and Congress that Arbenz had turned Guatemala into a Soviet satellite and that his land reform program was a Russian plot to destroy capitalism in Latin America. In 1954, the CIA orchestrated a coup. American planes bombed the capital city; the democratically elected president was overthrown and replaced by a brutal right-wing military dictator, Col. Carlos Castillo Armas.

The new government immediately reversed the land reform process, abolished taxes paid by the company, eliminated the secret ballot, and jailed thousands of Castillo's critics. A civil war erupted in 1960, pitting the antigovernment guerrilla group known as the Guatemalan National Revolutionary Union against the United States–supported army and right-wing death squads. The violence intensified throughout the 1980s, resulting in the slaughter of hundreds of thousands of civilians, mostly Mayas. Many more were jailed and tortured.

In 1990 the army massacred civilians in the town of Santiago Atitlán, located near the high-altitude Lake Atitlán, renowned as one of the most beautiful spots in Central America. Although just one of many massacres, this one made international headlines because it happened in a place popular among foreign tourists. According to eyewitness reports, it began when a group of Mayas marched to the gates of the military base. One of their neighbors had been abducted by the army and, fearing that he would join the ranks of the thousands officially classified as "disappeared," they demanded his release. The army opened fire on the crowd. Although exact numbers are disputed, dozens of men, women, and children were seriously wounded and killed.

My trip to visit Pepe Jaramillo came shortly afterward, in 1992. He wanted SWEC to partner with him and obtain World Bank financing. I knew that the Mayas believe the earth is a living spirit and that places where steam gushes from the land are considered sacred. I suspected that any attempts to construct a power plant over geothermal springs would result in violence. Based on the United Fruit experience—as well as more recent ones I was intimately familiar with in Iran, Chile, Indonesia, Ecuador, Panama, Nigeria, and Iraq—I believed that if a U.S. company like SWEC called for help in a place like Guatemala, the CIA would show up.

The violence would escalate. The Pentagon might send in the marines. I already had enough blood on my conscience; I was determined to do everything I could to prevent more mayhem.

A car had picked me up at my hotel that morning and driven me into the circular driveway of one of Guatemala City's more impressive modern buildings. Two armed doormen ushered me in. One escorted me on the elevator to the top floor. He explained that the building was owned by Pepe's family and all eleven floors were occupied by them: their commercial bank on the ground floor, offices for various businesses on two to eight, and family residences on nine, ten, and eleven. Pepe met me at the elevator door. After coffee and a brief introductory conversation, he gave me a quick tour of his building, except for floor nine, which he said was reserved for the privacy of his widowed mother (I suspected additional reasons). If the intent of the tour was to impress SWEC's representative, it succeeded. Following a meeting with him and several of his engineers on floor five to familiarize me with the geothermal project, we lunched with his mother, brother, and sister on eleven, then headed for the elevator and a visit to the proposed site. We boarded the elevator with the AK-47–bearing men.

The elevator door closed. The man in the leather jacket pushed the bottom button. No one spoke as the elevator descended. I kept thinking about the AK-47s. I realized they were there to protect Pepe and me from the Mayas, the very people I worked with through the nonprofit. I wondered what my Mayan friends would think of me now.

The elevator stopped. When the door opened, I expected to see the afternoon light through the portico where I had entered earlier. Instead, I saw an immense concrete garage. It was well lighted in the extreme and smelled of damp concrete.

Pepe's hand gripped my shoulder. "Stay here," he commanded in a soft voice.

16

Obsessed with Anger

Two of the guards stepped in front of Pepe and me, blocking the doorway, AK-47s aimed into the cavernous garage. The third, the leather-jacketed one, dropped to a crouch and moved out, his head and weapon swinging from side to side, scanning the area before him. Our two guards also stepped outside, each taking up a position next to the open elevator door.

I now had an unobstructed view of the garage. I was surprised to see that there were only six cars. All were U.S. made, Chevys and Fords. Five were black station wagons. The sixth was a red pickup truck. They were, in every way, nondescript.

Leather Jacket flashed a light inside each car and then under it. When he finished he once again scanned the entire garage. Apparently satisfied, he opened the door of one of the wagons, got in, and started the engine. Then he slowly drove it up to where we waited.

One of our two guards opened the wagon's back door. They both climbed in and moved to the third seat, which faced backward. Leather Jacket jumped out, AK-47 at his side. Pepe followed me into the second seat. Leather Jacket closed our door. He blew on a shrill whistle and then resumed his position behind the wheel.

The wagon ascended a steep incline. As it approached the top, a metal door rose up, exposing us to sunshine. Three men toting AK-47s stood at attention outside. They saluted as we drove past. The wagon stopped. One of the three opened the front door opposite the driver, Leather Jacket, and climbed in. He spoke into a walkie talkie. Moments later, two sedans, one white, the other silver, pulled up to the curb in front of us. Tinted windows made it impossible to see inside. The man next to our driver waved. The white car headed out into the street. We followed it and the silver one fell in behind us.

Pepe patted my knee and broke the silence. "Awful, isn't it, to have to live this way?"

"Unbelievable. But your guys seem to know their business."

"They're the best money can buy, all trained at your School of the Americas." He frowned. "Just last week, a car carrying my sister was attacked by a bunch of Mayans. Thank God our vehicles have bulletproof glass. That and the guards saved her life."

"Was anyone hurt?" I asked.

He shrugged. "The guards say they wounded two of the bastards, but their friends carried them off. Our men are smart enough not to chase them. That happened to a business associate of mine. His guards chased the attackers—and ran right into a trap. One was killed and one wounded." He looked through his window at the wide boulevard we were traveling along. "Used to be a nice city," he mused. "Most of the violence happened in the countryside." He turned to me. "Not anymore. These damn Mayans have gone berserk." He stared back at the world outside his car, then looked at me again and chuckled. "If you're a guy like me, who do you fear the most?"

"What do you mean?"

"Who's got the best chance of killing you?"

I remembered Panama's Torrijos and the rumors that one of his security officers had handed him a tape recorder booby-trapped with explosives just before he boarded that fateful flight on his Twin Otter. "Your guards."

"Of course." He relaxed back into his seat. "You got to find the best and pay them very well. We have a large security force. Before anyone makes it to our private household, like these guys . . ." He motioned at the cars in front of and behind us. "They spend years in that force—at one of our factories, banks, or haciendas. They don't get near me or my family until they've proven themselves."

"How do they do that?"

"Prove themselves?" He nodded and smiled. "They have to put their life on the line, shoot it out in a firefight, demonstrate they got the balls and the loyalty."

For me, his words brought to mind what had happened in Iraq that triggered the U.S. invasion a year earlier, in 1991. When I mentioned this, Pepe nodded. "Tell me more."

"Our jackals tried to take out Saddam, but his security forces were too good, loyal. Besides he had all those look-alike doubles. Imagine if you're one of his guards and you're tempted to accept a bribe. You know that if you shoot a double, you and your family will die horrible, slow deaths. That's why Bush sent in the army."

"That's a good one," he chortled. "I'll have to get the word out that we can arrange for slow deaths—in case any of my boys are ever tempted."

We left the city and headed toward a majestic volcano. The sky was a bright azure. It was only then that I realized that the capital had been enveloped in a mist of smog. Beyond the city, the day was brilliant. We passed a small lake and the car turned onto a dirt road. Pepe explained that all the trees had been cut by campesinos who burned them for their cooking fires and to heat their homes. The hillsides were scarred with gullies caused by the resulting erosion.

"You would think," he said, "they might have learned their lesson. Their ancestors destroyed themselves by cutting the forests and building pyramids. Now they do this. Stupid, hopeless people."

I was tempted to point out that the urban pollution was much more destructive in the long run, that the factories and cars he and I depended on were the worst culprits, and that it was our policies that forced the campesinos to burn their trees. But I figured that he would just write me off as an "Indian lover," a radical ecologist, and therefore someone who could not be trusted. I stared out the window.

The barren landscape reminded me of the time I had come to this country to talk with a Mayan shaman. The nonprofit organization had sent me to ask the shaman to perform opening ceremonies at an upcoming board meeting. I was accompanied by Lynne Twist, a fund-raiser (and author of *The Soul of Money*). We encountered a great deal of resistance as we tried to arrange meetings; it became painfully obvious that the persecution suffered by the Mayas at the hands of the government—which was supported by Washington—was blocking our efforts.

Finally, Lynne and I found ourselves in the small adobe house where a famous shaman lived. He was wearing blue jeans and a traditional embroidered shirt; a red bandana was wrapped around his head. His home carried the aroma of wood fires and herbs. It was high up in mountains that, like the ones we were passing, had been ravaged by erosion. He listened quietly while I outlined our desire to involve him in our meeting, to enlist his help so we could work more closely with his people. I spoke in Spanish to a translator who repeated my words in the local Mayan dialect.

When I finished, the shaman launched into an angry speech. He gestured passionately and shouted. "Why should I help you?" he demanded. "Your people murdered mine for five hundred years. Not just the Spanish during colonial times. Your government has sent secret agents and uniformed troops here throughout my lifetime, including right now. You attacked my capital city and overthrew Arbenz, the one president who tried to help us. You train Guatemalan soldiers to torture Mayas. Now you ask me to help you?"

"These Mayans," Pepe said, as though he had read my thoughts, "are obsessed with anger. They blame the rest of us for all their troubles. We give them work, they complain that we enslave them. When we don't hire them—my family imported Haitians who work for pennies—they riot and try to murder us. And it isn't just here. Similar things are happening throughout the hemisphere. In the Andes, the Amazon, Mexico, Brazil, Ecuador, Peru, Venezuela, Bolivia, Colombia. Name any country south of the Rio Grande. You gringos don't get it because you killed off all your Indians. We should've followed your example." He tapped my knee for emphasis. "Mark my words, the challenge of the next few decades will be to keep the indigenous people —the Indians—down. You can talk all you want about democracy, but these countries are going to need strong leaders to hold those Indians in their places. The Mayans don't care a damn about democracy. Nor do the Quechua. Or any of the others. Given the opportunity, they'd slaughter every one of us."

I did not tell him about my experience with the Mayan shaman who in the end agreed to work with us. The breakthrough came when I told him that the only reason I could think of for him to help us was so that together we could build a bridge between his people and mine. "Many of us in the United States," I said, "share your disgust for the ways our government treats your people. We want to change." I opened a bag containing Incan stones presented to me by Quechua shamans from Ecuador. "We're trying to do similar things in other parts of Latin America." After that, to my surprise, he switched to Spanish, which he spoke fluently.

By the time Pepe's caravan arrived at the geothermal site, I suppose I had already decided what I would recommend to SWEC. This project was not just about using World Bank funds to enrich the wealthy and leave the poor in deeper debt; it would also rob the Mayas of their sacred rights. When the three vehicles pulled to a stop, Pepe once again kept me inside while his men—totaling twelve now—searched the area. Outside, great clouds of steam bellowed from the earth.

As Pepe and I strolled around, he recited engineering statistics about pounds of pressure, kilowatts, and construction costs. We stood at the edge of a pool of bubbling water, inhaling sulfur fumes; he pointed through the steam down the hill to a valley and described the spa-resort his sister envisioned there.

I felt compelled to state the obvious. "The Mayans will certainly fight you tooth and nail."

"Aha," he said. "You're wrong there. They may be stupid, but they know me and my family . . ." His voice drifted off. He grinned. "I'm certain we can come to terms with them. And it won't cost much; just a pittance really. That's all they need. It's the reason you must have partners like my family. Bring in a gringo negotiating team, the party's over. We, on the other hand, can handle them." His eyes met mine. "I think you know what I mean."

I nodded and turned away. Of course I understood, and it infuriated me. I walked to the other side of the pool. I picked up a small stone. Throwing it into the bubbling water, I sent with it my respects to the Mayan spirits or whatever force it was that created such an amazing phenomenon.

Our return trip was so delayed by rush hour traffic that I missed my flight. It did not phase Pepe; he called his pilots. They picked me up at his building and drove me to his private jet. It seemed terribly ironic that two pilots and thousands of dollars of jet fuel would fly me all the way to Miami so I could squelch Pepe's project. At first I felt guilty accepting his plane, then exonerated; I figured the Mayan shaman and the geothermal spirits would be amused—and grateful.

––––––

One statement Pepe made haunted me for years: "Mark my words, the challenge of the next few decades will be to keep the indigenous people—the Indians—down." Those words took on new relevance as we approached and entered the third millennium.

Beginning in 1998, seven countries in South America, over 300 million of the continent's 370 million population, had voted for presidents who campaigned against foreign exploitation. Despite the proclamations by our press and politicians, the votes were not for communism, anarchy, or terrorism. They were for self-determination. Through the democratic, electoral process, our neighbors sent us a strong message: They do not seek our altruism; they simply want our corporations to stop abusing them and their lands.

Latin Americans are following in the footsteps of Paine, Jefferson, Washington, and all the courageous men, women, and children who stood up to the British empire in the 1770s. It is a fascinating twist of history that, marching at the forefront of today's revolution against empire, are the indigenous people. While our Founding Fathers based their new government on Iroquois principles and our Continental Army used Indians as scouts and soldiers, in the end our nation rewarded them with exclusion and genocide. For many South American countries they are the vanguard. A new generation of heroes is emerging. Although born of pre-Columbian cultures, these leaders view their constituency as the poor and disenfranchised, regardless of race, heritage, and religion or whether they live in crowded slums or on remote subsistence farms.

Nowhere is this more evident than in Bolivia.

As I followed the Bolivian presidential elections in 2005, I wondered what Pepe was feeling. How did he react when an indigenous farmer from the humblest of backgrounds—an Aymara Indian—won with an overwhelming mandate? Evo Morales's victory was the materialization of Pepe's nightmare. Watching TV coverage of the postelection celebrations, I was transported back to the time when I was offered one of the most powerful jobs in that country. The way it happened is illustrative of the corporatocracy's attitudes and actions.

17

Recruited as President of Bolivia Power

"Bolivia is emblematic of a land exploited by empires." Those words, uttered by a teacher at my Peace Corps training camp in Escondido, California, in 1968, stuck with me. The teacher had lived in Bolivia; he continually impressed upon us the toll that centuries of oppression had taken.

After I completed training, while serving as a volunteer in Ecuador, I often thought about Bolivia. I was fascinated by this landlocked country that on a map looks like the hole in a donut comprised of Peru, Chile, Argentina, Paraguay, and Brazil. During my Peace Corps tour, I visited all but one of Bolivia's neighbors, avoiding Paraguay as a personal protest against its ruler, Gen. Alfredo Stroessner, and his policy of sheltering Nazi SS officers. I also studiously skirted Bolivia because young North Americans we referred to as "on the Gringo Trail" who sometimes stayed with me described it as more brutal toward its Indians than Ecuador.

At that time it seemed impossible that any place could surpass Ecuador in this category. The indigenous people were considered by the country's wealthy elites as subhuman. Like African Americans in the United States a few decades earlier, they lacked civil rights. Rumors abounded about a "sport" played by rich young men. They would catch an Indian doing something illegal—like picking hacienda corn so his starving family could survive—order him to run, and then shoot him down. Oil company mercenaries in the Amazon carried out similar executions, although they justified them as fighting terrorists, not sport. Yet despite the oppression in Ecuador, Bolivia was apparently worse.

This point was brought home by the fact that Che Guevara, the

Argentine physician who decided to fight oppression, selected Bolivia as his battlefront. The ruling class solicited Washington's aid. Che was relegated to a classification worse than subhuman or terrorist; because he was supported by Cuba, he was categorized as a communist fanatic. Washington sent one of its most skilled jackals to hunt him down. CIA agent Felix Rodriguez captured Che in the jungle near La Higuera, Bolivia, in October 1967. After hours of interrogation, Rodriguez, under pressure from the Bolivians, ordered the Bolivian army to execute Che.[17] After that, the fist of the corporatocracy tightened around Bolivia. The donut squeezed the hole.

Before finally traveling to Bolivia as an EHM in the mid-1970s, I did my research. I discovered that repression there far exceeded anything I had expected, that my Peace Corps teacher and those gringo pilgrims had barely scratched the surface. The country had been plagued by violence since the beginnings of recorded history, the victim of one empire or ruthless despot after another.

Bolivia's indigenous cultures were conquered by the Incas in the thirteenth century. Spanish conquistadors arrived in the 1530s, subjugated the Incas, slaughtering thousands in cold blood, and ruled with an iron fist until 1825. In a series of wars throughout the 1879–1935 period, Bolivia lost its Pacific coast to Chile, its oil-rich Chaco region to Paraguay, and its rubber-growing jungles to Brazil. During the 1950s, a reformist government under Victor Paz Estenssoro initiated programs to improve conditions for the Indian majority and nationalized the oppressive tin mines. The international business community was outraged; the Estenssoro administration was overthrown by a military junta in 1964. Not surprisingly, the CIA was implicated. Coups and countercoups plagued the nation into the seventies.

Even the geography is oppressive. The country is divided by two parallel and exceedingly rugged Andean mountain ranges into three distinct regions: the arid, inhospitable high-altitude plateau, known as the Altiplano; semitropical valleys in the west; and lowlands and vast rainforests in the east.

The majority of Bolivia's nine million inhabitants are Indians who traditionally coax a living from subsistence farms clinging to windswept Andean slopes. Reflecting this ethnic diversity, Bolivia has three official languages: Quechua, Aymara, and Spanish. Although endowed with abundant natural resources—silver, tin, zinc, oil, hydroelectric power, and the second largest natural gas reserves in South America (after Venezuela)—Bolivia is one of the hemisphere's poorest countries.

It was also one of the first to implement the IMF's package of Structural Adjustment Programs (SAPs). I have to take some of the responsibility for that.

By the time I arrived in Bolivia in the middle of the 1970s, fear inspired by Che's legacy had convinced a coalition formed between the economic elite and the military to brutalize the country's indigenous community. My job was to explore ways we EHMs might induce that coalition to integrate more extensively with the corporatocracy. During meetings with a broad spectrum of Bolivians, I formulated ideas that were similar to those that later gelled into the SAPs accepted by many countries in the 1980s and 1990s. Like Indonesia's Suharto, Bolivia's rulers were predisposed to adopting programs that sold their country's resources to foreigners. They had a long history of yielding to and prospering from foreign mining companies; they had incurred excessive debts; and, feeling vulnerable to neighboring countries, their traditional enemies, as well as to their own indigenous populations, they desired to secure Washington's promises of protection, and grow rich in the process. They would follow Suharto's example by investing their fortunes in the United States and Europe, thus insulating themselves against future economic crises in Bolivia.

At those initial meetings in the 1970s, I concluded that Bolivia was ripe for privatization. La Paz's businessmen and politicians were eager to expand the model initiated by the mining companies. Although this amounted to a sellout of their nation's sovereignty, it relieved them from the burden of raising funds through taxation, capital markets, and their own bank accounts to develop water, sewage, and electrical facilities, transportation and communications networks, and even educational and penal systems. With my help, they also understood that they would receive lucrative subcontracting jobs and their sons and daughters would be rewarded with all-expense-paid educations in the States, along with internships at our most prestigious engineering and construction companies. They enthusiastically approved tax incentives for foreign investors and agreed to drop trade barriers against U.S. imports, while accepting ones we imposed on Bolivian products. In essence, Bolivia's economic elite–military coalition seemed ready to buy into what constituted a new form of colonialism, so long as it was couched in IMF language, such as "good governance," "sound economics," and "structural adjustments."

After the government passed legislation to permit joint ventures, attract foreign capital, and remove restrictions on currency conversions, it did not take long to privatize Bolivia's five largest state-held companies. Furthermore, the government announced plans in 1990 to sell as many as 150 state-owned companies to foreign investors. And, in an interesting turn of fate—symbolic of the revolving door that propels so many U.S. government decision makers into lucrative corporate positions—I was offered the presidency of Bolivia's most powerful utility company.

In 1990, Leucadia National Corporation, a U.S. company, contacted me and asked if I would be interested in becoming president of their wholly owned subsidiary, Bolivia Power Company (Compañía Boliviana de Energía Eléctrica—COBEE in Spanish). Leucadia had earned a reputation for buying troubled companies and turning them into profit centers. (Leucadia would become famous in 2004 when it sought antitrust clearance to buy more than 50 percent of the stock in MCI Inc., the nation's number-two long-distance carrier.) Corporate representatives informed me that I appeared uniquely qualified to run COBEE. In addition to the fact that I had helped structure Bolivia's SAPs, I also: 1) was CEO of my own successful independent power company in the United States (a company I had created after leaving the EHM ranks that benefited greatly from favors owed me for my EHM work);[18] 2) spoke Spanish and was familiar with Latin American cultures; and 3) as a former EHM, was in an ideal position to secure World Bank and InterAmerican Development Bank loans needed to expand COBEE's system.

Following interviews on the East Coast, Leucadia flew my wife, Winifred, seven-year-old daughter, Jessica, and me to the Salt Lake City mansion where the company's CEO, Ian Cumming, and his wife spent much of their time. After introductory meetings with several executives, we joined the Cummings in their formal dinning room for a gourmet five-course meal served up by the family's chef and staff. Ian and I then retired to his office for a private conversation. At one point an aide interrupted us and apologetically explained that he had received a fax from La Paz, that the Spanish translator had left for a doctor's appointment, and he hoped I might be able to help. As I read the message aloud in English, I could not help suspecting that my language abilities were being tested.

Apparently I passed that and other tests. Soon after the Salt Lake City visit, Leucadia arranged for the three of us to travel to Bolivia.

18

Maximizing Profits in La Paz

We landed at El Alto, one of the highest commercial airports in the world, located on a plateau at nearly thirteen thousand feet above sea level. Exiting customs, we were met by COBEE's about-to-retire president and his wife. They and the rest of the company's top executives treated us like royalty during our stay. They escorted us to colorful local markets, museums, colonial churches, the exclusive Americanized school Jessica would attend, the elite country club that was eager to welcome us as members, and scenic natural points of interest in the mountains surrounding La Paz, including the bizarrely eroded sandstone formations at the Valley of the Moon. They guided us through power plants and substations, and along proposed transmission line rights-of-way.

One cold, rainy afternoon, a company executive announced that he would show us "the heart and soul of our operation." I expected a state-of-the-art engineering marvel. Instead his chauffeur drove us through the freezing drizzle to a commercial bank in the center of La Paz.

A ragged line of Indians stretched down the side of the bank building and around the block. They huddled together against the soaking rain, many holding open newspapers above their heads. They were dressed in traditional clothes, woolen pants, skirts, and ponchos. I lowered the car window a crack and was greeted by a blast of cold air and the smell of wet wool and unwashed bodies. Like remnants of the days when conquistadors had lined them up to work the tin mines, they were silent, simply standing there, staring and occasionally taking a step forward, toward the massive doors of the bank where a cluster of armed guards watched over them. Dozens of ragged children were scattered along the line; many of the women carried babies wrapped in shawls that hung, dripping water, from their shoulders. "They've come to pay their electric bills," the executive explained.

"How barbaric," Winifred muttered.

"On the contrary," the executive corrected. "These are the lucky ones. Unlike their rural kin, they're privileged, connected to the grid. They've got electricity."

As we drove back toward the office, the executive turned from his seat next to the chauffeur and explained that COBEE sent bags of money to the States through the U.S. embassy on a regular basis—money the Aymara and Quechua had stood in line to deliver. "This company's a cash cow for Leucadia," he added gleefully.

I would later learn that although their electric usage might be limited to a single lightbulb, once a month they made a pilgrimage to the bank; lacking checking accounts or credit cards, they stood patiently in line and paid in cash.

That night, back in the seclusion of our hotel room, Winifred asked why the embassy should serve as a courier service for a private corporation. I had no answer, except for the obvious—that U.S. diplomatic missions around the world exist primarily to benefit the corporatocracy. We also wondered why the executive had gone out of his way to show us that line. "He seemed so proud of it," Winifred said. "What a warped sense of finance."

The next morning we were briefed on the Zongo River project. It sounded to me like the true heart and soul of COBEE. Famous among Latin American power industry executives, it consists of a series of hydroelectric sites that begin near the top of the Andes and descend down a deep gorge into a tropical valley—a model of efficiency and good environmental stewardship. Several engineers assured us that seeing it firsthand was well worth the grueling trip. One shook his head sadly. "It'll never happen again," he moaned. "We all love Zongo because it's a beautiful example of how things can be done. But no modern lender, least of all the World Bank, invests money in such small, exquisitely engineered projects. If they had it to do over again, they'd insist we build a huge dam and flood the entire valley."

COBEE's president and his wife offered to take us to the Zongo River. They picked us up at our hotel before dawn one morning in their four-wheel-drive station wagon. We drove out of the city and headed up to the Altiplano. A thin blanket of snow covered this barren plateau that resembles an arid version of the Arctic tundra. Suddenly, morning arrived and we witnessed a spectacular sunrise along the massive Cordillera Real. Nicknamed "The Himalayas of the Americas," this Andean range includes twenty-two ice-clad peaks that are nineteen thousand feet or higher.

Several hours later, as we crossed a mountain pass at about seventeen thousand feet, Jessica had the opportunity to see her first glacier. Alpacas roamed in the pasture separating us from the mammoth ice sheet. We pulled to a stop. When Jessica raced across the road to get a closer look, her lips blackened from lack of oxygen. She sank to her knees and vomited violently. Winifred and I hustled her back into the station wagon and we hurried down to lower altitudes, arriving in mid-afternoon at the first of the hydroelectric sites.

A small dam across the glacier-melt Zongo River created a retaining pond. From there the water flowed along canals cut deep into the mountainside, through tunnels, into a metal penstock, and eventually to a powerhouse where electricity was produced. This process was repeated several times, a system that was ingeniously designed to maximize the energy-producing potential of the river while maintaining the integrity of the natural landscape. As we wound through the gorge, surrounded on all sides by perpendicular cliffs, a fully recovered Jessica made a comment that verbalized my sentiments. "I'm glad they didn't build a big dam and flood this whole valley," she said. "It's so lovely."

Eventually we pulled up to a quaint cottage we were told would be our private retreat if I became president. After settling in, Winifred, Jessica, and I hiked to a nearby waterfall. At eight thousand feet, we felt positively energized after the thin air of La Paz and the mountain pass. We scaled a cliff next to the waterfall. Through the lush foliage we watched the sun setting behind the mountains across the narrow valley. Then we climbed down and joined our hosts back at the cottage. The caretaker served baked lasagna that tasted as though it might have arrived by courier from Rome.

That evening, as Jessica slept, we four adults chatted over cocktails. It was obvious that COBEE's president and his wife had enjoyed their Bolivian tour. It was also apparent that they were now eager for me to assume his position so they could return home. They repeated selling points we had heard before: We would live in a mansion; travel through the streets of La Paz in our own chauffer-driven car; be protected by armed guards; be pampered by private chefs, maids, and gardeners; and enjoy a deep-pocket expense account for entertaining Bolivia's aristocracy. They pointed out that I would be the second most power-ful person in Bolivia, after the country's president; whenever there was a coup, I would be the most powerful since I would control the flow of electricity to both the presidential palace and the military bases. The CIA would look to me to support their favored party.

As we lay in bed, Winifred praised the hydroelectric project. "I've never seen anything to compare," she said, adding, "I wonder if you could use it as the starting point for a sort of utility revolution in Latin America. Get rid of that horrid line those Indians have to stand in to pay their bills, make electricity available at low prices to rural communities, develop more projects like the one we saw today, in-stead of using World Bank loans to build big power plants, and commit the company to environmental stewardship."

I listened carefully to what she said. The next day, as we drove back to La Paz, and during the remainder of our stay, I mulled over this idea. On several occasions, I discussed it with COBEE's execu-tives and engineers. Many of them came from Argentina, Chile, and Paraguay, countries with long histories of military dictatorships that served at the pleasure of the corporatocracy. I should not have been surprised by their skepticism. Their comments echoed those of a Peruvian engineer who had worked at COBEE for more than a decade. "Leucadia expects its sacks of dough," he observed flatly.

The more I thought about this, the angrier I grew. Latin America had become a symbol of U.S. domination. Guatemala under Arbenz, Brazil under Goulart, Bolivia under Estenssoro, Chile under Allende, Ecuador under Roldós, Panama under Torrijos, and every other country in the hemisphere that was blessed with resources that our corporations coveted, and that had enjoyed leaders who were determined to use national resources for the benefit of their own people, had gone the same route. Every one of them had seen those leaders thrown out in coups or assassinated and replaced by governments that were puppets of Washington. I had played their game for ten years as an EHM. Another decade had passed since I had left those ranks. Yet I was still haunted by guilt. And anger. I had vacillated, detoured away from the principles I had been raised to respect, in my eagerness to serve the corporatocracy and gratify my own appetites. My personal prostitution infuriated me, as did the suspicion that any efforts on my part now to change a company such as COBEE would likely be thwarted. Nevertheless, I made a commitment to try.

When we returned to the United States, I called the Leucadia executive in charge of recruiting me. I informed him that I would consider accepting the job only if they allowed me to turn COBEE into a model for social and environmental responsibility. I explained that I was deeply impressed by the Zongo River hydroelectric project and that the company was uniquely positioned to be an agent of change, given that it had the opportunity to provide electricity to some of the poorest populations in the hemisphere.

There was a long pause. He informed me that he would check with Ian Cumming. "However," he said, "don't expect much. Our executives answer to our stockholders; a president of COBEE will be expected to maximize profits." Another pause. "Do you want to reconsider?"

His words strengthened my resolve. "Absolutely not."

I never heard from them again.

19

Changing the Dream

The longer I thought about the exploitation of Bolivia by foreign organizations and the role I had played in it as an EHM, the angrier and more depressed I grew. I considered flying back to La Paz or to Colombia or to one of the other Spanish-speaking countries and joining a resistance movement. It struck me that it was what Tom Paine would have done. Then I realized that rather than use a gun he would have taken up a pen. I asked myself how I could be most effective.

The answer began to materialize during one of my trips with the nonprofit organization that worked in Guatemala. Talking with a Mayan elder, I decided that I needed to return to Ecuador's Shuar territory, where I had lived as a Peace Corps volunteer more than two decades earlier. I was, I see now, extremely confused, torn between old loyalties to my EHM colleagues, a guilty conscience, a desire to expose the wrong I had done, and an addiction to that vice that so pervades our society, materialism. Someplace in my subconscious lurked the idea that the Shuar could help straighten me out.

A friend and the publisher of my books on indigenous cultures, Ehud Sperling, and I took an American Airlines flight to Quito, Ecuador, and a smaller plane down the Andes to Cuenca. We spent a couple of nights in that colonial city high in the mountains where I had lived following my tour in the rainforest. Then we rented a jeep and driver, left very early in the morning, and wound our way along treacherous mountain roads toward the jungle town of Macas.

The trip was spectacular; descending from the top of the Andes through an endless series of switchbacks, it was the old potholed road I remembered from two decades earlier, sheer cliffs rising on one side and a deep gorge of cascading water on the other. A few rickety trucks coming up out of the jungle forced us to pull over precariously close either to the rock wall or the drop-off. Otherwise, we had the place to ourselves. It was truly another world, far removed from our lives in the States. I wondered how I had ever managed to make the transition from this to EHM. The simple answer was that back then, a very young and frustrated man who had grown up in rural New Hampshire, I had craved the excitement and money that the profession offered. Like a fish seduced by a shiny lure flashing through the water, I had snatched it.

Around noon our jeep drove into a small community where the road had previously ended; now it continued on, rougher and muddier, soaked by rains that swept up from the Amazon basin, toward the town of Macas. I began to tell Ehud how I had felt when I first visited Macas in 1969. It got us to talking about the role our country has played in world history.

The United States exemplified democracy and justice for about two hundred years. Our Declaration of Independence and Constitution inspired freedom movements on every continent. We led efforts to create global institutions that reflected our ideals. During the twentieth century, our leadership in movements promoting democracy and justice increased; we were instrumental in establishing the Permanent Court of International Justice in the Hague, the Covenant of the League of Nations, the Charter of the United Nations, the Universal Declaration of Human Rights, and many U.N. conventions.

Since the end of World War II, however, our position as leader has eroded, the model we presented to the world undermined by a corporatocracy hell-bent on empire building. While a Peace Corps volunteer, I was aware that Ecuadorian citizens, as well as those in neighboring nations, were outraged by our brutality and baffled by our overt contradictions in policy. We claimed to defend democracy in places like Vietnam; at the same time, we ousted and assassinated democratically elected presidents. High school students throughout Latin America understood that the United States had overthrown Chile's Allende, Iran's Mossadegh, Guatemala's Arbenz, Brazil's Goulart, and Iraq's Qasim—even if our own students were unaware of such things. Washington's policies transmitted a confusing message to the world. Our actions undercut our most hallowed ideals.

One way the corporatocracy exerted control was by empowering autocratic governments in Latin America during the 1970s. These governments experimented with economic policies that benefited U.S. investors and international corporations, and generally ended in failure for local economies—recessions, inflation, unemployment, and negative economic growth. Despite mounting opposition, Washington praised the corrupt leaders who were bankrupting their nations while amassing personal fortunes. To make matters worse, the United States supported right-wing dictators and their death squads in Guatemala, El Salvador, and Nicaragua.

A wave of democratic reforms swept the continent in the 1980s. Newly elected governments turned to the "experts" at the IMF and the World Bank for solutions to their problems. Persuaded to adopt SAPs, they implemented unpopular measures ranging from privatization of their utilities to cuts in social services. They accepted outrageously large loans that were used to develop infrastructure projects that all too often served only the upper classes while leaving the country burdened with debt.

The results were disastrous. Economic indicators tumbled to new depths. Millions of people once hailed as members of the middle class lost their jobs and joined the ranks of the impoverished. As citizens watched their pensions, health care, and educational institutions decline, they also noticed that their politicians were buying up Florida real estate rather than investing in local businesses. The communist movements of the 1950s and 1960s never took hold, except in Castro's Cuba; however, a new wave of resentment against the corporatocracy and its corrupt Latin collaborators swept the continent.

Then, less than a year before Ehud and I headed to Ecuador, the first Bush administration made a decision that had a lasting negative impact on United States–Latin American relations. The president ordered the armed forces to invade Panama. It was an unprovoked, unilateral attack to unseat a government, ostensibly because it refused to renege on the Panama Canal Treaty. The invasion killed more than two thousand innocent civilians and sent waves of fear across every country south of the Rio Grande. The fear soon turned to anger.[19]

I mulled these things over and discussed them with Ehud on that drive to Macas. I asked him if he thought there could be any alternative to the corruption that plagued the continent.

"Of course there is," he assured me. "Critical mass. That's all you need." He asked how I had journeyed to Macas in those days, given that the road had not gone that far.

"You could slosh through the jungle for weeks. Or you could take a 'stopwatch flight' on an old World War II Army-surplus DC-3. That flight seemed almost suicidal, but it's what I did."

"Stopwatch flight?"

"Those planes couldn't make it over the top of the Andes; they had to follow the river valleys. No radar. The pilot never knew when clouds would sock him in, so as soon as he left the ground, he clicked on a stopwatch. After thirty seconds he took a ten-degree turn to the right, after another forty-five seconds a fifteen-degree bank to the left . . . Pretty scary. Lost a lot of planes in those days. But it was better—and safer—than trekking through the jungle."

"So they built the road." He paused. "Why?" His arched eyebrows gave me the clue.

"Critical mass?"

"Exactly."

People had demanded change. When the clamoring reached a certain level, it happened. In this case, that change had been on the side of commercial development opening up the Amazon basin. I knew that the critical mass had been heavily influenced by oil companies. Entering Macas, I saw that the road had transformed a sleepy jungle outpost into a bustling boomtown. Yet I could speculate that as more and more of us become aware of the threats to our future, the critical mass may shift to projects that emphasize peace and sustainability.

We checked into a hotel that had a couple of items I had never seen before in this part of the world: a flush toilet and shower. The latter greatly amused Ehud because of the electrical outlet next to the faucet.

"For electric shavers," I assured him.

"To execute yourself," he replied.

The next morning we boarded a small plane. Ehud asked the pilot about the stopwatch. "My uncle used one." The pilot grinned. "But I got radar."

The plane deposited us on a mud runway deep in the forest. A cluster of Shuar men were assembled at the edge of the clearing. They looked pretty much as I remembered them—muscular, buff, laughing, happy people, except now they wore old T-shirts and Dacron shorts the missionaries insisted they use to combat the sin of nudity.

As they unloaded supplies that had arrived with us, an old man approached me. When I announced my interest in helping his people save their jungle from destruction he reminded me that my culture, not his, was causing the problems.

"The world is as you dream it," he told me. "Your people dreamed of huge factories, tall buildings, as many cars as there are raindrops in this river. Now you begin to see that your dream is a nightmare."

I asked what I could do to help.

"That's simple," he replied. "All you have to do is change the dream . . . You need only plant a different seed, teach your children to dream new dreams."

Over the next few days, we heard similar messages from other members of the community. Both Ehud and I were impressed with the wisdom of these people and their determination to protect their environment and culture. After I returned to the United States, I set in motion procedures for creating an organization dedicated to altering the way we in industrialized countries see the earth and our relationship to it. I did not realize it at the time, but I was endeavoring to reverse the process I had promoted as an EHM.

Eventually we named the nonprofit corporation Dream Change, in recognition of the message delivered to me that day in Shuar territory. Through it, we organized trips and workshops. We took people to live with indigenous teachers and we brought those teachers to the United States. We produced books, tapes, CDs, and films aimed at bridging the gaps between these two worlds. The Pachamama Alliance, another nonprofit, was formed as a result of one of our trips. It has raised millions of dollars to help indigenous communities, much of it used to finance legal battles against oil companies.

Thanks to my experience with COBEE, I had launched myself on a new career. Throughout the 1990s and into the early years of the new millennium, I traveled frequently to Latin America. I spent most of the time there with indigenous people in the Amazon and the Andes. I was deeply impressed by their commitment to environmental stewardship and a spirituality that surpassed anything I witnessed among the world's major religions. These people appeared determined to make the world a better place.

As a Pachamama Alliance board member I also met with lawyers, politicians, and oil company employees. It was over dinner with such a group one night in Quito that I first learned about Venezuela's Hugo Chávez. The oil company representatives despised this fiery military officer who founded the anticorporatocracy Fifth Republic Movement, but the politicians had to admire his charisma. My indigenous friends were encouraged that his ancestors were Indian and African as well as Spanish, that he continually lambasted the wealthy, and promised to help the poor to better lives.

20

Venezuela's Chávez

Chávez's rise to fame began in February 1992, when, as a lieutenant colonel in the Venezuelan army, he led a coup against Carlos Andrés Pérez. The president, whose name had become synonymous with corruption, angered Chávez and his followers because of his willingness to sell his country to the World Bank, the IMF, and foreign corporations. Largely as a result of Caracas's collaboration with the corporatocracy, Venezuelan per capita income had plummeted by more than 40 percent and what had previously been the largest middle class in Latin America sank into the ranks of the impoverished.

Chávez's coup failed, but it set the stage for his future political career. After he was captured, he was allowed to appear on national television to persuade his troops to cease hostilities. He defiantly declared to his nation that he had failed *"por ahora"*—for now. His courage catapulted him to national fame. He served two years in Yare prison; during that time, Pérez was impeached. Chávez emerged with a reputation for boldness, integrity, a commitment to helping the poor, and a determination to smash the shackles of foreign exploitation that had enslaved his country and his continent for so many centuries.

In 1998 Hugo Chávez was elected president of Venezuela with an impressive 56 percent of the vote. Once in office, he did not bow to corruption like so many before him. Instead he honored men like Guatemala's Arbenz, Chile's Allende, Panama's Torrijos, and Ecuador's Roldós. They had all been assassinated or overthrown by the CIA. Now, he said, he would follow in their footsteps, but with his own vision and charismatic personality, and the staying power endowed on the leader of a country overflowing with oil. His victory and his continued defiance of Washington and the oil companies inspired millions of Latin Americans.

Chávez kept his commitments to the poor—urban and rural. Instead of re-injecting profits into the oil industry, he invested them in projects aimed at combating illiteracy, malnutrition, diseases, and other social ills. Rather than declaring huge dividends for investors, he helped Argentina's embattled President Kirchner buy down that nation's IMF debts of more than $10 billion and he sold discounted oil to those who could not afford to pay the going price—including communities in the United States. He earmarked a portion of his oil revenues for Cuba so it could send medical doctors to impoverished areas around the continent. He forged laws that consolidated the rights of indigenous people—including language and land ownership rights—and fought for the establishment of Afro-Venezuelan curricula in public schools.

The corporatocracy saw Chávez as a grave threat. Not only did he defy oil and other international companies, but also he was turning into a leader others might try to emulate. From the Bush administration's perspective, two intransigent heads of state, Chávez and Hussein, had evolved into nightmares that needed to end. In Iraq, subtle efforts—both the EHMs' and the jackals'—had failed, and now preparations were underway for the ultimate solution: invasion. In Venezuela, the EHMs had been replaced by jackals, and Washington hoped that they could solve the problem.

Using tactics perfected in Iran, Chile, and Colombia, jackals sent thousands of people into the streets of Caracas on April 11, 2002, marching toward the headquarters of Venezuela's state-owned oil company and on to Miraflores, the presidential palace. There they met pro-Chávez demonstrators who accused their organizers of being pawns of the U.S. CIA. Then suddenly and unexpectedly, the armed forces announced that Chávez had resigned as president and was being held at a military base.

Washington celebrated, but the jubilation was short-lived. Soldiers loyal to Chávez called for a massive countercoup. Poor people poured into the streets, and on April 13, Chávez resumed his presidency.

Official Venezuelan investigations concluded that the coup was sponsored by the U.S. government. The White House practically admitted to culpability; the *Los Angeles Times* reported: "Bush Administration officials acknowledged Tuesday that they had discussed the removal of Venezuelan President Hugo Chávez for months with military and civilian leaders from Venezuela."[20]

Ironically, the 2003 invasion of Iraq was a boon to Chávez. It sent oil prices skyrocketing. Venezuela's coffers filled. Suddenly drilling for the heavy crude oils of the country's Orinoco region became feasible. Chávez announced that when the price of oil reached fifty dollars a barrel, Venezuela—with its abundance of heavy crude—surpassed the entire Middle East as the world's number-one repository of petroleum. His analysis, he said, was based on U.S. Department of Energy projections.

The rest of Latin America watched closely to see how the Bush administration would deal with Chávez after the failed coup attempt against him. What they witnessed was a cowed U.S. president. The White House realized that it had to tread carefully. Venezuela was our second-largest supplier of petroleum and petroleum products (fourth-largest supplier of crude). Its oil fields were much closer than those of the Middle East. Through its ownership of Citgo, Venezuela impacted many American workers, drivers, and a multitude of corporations that sell to or buy from Citgo. In addition, Caracas had been our ally in breaking the OPEC oil embargos of the 1970s. The Bush administration's options for military intervention were limited by the wars in Iraq and Afghanistan, the Israeli-Palestinian debacle, the growing unpopularity of the royal family in Saudi Arabia, political problems in Kuwait, and a militarized Iran.

Luiz Inácio "Lula" da Silva's 2002 landslide victory in Brazil further bolstered nationalistic movements. A founder of the progressive Workers' Party in 1980, Lula was a politician with a long history of advocating social reform, demanding that Brazil dedicate its natural resources to helping the poor, and insisting on audits for Brazilian debts to the IMF that he claimed were illegal. In winning the election with more than 60 percent of the vote, Lula joined Chávez as one of the continent's new wave of living legends. Word spread to the most remote villages at the top of the Andes and deep into the rainforests that those previously considered as disenfranchised were coming into power.

Latin Americans took heart. For the first time in recent history, they saw the opportunity to slip out from under the U.S. yoke of domination.

Two countries were especially influenced by the successes of Chávez and Lula. They too had large indigenous populations and they possessed oil and gas resources coveted by the corporatocracy. They were also countries where I had strong and very personal connections: Ecuador and Bolivia.

21

Ecuador: Betrayed by a President

In *Confessions of an Economic Hit Man* I described my relationship with Jaime Roldós Aguilera, the university professor and attorney who in 1979 became Ecuador's first democratically elected president after a long line of corporatocracy-supported dictators. As soon as he took office, Roldós set about honoring his campaign promises to rein in the oil companies and apply his country's natural resources to benefit its poor people. At that time I feared that if he did not comply with the wishes of the EHMs, he would be targeted by the jackals. My fears materialized. On May 24, 1981, Jaime Roldós died in an airplane crash. Latin newspapers plastered their front pages with stories under headlines like CIA ASSASSINATION!

Now, a decade later, it appeared that all the circumstances in the country were different but the politics had not changed. Following the trip with Ehud to the Shuar and the formation of Dream Change and the Pachamama Alliance, I became increasingly aware of the turmoil that in the 1990s brewed beneath the surface. The jackals had taken Roldós out, but the United States did nothing to address the real problem. The gap between rich and poor, environmental destruction, and neglect of education, health, and other social services were exacerbated when Ecuador rose to become the region's number-two petroleum exporter to the United States (after Venezuela). The Indian populations were most severely impacted. The government and oil companies tried to force them off their lands. If they refused to leave, all too often they had to watch as their trees were replaced with oil derricks and their rivers flooded with pollution.

The pressure took many forms. One of them was clearly elucidated on an afternoon when I was visiting the Amazon. Tunduam, a young Shuar man, informed me that he was considering leaving his community. "I'm good at languages," he explained. "The experts at the oil company said so. They'll send me to school to learn English and pay me a fortune to work for them." Then he frowned. "But I'm concerned. Tsentsak did the same thing. Now his name is Joel, not Tsentsak. They told him to write newspaper articles against you, Dream Change, Pachamama, and the others who try to help us fight the oil companies. They told him to claim he was an elected representative of the Shuar people and to sign papers giving our land to the company. When he tried to refuse they said they'd put him in prison."

"What did he do?"

"What could he do? He's writing those articles and signing those papers."

I asked Tunduam whether he wanted that to happen to him.

He shrugged. "I'd like to learn English and earn a lot of money." He swept his arms out toward the forests. "All this is disappearing. The missionaries tell us we must become more modern, we can't live as hunters any longer."

Such stories strengthened my resolve to help the Shuar and their neighbors, the Huaorani, Achuar, Kichwa, Shiwiar, and Zaparo. The dilemma of these people also fired my interest in the 2002 Ecuadorian presidential campaign. For the first time since Roldós, a candidate appeared to take indigenous issues to heart while at the same time seriously opposing Big Oil.

I was in Shell, a jungle town named after the oil company, waiting for a plane to fly me and a group of Dream Change people into Shuar territory on a day when Lucio Gutiérrez was scheduled to visit. By this time, the presidential candidate had forged a unique alliance that included Ecuador's armed forces and the most powerful indigenous organizations. The former supported him because he was one of them, a retired army colonel; the latter because he had refused to order his soldiers to attack indigenous demonstrators when they swarmed the presidential palace in 2000, forcing President Jamil Mahuad to abandon his office. The colonel instead set up army food kitchens to feed the protestors and then allowed them to take over the congress building. By disobeying his president, Gutiérrez had abetted the overthrow of a man hated by the poor because of his overt support of IMF and World Bank policies, including the highly unpopular dollarization of Ecuador's currency—an act with severe negative consequences for every Ecuadorian except those wealthy enough to have already invested in overseas bank accounts, Wall Street stocks, and foreign real estate.*

Shell seemed a fitting place for the presidential candidate to meet people from the jungle. The town had been hacked out of the forest decades earlier to create a staging ground for oil operations. The indigenous communities had resisted, sometimes violently. Quito, with the Pentagon's support, sent thousands of troops and established a huge military base that began in the center of Shell and stretched back into the forests. Its paved runways were a rarity in this part of the world. Its buildings housed some of the most sophisticated eavesdropping equipment on the planet. It was said that U.S. and Ecuadorian communications specialists sitting in an office near Shell's main street could listen to conversations held in every council lodge in the upper Amazon. Rumors abounded about missionary groups accepting millions of dollars from oil-funded foundations in exchange for planting hidden microphones in the food baskets and medical kits they so generously distributed. Every

---

* The conversion of Ecuador's sucre to the dollar was a political issue of vast proportions. It was not only a blow to national pride; it also meant that Ecuadorians who held dollar accounts made windfall profits practically overnight while the rest of the population saw any savings they might have accumulated plummet. When Mahuad took office in 1998, an Ecuadorian with 6,500 sucres could purchase one dollar; in 2000 the official rate was pegged at 25,000 sucres to a dollar, which meant that the man who owned a dollar's worth of sucres two years earlier now had only 26 cents, while the man wealthy enough to have dollar accounts in an overseas bank had increased his riches, relative to the local population, by nearly 400 percent. This was a permanent change as the sucre was demonetized and replaced by the dollar.

time a tribal council decided to send warriors to disrupt an oil camp, army units, helicoptered out of Shell, seemed to arrive there first.

On this day when Gutiérrez was scheduled to visit, people crowded the muddy streets hoping to shake the candidate's hand. Shuar shamans in traditional toucan-feathered crowns mingled with U.S. Green Berets, oil drillers, and Ecuadorian commandos. The atmosphere was festive, old animosities set aside. The cavalry and Indians had apparently made a pact to ride side by side to the rescue of a nation demoralized by years of corruption, inflation, and exploitation.

My visit to Shell came only a few months after September 11, 2001. That tragic event, combined with the failure of the Bush administration to discredit and overthrow Chávez, was having a major impact on the Ecuadorian presidential campaign. A cartoon in one of the newspapers illustrated local attitudes. Based on the Old West theme of two men facing off for a gun duel, the first box showed a cowboy-hatted Chávez, holster and gun low on his hip, patrolling a Dodge City street. The second contained a gun-toting George Bush stepping out to confront Chávez. The next depicted Chávez from the back standing up to a Bush whose face was set in fierce determination. Behind the U.S. president: the ghostly image of two flaming towers. In the last box, Chávez was doubled over with laughter as Bush ran away, his feet kicking up dust, his hat lying in the street; Gutiérrez leaned against the wall of a saloon clapping.

Although our plane arrived and we had to leave Shell before Gutiérrez made his appearance, that short visit helped me better understand why this election was so important to Ecuador's indigenous people. Like their brethren in Bolivia, Brazil, and Venezuela, they had suffered for centuries from foreign exploitation; they were now determined to end that pattern.

Gutiérrez was elected president of Ecuador in November 2002. The indigenous people expressed surprise that their man had actually won. They seemed to anticipate more difficult times. The BBC reported:

> The victory of former coup leader Lucio Gutiérrez . . . follows closely on that of Brazilian Workers' Party leader, Lula, and seems reminiscent of the election of Hugo Chávez in Venezuela.
>
> Each of these men won democratic elections on programmes based on calls for change, for new strands of economic thinking and an end to corruption . . .
>
> In the first round of voting last month, Mr. Gutiérrez surprised everyone by taking the lead, thanks to a massive vote for change . . .
>
> But in a country beset by huge debt problems, a poverty level around 60% and an unstable and unpredictable political system, the odds seem to be stacked heavily against him.[21]

The new president, during his first month in office, flew to Washington to meet President Bush. He welcomed World Bank officials to Quito and opened negotiations with the oil companies. Simultaneously, relations between the companies and indigenous organizations grew increasingly tense. In December 2002, CGC (an Argentine company) accused an Amazonian community of taking a team of its workers hostage and suggested that the jungle warriors had trained with al-Qaeda. A startling fact emerged: The oil company had not received government permission from the inhabitants to begin drilling and yet it claimed the right to trespass on indigenous lands; the warriors maintained that they had simply detained the oil team long enough to assure their safe passage out of the jungle.[22]

I traveled to Ecuador again in early 2003. When I arrived in Quito I discovered that many Ecuadorians were convinced that Gutiérrez was cutting secret deals with the oil companies and that he had agreed to adopt World Bank and IMF SAPs. Photos of him holding hands with President Bush were plastered around the city. Indigenous leaders, incensed over the suggestion that they had joined an Islamic terrorist organization, pointed out that if Gutiérrez forced them to fight oil company mercenaries, such a rumor might become self-fulfilling.

"In the old days," one told me, "people who felt threatened by the U.S. could turn to Russia for weapons and training. Now there is no one, except those Arabs."

The situation continued to deteriorate throughout 2004. Rumors about oil company profiteering and government corruption proliferated. Then the government introduced measures reminiscent of those adopted in Bolivia as a result of World Bank pressures. According to the Associated Press, Gutiérrez's "left-leaning constituency soon fell apart after he instituted austerity measures, including cuts in food subsidies and cooking fuel, to satisfy international lenders."[23]

When Ecuador's Supreme Court threatened to interfere with his policies, Gutiérrez ordered its reorganization, in effect dissolving it. Ecuadorians stormed the streets, demanding his ouster.

"Gutiérrez has to go," an indigenous leader, Joaquin Yamberla, told me. "He was democratically elected. He broke his promises to the people. Democracy demands we throw him out of office."

People kept asking me to identify the EHM who was corrupting Gutiérrez. They had no doubt that Ecuador's president was capitulating to a combination of threats and bribes. Although I could not offer a name, I suspected they were correct. As detailed later in this book, I was subsequently contacted by a jackal who seemed to claim to be that very man.

Bolivians, however, were experiencing something very different.

22

Bolivia: Bechtel and the Water Wars

Bolivia, like Ecuador and Venezuela, began the twenty-first century with protests against foreign corporations that plundered its resources. Demonstrations, boycotts, and strikes halted commercial activities along the streets of La Paz and many other cities. Although spearheaded by Aymara and Quechua leaders, the indigenous people did not stand alone; labor unions and civil organizations supported them.

Unlike Ecuador and Venezuela, the immediate cause of unrest was not oil; it was water. During the 1990s it had become increasingly apparent that water would soon be one of the most valuable resources on the planet. The corporatocracy understood that by controlling water supplies they could manipulate economies and governments.

The turmoil in Bolivia once again was detonated by the World Bank and the IMF. In 1999 the two organizations insisted that the Bolivian government sell the public water system of its third largest city, Cochabamba, to a subsidiary of engineering giant Bechtel, as part of a new round of SAPs. At the World Bank's insistence, Bolivia further agreed to pass the costs associated with providing water on to all consumers, regardless of their ability to pay—an act contrary to indigenous traditions, which hold that all people have an inherent right to water, regardless of their economic status.

When I heard that Bolivia had bought into this EHM ploy, I was racked with guilt; the Every-Person-Pay (EPP) policy was an approach to rate structuring I helped formulate in the mid-1970s. At that time the idea was applied mainly to electric tariffs and was considered innovative. It contradicted a basic premise of most rate plans advocated for helping impoverished regions since the 1930s, including those adopted by the Rural Electrification Administration (REA) in the United States: that providing services such as electricity, water, and sewer to everyone was essential to general economic growth, even if such services had to be subsidized. Following the REA example, implementing this theory had proven highly effective in numerous countries. Despite the successes, the World Bank decided to experiment with something radically different.

As chief economist of one of the firms hired to promote Bank policies in the 1970s, I was pressured to develop econometric models that would prove the validity of EPPs. Econometrics makes it easy to justify just about anything and I had a brilliant staff of economists, mathematicians, and financial experts; so technically it was not a problem. However, there were two issues that tore at me. The first was the obvious moral one. The second was pragmatic, a recognition that the old theory had demonstrated its efficacy time and again. So, I asked myself, why tinker with success, why risk increased poverty and social unrest, why advocate EPPs?

The answer was evident: the EPP approach would transform government-subsidized bureaucracies into profitable "cash cows" ripe for privatization (as I would later discover in Bolivia at COBEE). EPPs evolved out of the same mentality as infrastructure loans that benefited foreign construction companies and the local rich while leaving the poor with nothing, other than huge debts. On a trip to Argentina, I learned of another reason.

"These countries are our future security," Gen. Charles Noble told me as we rode together in a chauffeur-driven car through the streets of Buenos Aires in 1977. "Chuck" was a vice president at MAIN (who would later be promoted to president). A West Point graduate with a master's degree in engineering from MIT, he had a distinguished military career, having served as commanding general of the U.S. Army Engineer Command in Vietnam and president of the Mississippi River Commission. Now he was in charge of MAIN's water resource studies for Argentina, including those relating to the massive Salto Grande hydroelectric project the country was building in partnership with Uruguay, which would produce nearly two thousand megawatts, create a vast lake, and flood a town of twenty-two thousand inhabitants.

"We lost Vietnam because we didn't understand the communist mind. We gotta do a whole lot better here in Latin America." Chuck gave me his best smile, one that was shockingly gentle for a man with his reputation for toughness. "Don't ever let the socialists talk you into believing that offering a free lunch buys anything but disrespect. People have to pay for what they get. Only way they appreciate it. Besides, it teaches them capitalism, not communism. Look at that." He pointed at a pond in a park we were passing. "Water's the future gold and oil combined. We need to own as much of it as possible. That'll give us leverage, power."

More than two decades later, I thought about Chuck Noble when the announcement was made that a single company had been granted the exclusive right to purchase Cochabamba's water system, known as SEMAPA. A forty-year privatization lease was granted to Aguas del Tunari, a partnership led by a subsidiary of the infamous Bechtel Corporation. Awarding such a license-to-exploit to a U.S. company had to make the general very happy. But people in Latin America felt differently. The San Francisco–based firm had earned a reputation as an organization that managed to win favors from just about everyone in high places. It had a long history of securing lucrative contracts from the World Bank and the U.S. government. Because it was a private corporation, controlled by a single family, it did not have to open its books to the SEC or other watchdog organizations and adamantly refused to do so.

"If Bechtel wants the job, don't even bother to bid," I had been told during my EHM days on different occasions by government officials in Indonesia, Egypt, and Colombia. Not long after my trip to Argentina with Chuck Noble, an Ecuadorian contracting officer, a personal friend from my Peace Corps days, allowed me to take him out to dinner at the most expensive restaurant in Quito and then confided that he would save me thousands of times the price of that meal by advising me not to spend the next several months preparing proposals for a project he knew Bechtel was slated to get. He rubbed his thumb and forefinger together. "Everyone will grow rich," he said. "Me, the mayor, the president, the boys from San Francisco." He grimaced. "Except you—and the other poor suckers who think this is a competitive bidding process."

Bechtel's ex-officers and executives include such luminaries as George Shultz (Bechtel president and board member, Secretary of the Treasury under Nixon, and Secretary of State under Reagan), Caspar Weinberger (Bechtel vice president and general council, and Secretary of Defense under Reagan), Daniel Chao (executive vice president and managing director of Bechtel Enterprises Holdings, Inc. and member of the advisory committee for the Export-Import Bank of the United States), and Riley Bechtel (Bechtel CEO and member of George W. Bush's President's Export Council). Bechtel's management also included my father-in-law, who, before he retired, had been the company's chief architect and then was brought out of retirement to serve as project manager of a huge Bechtel job to build cities in Saudi Arabia. My wife had started her career at Bechtel. I knew the company well—from many angles.

Almost immediately after the lease for SEMAPA was granted to Bechtel, water rates skyrocketed. Some Cochabambans experienced an escalation in their bills of more than 300 percent. This was catastrophic for the city's inhabitants, who ranked among the continent's most impoverished people.

"They're faced with the choice between food and water," a Quechua organizer told me. "The gringos want more profits. Bolivians are dying of thirst. They're told they can't even collect rain water, that their contract with SEMAPA requires them to pay Bechtel for any and all water they consume."

The citizens of Cochabamba rebelled. Boycotts shut down the city for four straight days in January 2000. Mobs threatened to storm SEMAPA's offices. Bechtel demanded protection. Bolivian

President Hugo Banzer acquiesced and mobilized the army. In the violence that followed, dozens of Aymara and Quechua were wounded and a seventeen-year-old boy was shot to death.

Fearing a full-blown revolution, President Banzer finally imposed martial law. Then, after reportedly meeting with U.S. embassy officials, he announced that he would nullify the Bechtel contract. In April 2000 Bechtel abandoned its operations at SEMAPA.

The people of Cochabamba celebrated their victory. They shared cups of water in the streets. They offered toasts to their new Aymara and Quechua heroes and wrote songs proclaiming this triumph as the beginning of a new era. However, soon it was apparent that they also faced a dilemma. They found that there was no one left with adequate experience to run SEMAPA. Many of the former managers had retired, relocated, or accepted other jobs.

The community elected a new board of directors and established a set of governing principles that identified social justice as SEMAPA's guiding commitment. The water company's most important objectives would be to supply water to the poor, including those who had not previously been connected to the system; provide adequate compensation to its workers; and operate efficiently and without corruption.[24]

Meanwhile, Bolivia's government still had to deal with the corporatocracy. Bechtel was not about to give up its cash cow—and set a precedent that might encourage other countries to follow Bolivia's example—without a fight. In a classic case that demonstrates the corporatocracy's willingness to manipulate international law in order to achieve its goals, Bechtel enlisted one of its Dutch holding companies. Drawing on a 1992 Bilateral Investment Treaty (BIT) between the Netherlands and Bolivia (since none existed between the United States and Bolivia), the Dutch subsidiary filed a $50 million lawsuit against the Bolivian people, half for profits it claimed would be lost from its "expropriated investment" and half for damages.

This incredible story of corporate intrigue, greed, and insensitivity was largely ignored by the U.S. media. However, the Latin press covered it extensively. As I followed reports posted on their Web sites, I kept thinking about the people at COBEE. I recalled that most of the key executives and engineers at Bolivia's most powerful electric utility—the one that supplied power to both the presidential palace and military headquarters—were citizens of other countries (the United States, the United Kingdom, Argentina, Chile, Peru, and Paraguay). This dependency on foreign nationals was, I realized, a calculated strategy, virtually ensuring that the utility would never be nationalized.

I also discovered that Leucadia no longer owned COBEE. The electric company had been bought and sold several times since the early 1990s, always by foreign corporations. Leucadia and the others had reputations for merchandising companies at a profit. Cash cows were a good thing; but the quick, high-return sale was even better, especially since it kept local populations off balance.

From all the turmoil, a new leader emerged. Following a pattern that seemed to be turning into a trend, Evo Morales rose out of the indigenous community. An Aymara activist, he joined the Movimiento al Socialismo (MAS) party. His was a strong voice that opposed privatization and what euphemistically was referred to by corporatocracy supporters as "liberal" or "free market" economic reforms—policies that would prevent Bolivia from protecting its farmers and businesses while at the same time forcing it to accept protectionist barriers from the United States. He denounced the Washington-driven Free Trade Area of the Americas as a plan "to legalize the colonization of the Americas." His popularity grew and he was elected to Congress.

Almost immediately, the corporatocracy labeled him a terrorist. The U.S. State Department described him as an "illegal coca agitator."[25] Although Morales had been part of the *cocalero* movement—a coalition of coca leaf–growing campesinos who resisted U.S. efforts to eradicate coca farms—he pointed out that the plant was used by Andean people as a dietary supplement and medicine long before it was made into cocaine. A remedy for altitude sickness, muscle aches, hunger pangs, and other digestive disorders, coca tea had been drunk by many dignitaries, including Pope John Paul II and Britain's Princess Anne. Nevertheless, Morales was forced out of his congressional seat in 2002 on charges of terrorism. The Quechua and Aymara accused the CIA of masterminding his removal. Within months, his eviction was declared unconstitutional.

U.S. Ambassador Manuel Rocha warned, "I want to remind the Bolivian electorate that if you elect those who want Bolivia to become a major cocaine exporter again, this will endanger the future of U.S. assistance to Bolivia." Rather than deterring Bolivians, Rocha inflamed them. Morales declared that the ambassador's words had helped to "awaken the conscience of the people." MAS plastered posters onto walls around the country; above an enormous photo of Morales, huge letters asked: "Bolivians: You Decide: Whose in Charge? Rocha or the Voice of the People?"[26]

In the 2002 presidential elections, MAS finished only a couple points behind the leading party. Morales refused to endorse the new president, a millionaire raised in the United States, Gonzalo Sánchez de Lozada. Instead MAS opted to play the role of opposition. Like Chávez after his failed coup attempt, Morales's reputation was bolstered by what on the surface appeared to be a defeat.

President Sánchez buckled to IMF and World Bank demands. In 2002 he decreed a huge tax increase. As so often happens in such circumstances, those who could least afford to pay taxes ended up hardest hit. Amid ensuing riots, thirty people were killed. Road blocks and demonstrations brought the country to a standstill. Sánchez's plans to export natural gas at low prices to the United States and other countries instead of distributing it to needy Bolivians further inflamed indigenous communities. Bloody fighting resulted in another twenty deaths. Finally, Sánchez was forced to flee the country. He now lives outside Washington, D.C.; the United States has refused Bolivia's requests to have him returned for trial.

Bolivians had defied the World Bank and they had defeated

Bechtel, one of the most powerful organizations on the planet. Now one of their "original people," one of those who had been so brutally subjugated for generations, had risen phoenixlike from the ashes of his culture's ruins.

In a way, it seemed to me that the real message here was not just for Bolivians and Latins; it was also intended for Bechtel and the rest of the corporatocracy. It was a pro-democracy, pro-justice message that served to inspire the younger generations in Bolivia, the United States, and the world.

I often found myself thinking about Jessica's comment as we wound through the Zongo River gorge. "I'm glad they didn't build a big dam and flood this whole valley," she had said. "It's so beautiful."

There was nothing beautiful about any aspect of U.S. foreign policy and CIA skullduggery I encountered during a trip to Brazil— Washington's attempt to counter the message sent by the new wave of Latin leaders.

23

Brazil: Skeletons in the Closet

By the time I arrived at the World Social Forum (WSF) in Brazil in January 2005, the continent was caught up in what amounted to a revolution against the corporatocracy. In addition to Chávez, Lula, and Gutiérrez, Néstor Kirchner and Tabaré Ramón Vázquez had won elections in Argentina and Uruguay respectively. Regardless of whether some might be bending under pressure, all had run populist campaigns that denounced U.S. intervention and exploitation by foreign corporations. The North American press could denounce them as "leftists," "friends of Castro," and even "communists," but in Africa, Asia, and Europe, as well as Central and South America, people knew that these adjectives were irrelevant; each of the new presidents had campaigned as a nationalist determined to see his country's resources used to help its citizens rise out of poverty.

Something extraordinary was also happening in Chile. Published reports and recently declassified U.S. government documents confirmed rumors long held that the Nixon administration and the CIA had coordinated efforts with U.S. companies and the Chilean military to overthrow and assassinate democratically elected president Salvador Allende in 1973. Allende's "crime" had been to honor his campaign promises that Chilean resources should belong to Chileans, and, after election, to nationalize the foreign-owned copper, coal, and steel industries, and 60 percent of the private banks. As in Iran, Iraq, Guatemala, Indonesia, and so many other places before, the United States backed a man to replace him whose personality matched the profile of a bloodthirsty despot: Gen. Augusto Pinochet. Now, two decades later, the WSF was abuzz with the news that U.S. congressional investigators and a Chilean judge had uncovered secret

Pinochet bank accounts at Riggs Bank in Washington and other foreign banks totaling at least $16 million and that Pinochet himself would finally be brought to justice for the estimated two thousand people killed by police and army units under his command.

Rumors also abounded at the WSF that a Chilean woman whose air force general father had died in prison for opposing Pinochet was a strong possibility for the 2005 presidential elections. Michelle Bachelet had already established herself as a very competent head of Chile's health and defense ministries; she had demonstrated that she was a nationalist with the courage to stand up to the corporatocracy. If she won, it would mean that more than 80 percent of South America had voted for anticorporatocracy presidents, that 300 million people (roughly the population of the United States) had chosen the candidate who opposed the empire to the north.

The WSF is a symbol of the changes sweeping our planet. It was established at the beginning of the third millennium as a response to the World Economic Forum, where government and business leaders collaborate, strike deals, hammer out trade policies, and coordinate other corporatocracy strategies. More than 150,000 participants from more than 130 countries flocked to the WSF in Porto Alegre, Brazil, in January 2005 to discuss economic, social, environmental, and political issues and to formulate alternatives to failing systems. Presidents Lula of Brazil and Chávez of Venezuela, among other luminaries, attended the WSF.

I had been asked by a Swedish nonprofit organization, the Dag Hammarskjöld Foundation, to give a keynote address entitled "Confessions of an Economic Hit Man—What Next for the World?" A huge tent was provided for my talk. Rights to the book had been sold in many languages, but most had not been published yet. It did not seem to matter; the English version circulated widely. The crowd that showed up filled the hundreds of chairs and expanded out through the tent's doorway. Following my talk, dozens lined up at the microphone to ask questions and make their own comments. I personally was particularly moved by a young Brazilian man who launched into a critique of his own government; he accused Lula of succumbing to the EHMs and backing down from his campaign promises. His brief speech reminded me of similar criticisms against Gutiérrez I had heard in Ecuador.

My speech opened a door. I was approached by groups of people from Africa, Asia, and Latin America, and by a number of individuals. They all wanted to share their stories and ideas, as well as hear more of mine.

One man who was more elegantly dressed than most handed me a business card identifying him as a top advisor to President Lula of Brazil. He asked me to meet him in a small park near my hotel. "Please keep this confidential, just between us," he added.

At the designated time, I walked to the park. I was a bit anxious; I wondered if I had somehow displeased the Brazilian administration. I could not see how; yet to be approached by a government official and to meet in this clandestine manner seemed very strange.

I stood at the edge of the park for a few minutes, trying to relax. Horns honked and raucous music with a head-pounding beat blared from a passing car. I bent over a flowering bush to smell its fragrance, but the only odor was that of car exhaust. I thought about this city. Porto Alegre is an industrial center with a population of nearly 1.5 million but few people I had talked with in the United States had ever heard of it. I straightened and walked into the park.

"José" was sitting on a bench under a tree. He had exchanged his pressed shirt and creased slacks for a polo shirt and blue jeans. He sported oversized sunglasses that gave him a dragonfly appearance and wore a floppy straw hat pulled low over his forehead. When I approached, he stood up, peering nervously around, and shook my hand. "Thank you for coming," he said. Still standing, he explained in flawless English that if anyone should interrogate him about our rendezvous he would simply tell them he was trying to learn more about me and my book before its impending publication in Portuguese. "But I hope it doesn't come to that," he added, once again scanning the park. "One never knows though, these days . . ." His voice trailed off and he motioned to the bench. "Please." We sat down side by side.

He asked questions about some of the people in *Confessions*, focusing particularly on the Iranians "Yamin" and "Doc" who in 1977, at great personal risk to themselves, shared with me information about the shah and the mullahs' determination to overthrow him (something that happened nearly two years later). José expressed his relief over my assurances that Yamin and Doc's true identities would never be disclosed. He said that he wanted his message to reach the people of the United States, but that I had to guarantee to keep the source confidential. He invited me to take notes, as long as I did not disclose his name. During our conversation, he mentioned that he had been twenty-six years old at the time I graduated from college in 1968.

He told me that he had read my book and appreciated the things I had exposed. However, he said, "It is only the tip of the iceberg. I'm sure you know this, but I feel I must say it. Even your book misses the real story."

José described the tremendous pressure being exerted on his boss, Lula. "It's not just about bribes and the threat of coups or assassinations, not just about striking deals and falsifying economic forecasts, not just about enslaving us through debts we can never repay. It goes much deeper."

He went on to explain that in Brazil and many other countries, the corporatocracy essentially controls all political parties. "Even radical communist candidates who appear to oppose the United States are compromised by Washington."

When I asked him how he knew all this, he laughed. "I've been around a long time," he said. "I've always been involved in politics. From Johnson to Bush, both Bushes, I've seen it all. Your intelligence agencies, as well as your economic hit men, are a lot more efficient than even you imagine."

José described how students are lured in while they are naïve and vulnerable. He talked about his own personal experiences as a young man and the way women, booze, and drugs were used. "So you see, even when a radical opponent of the U.S. gets into office, and assuming that at this point in his life he sincerely wants to stand up to Washington, your CIA has what you call 'the goods' on him."

"Blackmail."

He chuckled at this. "You might call it that, or you might call it 'modern diplomacy.' It isn't just the U.S. of course. Surely you've heard the rumors about why Noriega was taken down and today rots in a U.S. prison."

"I've heard that he had cameras on Contadora Island." It was an infamous resort off Panama's coast, a "safe haven" where U.S. businessmen could treat politicians to every conceivable vice. I had visited—and used—Contadora several times during my EHM days.

"You heard who got caught by those cameras?"

"Rumors that George W. was photographed doing coke and having kinky sex during the time his father was president." There was a theory in Latin America that Noriega had used incriminating photos of the younger Bush and his cronies to convince the older Bush, the president, to side with the Panamanian administration on key issues. In retaliation, H. W. invaded Panama and hustled Noriega off to a Miami prison. The building housing Noriega's confidential files had been incinerated by bombs; as a side effect, more than two thousand innocent civilians were burned to death in Panama City that day in December 1989. Many people claimed that this theory offered the only logical explanation for violently attacking a nation without an army and that posed no threat to the United States.

José nodded. "From where I sit, those rumors ring awfully true. I've experienced things that take them out of the realm of fantasy." He cocked his head. "So have you." He paused, looking around. "And it terrifies me."

I asked whether Lula had been corrupted and for how long. It was obvious that this question made him extremely uncomfortable. After a long pause, he admitted that Lula was part of the system. "Otherwise, how could he have risen to such a position?" However, José also professed his admiration for Lula. "He's a realist. He understands that in order to help his people he has no choice . . ." Then he shook his head. "I fear," he said, "that Washington will try to bring Lula down if he goes too far."

"How do you think they'd do it?"

"Everyone has—as you say—skeletons in his closet. Every politician has done things that can look bad, if brought into the light in a certain way. Clinton had Monica. She wasn't the issue, though. Clinton went too far in his efforts to revise world currencies and he posed a huge threat to future Republican campaigns—he was just too young, dynamic, and charismatic. So Monica was marched into the spotlight. Don't you believe that Bush has a few women in his background too? But who dares talk about them? Lula has skeletons. If the powers that run your empire want to bring him down, they'll open the closet door. There are many ways to assassinate a leader who threatens U.S. hegemony." He gave me a look that I would remember several months later when four senior officials from Lula's party resigned amid accusations that they had masterminded a multimillion-dollar scheme to pay legislators in return for votes and it looked as though Lula's political career would end as a result of the scandal.

In response to my question about how we might rein in the empire, he said, "That's why I'm meeting with you. Only you in the United States can change it. Your government created this problem and your people must solve it. You've got to insist that Washington honor its commitment to democracy, even when democratically elected leaders nationalize your corrupting corporations. You must take control of your corporations and your government. The people of the United States have a great deal of power. You need to come to grips with this. There's no alternative. We in Brazil have our hands tied. So do the Venezuelans. And the Nigerians. It's up to you."

The euphoria I felt over the reception of my book and the speech I gave at the WSF was dampened by that conversation with José. Wandering around the streets of Porto Alegre, I became increasingly dejected. This, I suppose, made me more vulnerable to the stunning Brazilian woman who claimed to be a journalist.

24

The Beautiful Carioca

I could not help but notice her sitting in the front row of the tent, just below the podium, as I gave my presentation. The auburn hair tumbling about her shoulders, the long legs exposed by the short skirt, the high cheekbones that bespoke indigenous blood, and the smile that seemed intended exclusively for me—all these set her apart even in this country that is famous for its beautiful women.

After my speech, she was the first to the podium. She shook my hand warmly and offered me a card with her name, Beatriz Muchala, a list of several magazines, and a Rio address. "I must interview you," she said. "My readers simply have to know more. I'm Spanish by heritage, born in Argentina." She smiled. "But Carioca at heart."

The way she expressed it, as well as the words themselves, put me on alert. Cariocas, women from Rio de Janiero, were legendary for their ability to please men. But Beatriz struck me as different. Perhaps it was the strategy of where she had sat, her posturing and clothes, or that she was just a bit too beautiful. My instincts warned me away. I told her that my schedule was full.

Later that day I recalled a retired CIA agent who shared with me his version of Clinton's impeachment. It was consistent with the things José had described. "Linda Tripp was assigned to destroy a president feared as a reformer who might undermine the corporatocracy," the CIA man said. "As you know, guys like me always look for 'innocents' to do our dirty work. Less risk, no evidence. Linda found her innocent in Monica Lewinsky. She told Monica, 'Poor Bill doesn't get any TLC at home. You could do him a favor.' The rest is history."

Beatriz approached me several times later that day as I met with groups from Africa and Europe. I remained resolute. Amazingly, our paths crossed again after my discussion with José as I wandered around the city, dazed by what I had just heard. She gave me another card. This time she was less persistent, perhaps sensitive to my emotional state. Or hurt to discover that my schedule was not full—I was out for a walk. This latter gave me a pang of guilt. Why had I been so suspicious?

After that I found it hard to take my mind off her. I suppose my discussion with José should have warned me to be cautious. But, in fact, it had the opposite effect. I felt discouraged, dejected. Now I kicked myself for not agreeing to the interview. Spending time with a beautiful woman might be just what I needed. After all, she was a journalist and I had come to Brazil to spread the message of my book. What harm could a meeting with her have done?

I was relieved to find a message from her waiting at the front desk of my hotel. I called her and agreed to join her at her hotel that evening—in a very public place, the lobby.

Beatriz and I sat near the main door of the Plaza Hotel. The mini-skirt had been replaced by designer jeans. She requested that we conduct the interview in Spanish, explaining that her English was inferior to my Spanish. The articles would be published both in Argentina and Brazil; she would translate them into Portuguese. She shared a little of her background growing up in Argentina and I told about some of my experiences in Buenos Aires. She joked about the difficulties of being an Argentine woman amid the beauties of Rio.

After perhaps fifteen minutes, she requested my permission to use a tape recorder. I agreed. She pulled one out of a large knit handbag, set the microphone up on the table between us, and asked me several questions about EHMs. Then she checked the recorder, rewinding the tape and listening to it with earphones. She frowned and shook her head. "Too much background noise." She returned to the handbag, shuffled through it, removed a pen and notebook, apologized, and asked me to repeat the answers I had just given. I did so.

When we finished, she relaxed back into her chair, bit at the end of her pen, and mentioned my previous books on indigenous cultures. "My readers need to understand better about the people living in our vast rainforests. Can we move on to that subject?"

Overloaded with EHM conversations, I welcomed the opportunity to discuss my earlier writings.

She gave her tape recorder a wistful look. "I'd really like to have this on tape," she said. "How about getting away from this noise? My room is just an elevator ride away."

By now, I had bought into the idea of discussing indigenous cultures. I was impressed with Beatriz's professionalism and was enjoying our banter. Given my background, perhaps I should have been more wary, but my guard was lowered.

Following her down the long corridor from the elevator to her room, it was impossible not to be reminded of her physical beauty. Her high heels, tight jeans, and flowing auburn hair accentuated the walk that had made the beaches at Copacabana and Ipanema famous.

Once in the room, she sat me down on a sofa and busied herself positioning the tape recorder on a small table in front of it. Then she offered me a glass of wine. Although I seldom drink anything but beer, I accepted. She poured us each one and joined me on the sofa. "Let's get right to it," she said.

As I responded to her questions, I became aware that our bodies were touching. She moved closer. She reached down and, turning off the recorder, handed me my glass. Her fingers brushed against mine. Our glasses clinked. I watched her sip hers. Then suddenly I remembered her earlier in the day standing alone on the street between my hotel and the park where I had met José. How likely was such a "chance" encounter in a city the size of Porto Alegre? It hit me in the gut. I was pretty certain that Beatriz's motives were not simply to have sex with a best-selling author. Her eyes met mine, as she sipped her wine. I set my glass down, untouched, wondering if maybe it had been doctored.

"I'm old enough to be your father." I glanced around the room, searching for a hidden camera. "And I'm married." I stood up.

"In Brazil we have an expression: Older men know how to please a woman; married men are discreet."

"I've got to go," I said.

"It's so early."

I made my way to the door. "Let's end tonight as friends."

She rose from the couch and walked toward me.

I opened the door. "Please send me a copy of the EHM interview." By now I was backing into the corridor.

"If you change your mind, you can call." She smiled sweetly. "I'm here—all night. In any case, I will send you a copy."

But she never did.

25

Taking on the Empire

Not long after I returned from Brazil, its neighbor Bolivia entered a new period of political strife. The man who replaced deposed president Gonzalo Sánchez de Lozada, Carlos Mesa, was viewed as weak at best, and as a corporatocracy collaborator at worst. Evo Morales's MAS party and the indigenous organizations demanded land rights, subsidized cooking fuel for the poor, and nationalization of the oil and gas industries.

As I read reports streaming across the Internet and talked with friends in Latin America, I often visualized that long line of women, men, and children standing in the freezing rain waiting to pay their electric bills. What were they thinking now? They had seemed so docile, downtrodden, like the slaves who had worked the Spanish tin mines. But something had sparked them. They had fallen out of line and flooded the streets. They had swarmed the offices of the water company. They had surrounded the presidential palace. They had stood up to the World Bank, defied the corporatocracy, incurred the wrath of history's mightiest empire. They had died for their cause. What had it taken to make all that happen?

There are always a number of answers to such questions, but in this case, one of those answers was especially significant: a single man, Evo Morales. He was, of course, just one of a handful of leaders behind this new movement, but he was the one who became a congressman and then declared himself a candidate for the presidency. Above all else he was a symbol and a catalyst. Like George Washington, Simón Bolívar, and all great leaders before him, Evo Morales was both visionary and activist. He was the hope for Bolivia and also for the rest of us, because his rise was the materialization of a dream we all share: that at times of grave crises a human being will emerge to lead his people out of the darkness and into the light.

Morales owed a great deal to that other modern Latin leader, Hugo Chávez, the president who, like the cartoon gunfighter, had stood up to the most powerful ruler in the world and backed him down. The fact that millions of Latin Americans saw George W. Bush not as a legally elected representative of a democracy but rather as a despot who had stolen an election served both Chávez and Morales well. If great leaders need hostile adversaries, these men had theirs.

Events in another country also bolstered Morales. For very different reasons, the ongoing politics of Ecuador were working in the Aymara leader's favor. Accusing Lucio Gutiérrez of cutting deals with the EHMs, the Ecuadorian people demanded his resignation. On April 20, 2005, lawmakers in Quito voted to remove Gutiérrez from office; they swore in Vice President Alfredo Palacio to temporarily replace him.

It did not take long for the new Ecuadorian president to identify the transgressions of his predecessor as stemming from his willingness to cater to the IMF, the World Bank, Washington, and Wall Street. Two days after the ouster, *The New York Times* reported that Palacio and his economic minister, Rafael Correa, criticized the former president's "ties to the international lending institutions" and "called it immoral for a country to use 40% of its budget to service its debt." Stating that "his new government may reconsider the direction of trade talks now under way with the United States," *The Times* said Mr. Palacio indicated that he "would like to use oil money earmarked for the public debt to pay for social spending."[27]

In Bolivia, Morales read the Ecuadorian situation as an endorsement of the policies he advocated, another sign that the Andes was ready for change, and proof that the time was right for a person with his background (which by modern materialistic standards was impoverished) to take the helm. The official U.S. reaction to him was hostile; however, from a Latin standpoint, that served as another form of confirmation. Reflecting Washington's position, *The New York Times* reported:

> For the Bush administration, the prospect of Mr. Morales in the presidency is seen as a potentially serious setback in the war on drugs, one which could jeopardize hundreds of millions of dollars in American anti-drug, economic and development aid.[28]

Bolivians and other Latins understood that the White House and the mainstream U.S. media would stoop to any level to vilify Morales. This tactic might fool the U.S. electorate, but, as Ambassador Rocha had demonstrated earlier with his statements about withholding U.S. aid if a candidate like Morales were elected, such threats had the opposite effect in Bolivia.

At a party attended by a number of Latin American students in the United States I heard a joke.

"Who was Hugo's number-one publicist?" (Pause.) "George Bush. Who is Evo's number-one publicist?"

Answer: "George Bush?"

"Nope. He's number three. The *Wall Street Journal* and *New York Times* beat him out."

26

Kindred Spirits

For many Latin Americans, Evo Morales symbolized the anti-corporatocracy, pro-poor people movement. Dressed in traditional Andean sweaters, ponchos, and woolen caps, he dared to flaunt his humble roots. He unabashedly proclaimed the greatness of his people to the world, saying that just because they had been subjugated for centuries did not mean they would not now fight for their lands and their pride. Exploitation did not equal inferiority. Materialistic poverty was not a sign of moral inadequacy.

Announcing that he would run for president, he promised to fight foreign corporations determined to plunder resources and to defy the United States' demand that his country destroy its coca crops. Emphasizing that the plant only becomes a problem after it is processed into cocaine and shipped outside Bolivia, he insisted that the drug issue be handled at the consumer end.

In December 2005 Evo Morales won a landslide victory to become Bolivia's first Indian president. He immediately announced that he would cut his salary in half, mandated that no Cabinet minister would be paid more than he, and earmarked the money saved for hiring more public school teachers. His vice president, Álvaro García Linera, had been a guerrilla leader in Bolivia's anticorporatocracy revolutionary movement, spent four years in prison, was educated as a mathematician in Mexico, and then became a sociology professor at Mayor de San Andrés university in La Paz, where he was praised as an intellectual and political analyst. The minister of justice, a woman, had worked as a maid. The leader of the senate was a rural school teacher. Although indigenous, Morales said his commitment was to all of Bolivia's poor and disenfranchised, whether they lived in city slums, high in the Andes, or deep in the jungles.

The mainstream press in the United States openly deceived its U.S. audiences. In a campaign eerily reminiscent of the one launched against Guatemala's Arbenz before we invaded that country, the media conveyed the impression that Morales was a "Communist" and "agent of Castro."

Bechtel dropped its legal suit against Bolivia in January 2006, the month after Morales's election.

Less than four months later, on May 2, 2006, President Morales ordered the Bolivian military to occupy oil and gas fields around the country and place them under state control. Giving corporate executives 180 days to renegotiate existing contracts with the government, he proclaimed, "The looting by the foreign companies has ended." Rather than sharing profits in the ratio of roughly 80 percent to foreign corporations, 20 percent to Bolivians, he demanded a reversal in those numbers.[29]

Some saw the Bolivian move as a swing away from a united Latin front; they pointed out that Brazil and Argentina would be most significantly impacted since they import large quantities of Bolivian natural gas. However, Chávez vehemently defended Morales, saying, "We support a Bolivia that is pointing the same direction that Venezuela is pointing. We have recovered the control of our natural resources and our mineral riches in a very long and difficult process that even cost us an attempted coup. (In Bolivia) I am sure that everything will turn out well."

Morales himself made his policies very clear; he favored nationalism and also a united front when it came to Latin America versus the United States; he opposed corporate exploitation, regardless of where the corporations were headquartered:

We're going to defend the natural resources. If before, Bolivia was no man's land, now it is someone's land. It is the land of Bolivians, especially the indigenous and original people. Private companies, oil companies, transnational companies, if they want to come here and they want to respect Bolivian laws, they are welcome . . . but the companies that don't want to respect Bolivian laws, that don't want to subordinate themselves to the state, the law—may bad things come to them![30]

In January 2006, Chile followed in the footsteps of Argentina, Bolivia, Brazil, Ecuador, and Uruguay when Michelle Bachelet won her bid for the presidency on a platform that emphasized self-determination. The first woman ever to hold this position, she immediately fulfilled a campaign promise by naming women to half her Cabinet posts.

While these leaders could trace their heritage back to heads of state who had courageously opposed empires in the past, something different was happening in the first decade of the new millennium. And that difference had global implications.

Never before had so many voters sent to the highest office at the same time leaders who so strongly defended the rights of their people against the moneyed interests of the United States. Never before had there been such unanimity. Never before such a show of support for the poorest of the poor—both urban and rural. Or for indigenous populations. Never had colonized countries delivered such a powerful and unanimous message to their colonizer. It had not happened in the western hemisphere. Not in Africa or Asia. Although the Middle East also resisted the grip of empire, the struggles there took a terrible toll on the region's own people. The Latin American revolution, on the other hand, was not just aimed at expelling foreign exploiters; it was a positive movement toward greater equality, freedom, and social reform. For the most part, it was peaceful. Its impact reached around the planet and was setting an example; it accomplished concrete goals and inspired people on every continent.

The newly elected presidents also began something completely unprecedented in the history of the hemisphere. They agreed to defend each other. United not by a single leader (as in the time of Bolívar) but through mutual consent, they expanded their stance against the IMF, the World Bank, and the U.S. government to include self-defense. Countries like Brazil, Argentina, Chile, Peru, and Venezuela led efforts to switch their military objectives from protecting multinational corporations to defending their countries against foreign intervention. And they began to seriously discuss the possibility of extensive military cooperation.

In addition to strengthening the bonds with one another, Latin American countries began aggressively developing relationships with India, China, and other nations that share a distrust of U.S. empire building. In a highly significant November 2005 trip to the continent, China's President Hu Jintao visited Argentina, Brazil, Chile, and Cuba, and conducted bilateral meetings with Mexico's President Vicente Fox and Peru's President Alejandro Toledo. Chinese businesses have quietly beaten out U.S. corporations in a number of areas that previously were considered U.S. turf. A Chinese company effectively controls the "anchor ports" at both ends of the Panama Canal. China and Brazil launched their Earth Resources Satellite program in 1998. While Washington's attempts to create trade pacts that favor U.S. corporations have met with repeated resistance from Latin leaders, less onerous overtures by the Chinese have been embraced. This may seem contradictory given China's potential as an emerging empire; however, Latins understand that China, unlike the United States, does not have a history of meddling in their affairs. Similar to the U.S.S.R. in the sixties, seventies, and eighties, China today is seen as a place that offers balance, a protector against U.S. aggression.

That Latin emissaries are fanning out across the world reflects a determination to increase commercial relationships; however, it is also part of the anti-corporatocracy movement and a clear indication

that our southern neighbors are determined to oppose U.S. hegemony.

Latin fears of U.S. intervention are justified by covert activities,
as well as by Washington's pronounced policies. This became clear
to me when I was approached by several jackals who wanted to
"come in from the cold" and confess their recent sins.

27

A History of Assassinations

I walked into El Presidente's office two days after he was elected and congratulated him.

He sat behind that big desk grinning at me like the Cheshire Cat.

I stuck my left hand into my jacket pocket and said, "Mr. President, in here I got a couple hundred million dollars for you and your family, if you play the game—you know, be kind to my friends who run the oil companies, treat your Uncle Sam good." Then I stepped closer, reached my right hand into the other pocket, bent down next to his face, and whispered, "In here I got a gun and a bullet with your name on it—in case you decide to keep your campaign promises."

I stepped back, sat down, and recited a little list for him, of presidents who were assassinated or overthrown because they defied their Uncle Sam: from Diem to Torrijos—you know the routine.

He got the message.

Brett sipped on his beer. "That's it," he said, turning to watch a bikinied blonde hop onto a boat at the Waterway Café in Palm Beach Gardens, Florida. "That about says it all."

When Brett first contacted me, he identified himself as a jackal who wanted "to talk about Ecuador and other Latin American countries." He refused to be more specific over the phone or by e-mail. We met on a beach near my Florida home. Then, later, at several restaurants. Although still in the EHM business and therefore unwilling to publicly share his identity, he was distressed by the attitudes of those who hired him. "Too arrogant," he said. "And corrupt. Our citizens should know about our elected officials and how their attitudes turn lots of old friends against us." He admitted to making "around a half million dollars a year tax free." He had started, according to him, because growing up in a Cuban family that lost millions when Castro overthrew Fulgencio Batista, he feared communism. "The Commies are gone," he lamented. "This is still my job. I'm damn good at it too. I just don't like the fact that these jerks in Washington are creating a very bad impression."

Everything about Brett looked and felt the part. He was muscular with cropped hair. Unlike Neil, the man who headed security operations in tsunami-devastated Indonesia, he had the appearance of a cop. His accurate descriptions of people and places, including Panama and Torrijos in the late 1970s when he said he was just beginning his trade, were consistent with my recollections. Talking with him about his contemporary exploits took me back to those days. He would not identify his subject president by name, his most recent endeavor to turn an elected leader against his own stated policies, telling me instead that he wanted me to present that story as one of several examples of his work.

Nothing that he said surprised me. I always suspected that most of the presidents in those seven countries had been approached by someone who had my old job as an EHM. Not unknown to the president, this person had hung around the centers of power for some time, as a World Bank staffer, a U.S. embassy or USAID employee, or a consultant. Only after the election did he expose his most essential function.

When skeptics sometimes tell me they know that assassinations happen but ask why they should believe that people like EHMs, like Brett, exist, I point out the obvious. No sane person assassinates a head of state without first trying to bring him around. No politician or CIA agent would consider it. Not even the most hardened mafioso would do that. It is simply too risky. And too messy. There are so many possibilities for error. You always send emissaries first. They offer the carrot of corruption and then, if that does not work, they threaten the stick of coup or assassination.

When I was sent on similar assignments, I was more subtle than

Brett. I always assumed that hidden tape recorders captured conversations in government offices. However, the meaning of the message was the same. The president was left with no doubt: He could remain in power and get rich if he cooperated with us or he would be thrown out, alive or dead, if he did not.

President Chávez spoke about his own contacts with EHMs and jackals on Venezuelan radio. The BBC reported one of several of his talks on this subject:

> The president referred to the book *Confessions of an Economic Hit Man* by John Perkins, saying that these economic hit men approached him at one point. He said he was offered funds from the IMF if he agreed to surveillance flights and the presence of U.S. advisers . . . Even though he refused their offers, he said, these economic hit men did not give up and tried to exert pressure through "weak" government officials, legislatures and even military officers around him. Chávez said that as Perkins explains in his book, the jackals step in and stage coups d'etat and assassination plots when the economic hit men fail in their mission. "We have defeated the economic hit men and the jackals, and if they even consider coming back, we will defeat them again," he stressed to cheers from the crowd.[31]

Following President Gutiérrez's removal, I was contacted by Ecuadorian journalists. I discussed my conversations with Brett and suggested that the former president might have been visited by such a person. Whenever the opportunity arose during these interviews, I pointed out that my purpose was not to criticize any Latin politicians, but rather to ask the people of the United States to insist that our government and our corporations abstain from trying to impede democracy.

At least one of my interviews was picked up by the Ecuadorian press. On March 3, 2006, I received an e-mail from Bill Twist, chairman of the Pachamama Alliance, a nonprofit on whose board

I sit. Attached was an e-mail from a staff member in the organization's Ecuadorian office, along with an article from Quito's daily newspaper, *El Comercio*, that carried the headline, LUCIO GUTIÉRREZ INDICTS PERKINS FOR DEFAMATION (March 1, 2006). The staff member's e-mail summarized that article: "John's interview . . . is really causing a ruckus down here! . . . In today's *Comercio*, the director of Gutiérrez' political party announces that the ex-president will present criminal charges for defamation against him. This is pretty hot stuff because it's election season and the survival of Gutiérrez' fledgling political party is on the line."

El Comercio phoned me for a follow-up interview. I emphasized to the reporter my conviction that I had no right to participate in Ecuadorian politics, that my intention had never been to vilify Gutiérrez, that my goal was instead to convince the U.S. public that our government and corporations frequently overstep their authority, and that we must demand an end to such abuses of power. I said that while I had no proof that an EHM visited Gutiérrez, I personally had exerted that type of pressure on government officials in the past.

I heard no more from Gutiérrez. However, as a result of *Confessions* and the articles in *El Comercio*, several members of the U.S. armed forces approached me with accounts of maneuvers on Colombian soil aimed at a military invasion of Venezuela. Like Brett, they were deeply concerned about the course their country was taking; they did not dare go public but they wanted the American people to hear about their experiences.

Colombia is the glaring exception to the hemispheric anti-corporatocracy movements. It has maintained its position as Washington's surrogate. Shored up by massive U.S. taxpayer assistance and armies of corporate-sponsored mercenaries, as well as formal U.S. military support, it has become the keystone in Washington's attempt's to regain regional domination. Although official justification for U.S. involvement centers on drug wars, this is a subterfuge for protecting oil interests against grassroots opposition to foreign exploitation.

Raúl Zibechi, a member of the editorial council of the weekly *Brecha de Montevideo* and a professor at the Franciscan Multiversity of Latin America, points out that Colombia is now the world's fourth-largest beneficiary of U.S. military aid, behind Israel, Egypt, and Iraq (the Associated Press ranks it as number 3)[32] and that the U.S. Embassy in Bogota is the second largest in the world, after Iraq. He states that he and other analysts have concluded that Washington is creating a South American unified armed force, commanded by the Pentagon, that is a military version of the proposed Free Trade Area of the Americas (FTAA) and is headquartered in Colombia.[33]

The men who contacted me—two army privates and a second lieutenant—substantiated Professor Zibechi's allegations. They asserted that the real reasons they had been stationed in Colombia were to establish a U.S. presence and to train Latin soldiers as part of a United States–commanded Southern Unified Army (a term two of the three used).

"Everything we do in Colombia just makes it more attractive for the drug business," the lieutenant told me. "Why do you think the situation keeps getting worse there? Because we want it to, we're behind the drug trafficking. The CIA is—just like it was in Asia's Golden Triangle. And in Central America and Iran during Iran-Contra. And the British with opium in China. Coke provides illicit money, in the billions—for clandestine activities—and an excuse to build up our armies. What more can you ask? We're there, men like me in the legit army, to protect oil and to invade Venezuela. The drug game is a smokescreen."

A former U.S. Green Beret officer told me that a mercenary army was being assembled in Guyana, along the Venezuelan border. He said that all the men were combat-hardened paratroopers, training for jungle warfare and learning Spanish.

"We got wars under way in Afghanistan and Iraq. No jungles there. No Spanish. So what's the point? But guess where there's lots of jungle? Venezuela. And they speak Spanish in Venezuela.

In addition to guys like me—U.S., British, and South African mercenaries—there's a lot of guys in Guyana from Latin militaries, mostly WHINSEC graduates."

The Western Hemisphere Institute for Security Cooperation (WHINSEC), formerly the School of the Americas (SOA), trains Latin soldiers in combat, counterinsurgency, interrogation, torture, spying, communications, and assassination. Its graduates include some of the continent's most notorious generals and dictators. SOA was located in the Panama Canal Zone until Omar Torrijos insisted on its removal. The fact that Manuel Noriega would not allow it back after Torrijos's death is one of the reasons the United States placed him on its "Most Wanted" list. Both Torrijos and Noriega were SOA graduates and both understood the power it wielded as an antidemocratic institution. It was moved to Fort Benning, Georgia, and in 2001 its name was changed in an attempt to dampen growing criticism.

One morning during the time of the controversy over the articles in *El Comercio*, Marta Roldós e-mailed me from Ecuador. She said she would be traveling to the States and hoped to talk with me about the death of her father, Jaime, the Ecuadorian president who refused to be corrupted by me and other EHMs, and who died in a plane crash on May 24, 1981. According to news reports, his plane hit a mountain. However, credible sources confirmed my belief that it was not an accident; that he had been assassinated by the CIA. In *Confessions* I wrote: "In addition to the fact that Washington and the oil companies hated him, many circumstances appeared to support these allegations." Marta said she wanted to discuss those circumstances.

She flew into Miami and drove north to a restaurant near my home in Palm Beach County on March 16, 2006. My daughter, Jessica (by then, twenty-three years old), and I met her at a restaurant with an outdoor patio where we spent several hours conversing. Marta explained that she had come to the United States primarily to seek help in setting up a Jaime Roldós Library. It would be the first of its type in her country, a memorial to a popular president who had died tragically while in office. "Like the JFK Library," she said, beaming. She confided that it would house information never before made public about her father's death, adding, "I firmly believe that it was an assassination. The pilot was one of the best in the Air Force and my father's friend. He had a family and children and cared deeply for my mother, who was also on board; he would not have done anything foolish, as the report said. Contrary to press reports, the route that the airplane was supposed to take was not rugged country by Ecuadorian standards and the weather was not bad at all. The airplane inexplicably went off the route."

Marta then went on to describe details that had been concealed from the public at the time. The site had been sealed off immediately after the crash; local police had been kept out; only Ecuadorian and U.S. military personnel were allowed in. Two key witnesses had been killed in car accidents before they were supposed to testify in hearings concerning the cause of the crash. One of the plane's engines had been sent to a Swiss laboratory and tests there indicated that it had stopped before it "hit the mountain." Marta was only seventeen on the day of the tragedy. Both her parents had died in that crash. She had been devastated, and for years unable to take action. Then when she turned forty-one she realized that she had reached her father's last year; it was time to act.

"You talk in your book," she continued, "about the impact my father's death had on Omar Torrijos. I know that to be true too. I married Omar's nephew; he's the father of my ten-year-old daughter. My dad's assassination haunted Omar. He told my husband and many others that he expected to be killed just like my dad was. He said he was ready to die because he had succeeded, he had put the Canal in Panamanian hands and had thrown the School of the Americas out of his country."

Omar Torrijos died in a plane crash a little more than two months after Jaime Roldós, on July 31, 1981.

After returning home from that meeting with Marta I typed the above record of our conversation. I ran it by Jessica, sat on it for a week, reviewed it again, and then when I believed Marta was back in Ecuador e-mailed it to her. I did not hear back from her. I tried several more times. In June my wife and I moved to our summer residence in New England. I e-mailed Marta from there, a brief message asking her to confirm that I had her correct address. "Yes," was the reply, "this is me, Marta." Again I e-mailed her the record of our conversation, asking whether she wanted to add anything or modify it in any way. I never heard back. About two weeks later, I logged on to my e-mail and saw one from her address. Excited, I opened it, to find that I was on a list of many people being informed about a theater schedule in Ecuador! I hit the "reply" button and again requested her comments on my typed record. Not a word came back.

I accepted an invitation to give a commencement address on June 11, 2006, at a high school near Northampton, Massachusetts. As a result, I became friends with the school's Spanish teacher, Juan Carlos Carpio, a native of Ecuador whose uncle, Dr. Jaime Galarza Zavala, is a highly respected Ecuadorian intellectual, author of many important books, including *Who Killed Jaime Roldós*, and currently president of the Casa de la Cultura Ecuatoriana (one of the country's foremost cultural institutions) in El Oro province, Ecuador's main banana-exporting region. In August 2006, Juan Carlos called to inform me that his uncle was attending a conference in New York City and would like to meet with me.

On August 14, my wife, Winifred, and I drove to La Cazuela, a restaurant in Northampton. When we walked in I spied Juan Carlos and his uncle. It was a Sunday evening and the restaurant was nearly empty, yet they had selected a table in a back corner, removed from other diners. I wondered whether this was coincidence or a precaution against prying ears.

After chatting for a while, Jaime told me that *Confessions* had made a lot of waves in Ecuador and that it was practically impossible to purchase it there. "As soon as it arrives in bookstores, someone buys up all the copies." He smiled wryly. "This also happened to some of my books, including the one on Roldós's assassination, which implicates the CIA, the Israel government, top Ecuadorian army officials, and the Ecuadorian political right wing—all as accomplices." Like Roldós, Dr. Galarza had been a professor at the University of Guayaquil and "a good friend of Jaime's." He said that after being elected president Jaime had confided his fears of assassination to him. Then he said he would tell me about an event that I might find interesting.

"Jaime flew to a secret meeting with oil company executives in Houston in May 1981. Several top government officials joined him. He thought one of them would be especially helpful because he previously had worked for the oil companies. Jaime figured he'd make a good ally." Dr. Galarza shook his head sadly. "How mistaken he was. In any case, that was it—just the Ecuadorians and the oil men, who insisted on secrecy. No press, no announcements. The Americans presented the Ecuadorians with their offer. They knew that Jaime had promised to rein them in during his campaign, but they demanded the same sort of deal they had received previously in Ecuador and were getting in other countries. Their companies would conduct initial explorations and Ecuador would pay in dollars or crude.

"Jaime assured them that he did not mind paying a reasonable price for services rendered in dollars, but would not consider doing so in crude. 'I intend to build petrochemical complexes in my country, so my people can benefit from the value added,' he said. 'We want to retain all our crude.' This infuriated the executives. It was not the deal they had enjoyed with previous administrations and was contrary to their global policies. Discussions grew heated. According to what Jaime told me later, the meeting turned ugly. Finally, he'd had enough. He got up and walked out, expecting the other Ecuadorians to join him. They did not.

"Our president, my friend Jaime, flew back to Quito and called a meeting with his closest advisors. They told him they felt he was in a very precarious situation, that his life was in danger. But it didn't deter him. He continued to speak out. He went on TV and said he would nationalize foreign companies unless they implemented plans to help Ecuador's people. He gave a speech at Atahualpa Olympic Stadium, where he talked extensively about the sovereign rights of a nation to take care of its people, especially the poor. Not long after that, he and his wife boarded their small plane and headed for another destination. They never made it. They both died in that crash, on May 24, 1981, less than a month after the secret Houston meeting. There is absolutely no question that Jaime Roldós was assassinated."

The four of us sat in that Massachusetts restaurant without speaking for several long moments. I had an image of Jaime Roldós Aguilera on the day I first met him at a reception in Quito. I had been deeply impressed by his vigor, charm, sense of humor, and determination to pull Ecuador out of its position as one of the most impoverished countries in the hemisphere. Finally, I turned to Dr. Galarza and told him about my March meeting with Jaime's daughter, Marta. I summarized some of her allegations, which confirmed his own version of the assassination.

Dr. Galarza turned to his nephew. "Yes, isn't it amazing? In our country, our police were kept away from the crash site where our president died. U.S. authorities were allowed in, but not Ecuadorian police investigators. Figure that one out."

I then mentioned that I had tried to contact Marta by e-mail several times since our meeting. "I wanted to share with her what I wrote about our conversation and see if she had anything to add, but she never responded."

He laughed. "She won't either," he said. "Her uncle León, Jaime's brother, is running for president and, since the time when you talked with her, she has also decided to run for public office. You know, after her father and mother died, she and her brother looked to León as a sort of foster dad. All of them were traumatized, shook up, scared—as well they might have been. A lot has happened in

Ecuador during the months since you and your daughter lunched with Marta. My country is in turmoil. Gutiérrez was replaced by his vice president, Palacio, and Palacio is a man of contradictions. No one knows where anyone else stands. People like León and Marta are frightened. They know that behind the assassination of Jaime Roldós there are powerful global interests. She's not going to talk with you about these things now."

28

Lessons from Latin America

I was invited to Bolivia in December 2006. Philippe Diaz and Beth Portello of Cinema Libre Studios asked me to participate in a documentary they were making about the roots of poverty. I saw the trip as an opportunity to gain insights into how Bolivians felt one year after Evo Morales took office. I had read many of the president's speeches and interviews, but now I would have a chance to listen to both his supporters and opponents.

I talked with shopkeepers, taxi drivers, waiters and restaurant owners, landless peasants, ex-miners, organizers of strikes that brought down President Sanchez, a well-known actress, Carla Ortiz, who was closely connected to indigenous activists, and one man who had watched his brother die an agonizing death from a soldier's bullet. I met on-camera with pro–Morales government officials, disgruntled businessmen, and an ex-president, Jorge "Tuto" Quiroga Ramirez, who now led the opposition against Morales.

It became apparent that the new president faced a myriad of challenges. Most members of the commercial and upper classes were determined to quash his economic and social reforms. His supporters, including the indigenous communities, expected a quick reversal of policies whose roots reached back hundreds of years. I had no doubt that, on top of all the local pressures, Morales was also drawing threats and bribes from EHMs. He had to know that the jackals were waiting in the wings.

One afternoon I sat in a large salon in the Presidential Palace and chatted with Vice President Álvaro García Linera. I had learned that, although Morales presented the public face, the vice president was the power behind the scenes; he was responsible for turning rhetoric into policy.

The room could have been located in the Royal Palace of Madrid. The ceiling was two stories high. The three distinct sitting areas were each furnished with matching eighteenth-century French Baroque chairs, couches, and Persian carpets. Here I was, meeting with a man who had earned his reputation as a guerrilla warrior and who had suffered through four years in prison—in a hall designed for kings.

García Linera's appearance reinforced the irony. Slight of build, he wore pressed black slacks, a black shirt open at the collar, and a tailored gray sports jacket. His elegant hands appeared more suited to a piano's keyboard than a revolutionary's rifle.

After discussing specific aspects of the administration's policies, we moved into the topic of Bolivia's role as a model for other countries. "Either everyone must be free or no one is free," the vice president declared. "For people in your country and mine to have stability we need to make sure that everyone around the world has stability." He described what he called "a post-capitalist society" as one that sets for its primary goal a decent living for all its citizens. "No longer should the state serve the rich and the big corporations. It must serve all the people, including the very poor."

In interview after interview during my days in Bolivia, I heard people express the opinion that, given the political changes sweeping the continent, things would never return to the way they had been in the past. "I used to be ashamed of my Aymara heritage," one woman told me. "Not anymore. Evo has made us proud."

"We won't accept slavery again," her husband added. "Not from Spanish hacienda owners—or U.S. corporations."

However, a darker side also emerged. Many of Morales's supporters fear that he has buckled to pressure from Washington and, as a consequence, has not honored his campaign promises. "He's no Chávez," was a frequent refrain. His opponents are equally concerned that he is growing too cozy with the Venezuelan president.

They believe that Morales is allowing himself to be used as a stepping stone for what they see as Chávez's ambitions to assume leadership of the entire continent. "First Bolivia, then Ecuador; after that Peru and Colombia," one confided. "Chávez wants to control all the oil and gas in South America. He thinks he's a modern-day Bolívar."

I celebrated the arrival of the New Year in the Presidential Palace. Evo Morales strolled in shortly before midnight. He had promised to welcome 2007 by holding a press conference to outline some of his new programs. As he stepped before the television cameras, I glanced around at that sumptuous building; I looked at the members of the press—a woman from England's *The Economist* magazine, a man from the United States representing the Associated Press, and reporters from many Latin American countries. Morales appeared to be exhausted. I wondered what he was feeling, standing there alone, this man who had risen from such humble beginnings and now was making news across the entire planet. One thing seemed certain: His presidency would not be an easy one.

Flying from La Paz back to Miami on the first day of 2007, I thought about my experience in Guatemala with Pepe Jaramillo in 1992. It had turned out to be much more significant than I could possibly have realized at the time. I had traveled there as the representative of a U.S. corporation, to explore the prospects of exploiting Mayan resources, but I was also working closely in those days with a nonprofit organization dedicated to helping the Mayas protect their lands and sustain their culture. I did not fully appreciate my dual role; nor did I understand the contradictions in my life—contradictions that reflected those of my country.

Now, on this flight from Bolivia, like then, I was returning to a culture that professes to respect human rights and yet enjoys a materialism that is built on exploiting workers in other lands. I live in a nation that has less than 5 percent of the world's population, but manages to consume over 25 percent of its resources, a society that espouses ecological principles and produces more than 30 percent of the planet's worst pollution. My plane was burning fuel that had been drained from someone else's country. Some of my clothes had been manufactured in sweatshops.

My life was a perfect example of the picture that old man painted for me when I arrived in Shuar territory with Ehud Sperling in 1991. "Your people dreamed of huge factories, tall buildings, as many cars as there are raindrops in this river," he said. "Now you begin to see that your dream is a nightmare."

In 1992 Pepe feared the indigenous people. That decade and the next would prove that his fears were justified. The old man in the rainforest had given me a glimpse of the future when I asked him how I might help make things better. "That's simple," he had replied. "All you have to do is change the dream . . . You need only plant a different seed, teach your children to dream new dreams."

The Latin Americans have taken that idea seriously. Led by indigenous people, the urban poor, and rural campesinos, they changed the dream through both words and actions. They organized movements to protect their cultures and their lands. They threw out the old dictators and voted in presidents who demanded that local resources be used to benefit local people. And in an odd sort of way they protected us in the United States from ourselves. By defying the corporatocracy, they forced us to look at what we are doing in the world. They set an example for us and others to follow.

The Latins did something else too. Not south of the Rio Grande, but right here in the United States. While most of us complained about cuts in budgets for pensions, education, Social Security, and Medicare, the mounting costs of the Iraq War, and the government's betrayals in New Orleans, they took to the streets to protest what they saw as unfair immigration laws. We sat in our homes, bemoaned the state of government, flicked on the TV, and did nothing; they exercised the rights granted to them by our Constitution.

They spoke out and marched on Washington, D.C. Whether you supported their cause or not, you had to take notice, to respect their courage and their willingness to act.

People in the Middle East were also taking action. However, their approach to dealing with the empire-building sprouted from a historical perspective that is radically different from that in Latin America.

Part 3: The Middle East

29

A Bankrupt United States of America

Petroleum distinguished itself as history's all-time most valuable resource during the first half of the twentieth century. It became the driving force behind modernization. Procuring reliable supplies formed the cornerstone of foreign policies. Japan's petroleum obsession was a major factor in the decision to attack Pearl Harbor. World War II elevated oil to even higher status. It fueled tanks, airplanes, and ships; a combatant country without oil was doomed.

Oil also evolved into the single most powerful tool of the corporatocracy.

After peace was declared, U.S. oil company executives formulated a plan that would change the course of history. They decided that it was in their best interests (and therefore the country's!) to convince the president and congress to save U.S. reserves for future wars and other emergencies. Why drain domestic oil fields when those of other continents could be exploited? In collaboration with U.K. and European companies, they persuaded governments to grant them tax breaks and other incentives they claimed were required to ensure domination of global petroleum supplies.

This decision—which has been endorsed by every president and congress since—led to policies that have redefined national borders, created kingdoms, and brought down governments. Like gold, oil turned into a symbol of power and the basis for valuing currencies; unlike gold, it is essential to modern technologies—to the plastics, chemical, and computer businesses.

At first, it appeared that the oil executives' plan would heap wealth on Third World oil-producing countries. However, following in gold's footsteps, oil became an albatross. Petroleum-rich countries were similar to prospectors in the boomtowns of the Old West; as soon as they filed claims, they became the targets of scoundrels and robber barons.

At roughly the same time that oil was emerging as the key to the modern age, the Soviet Union surfaced as Public Enemy #1. Historians recognize that empire builders require external threats; the U.S.S.R. conveniently played this role for the United States. Moscow's nuclear arsenal gave credence to the corporatocracy's claims that the Cold War demanded novel approaches to international diplomacy.

It is not surprising that the first real Cold War showdown over oil occurred in that part of the world containing the most oil, the Middle East. Demanding that his people share in petroleum profits from their lands, the democratically elected and highly popular Iranian prime minister Mohammed Mossadegh (*TIME* magazine's man of the year in 1951) nationalized a British petroleum company's assets. An outraged England sought the help of her World War II ally, the United States. Both countries feared that military intervention would provoke the Soviets into pulling the nuclear trigger. Instead of the marines, Washington dispatched CIA agent Kermit Roosevelt Jr. (Theodore's grandson). With a few million dollars, Roosevelt organized violent demonstrations that eventually overthrew Mossadegh; the CIA replaced this democratically elected leader with Mohammad Reza Pahlavi (the "Shah"), a despotic friend of Big Oil.

As discussed in *Confessions*, Roosevelt's success generated a whole new profession, the one I followed, that of EHMs. The lessons of Iran were clear: An empire could be built without the risks of war and at far less expense. The CIA's tactics could be applied wherever resources existed that the corporatocracy wanted. There was only one problem. Kermit Roosevelt was a CIA employee. Had he been caught, the consequences would have been dire. The decision was made to replace government operatives with agents from the private sector. One of the companies enlisted was mine, MAIN.

Very soon we EHMs discovered that we did not need to wait for countries to nationalize oil fields as an excuse to manipulate their politics. We turned the World Bank, the IMF, and other "multinational" institutions into colonizing tools. We negotiated lucrative deals for U.S. corporations, established "free" trade agreements that blatantly served our exporters at the expense of those in the Third World, and burdened other countries with unmanageable debts. In effect, we created surrogate governments that appeared to represent their people but in reality were our servants. Some of the earliest examples: Iran, Jordan, Saudi Arabia, Kuwait, Egypt, and Israel.

In tandem with EHM efforts to dominate global politics, the corporatocracy launched campaigns to increase oil consumption. Like drug dealers, public relations experts fanned across the planet, encouraging people to buy goods sold by corporatocracy organizations—often petroleum-based and produced in Third World sweatshops, under appalling conditions.

During the decades after the Iranian coup, economists frequently cited examples of rapid economic growth as proof that poverty was declining. However, as we saw in Asia, the statistics deceived. In addition to ignoring social and environmental degradation, the statistics failed to address long-term problems.

A good example of these "unintended consequences" is provided by events resulting from Roosevelt's Iranian adventure. The coup may have brought an oil-friendly dictator to power, but it also institutionalized anti-American movements in the Middle East. Iranians never forgave the United States for overthrowing their popular, democratically elected prime minister. Nor have people in neighboring countries. Scholars of political history wonder what might have happened had Washington supported Mossadegh and encouraged him to apply oil revenues toward helping Iran's people pull themselves out of poverty. Many conclude that this would have encouraged other countries to pursue democratic approaches and might have prevented the terrible violence that has plagued the region ever since. Instead, the United States served notice that it was not a country to be trusted, not the defender of democracy we portrayed ourselves to be, and that our aim was not to help the Third World. We simply wanted to control resources.

The United States experienced severe problems at home during this same period. The process of expanding the corporatocracy's power base plunged our nation deep into debt. Increasingly, the factories that produced our products, as well as the oil fields, were located in other countries. Foreign creditors demanded payments in gold. The Nixon administration responded in 1971 by revoking the gold standard.

Now Washington was confronted with a new dilemma. If our creditors turned to other currencies, the corporatocracy could be forced to pay their loans off at the value they had held relative to gold when those debts were incurred. This would be calamitous, because corporatocracy coffers no longer contained funds sufficient to buy down the debt. The lone sentinel barring the bankruptcy door was the U.S. Mint, with its capacity to print dollars and dictate their value. It was imperative that the world continue accepting dollars as the standard currency.

In the Prologue of this book I summarized the solution as revolving around Saudi Arabia. That is the short version. The longer story includes two other unwitting allies who came to Washington's rescue—both of them in the Middle East.

30

King Dollar

"What's going to happen to the dollar?" MAIN president Jake Dauber asked rhetorically, not long after that momentous 1971 decision to abandon the gold standard. "In the end, I suspect its value will be determined by oil."

I had been invited to join the Daubers for dinner at the Hotel Intercontinental Indonesia, a stopover for them on their way to the Middle East.

"Nixon's got a pretty smart team in Kissinger, Shultz, and Cheney." Jake squeezed his wife's hand and looked into her eyes. "I anticipate the day when you and I'll sit back on our sofa and say we were part of this great adventure. The U.S. is launching a new period in world history and we've got front-row seats."

Jake did not live to see the day he had hoped to share with his wife. He died not long after that trip—and was replaced as MAIN's president by his protégé, Bruno Zambotti. However, his analysis of the dollar's future turned out to be accurate. Nixon's team was not merely smart; it was cunning.

Washington's first ally in the struggle to defend the sovereignty of the dollar was Israel. Most people, including the majority of Israelis, believed that Tel Aviv's decision to launch attacks against Egyptian, Syrian, and Jordanian troops along its borders in what came to be known as the Six-Day War of 1967 was driven by Israel's determination to protect its borders. Territorial expansion was the most obvious outcome; by the end of that bloody week, Israel had quadrupled its land holdings, at the expense of people living in East Jerusalem, parts of the West Bank, Egypt's Sinai, and

Syria's Golan Heights. However, the Six-Day War served another purpose.

Arabs were humiliated and infuriated by the loss of their territories. Much of their anger was aimed at the United States; they knew that Israel could never have succeeded without American financial and political support, as well as the not-so-veiled threat that our troops were standing by in the unlikely event that Israel needed them. Few Arabs understood that Washington had motives that were far more selfish than defending the Jewish homeland, or that the White House would turn Arab anger to its advantage.

Nixon's second, and wholly unsuspecting, ally was the entire Islamic Middle East. In response to the Six-Day War of 1967, Egypt and Syria simultaneously attacked Israel on October 6, 1973 (Yom Kippur, the holiest of Jewish holidays). Knowing that strategically he was on shaky ground, Egypt's President Anwar Sadat pressured Saudi Arabia's King Faisal to strike against the United States (and therefore Israel) in a different way—by employing what Sadat referred to as "the oil weapon." On October 16, Saudi Arabia and four other Arab states in the Persian Gulf announced a 70 percent increase in the posted price of oil; Iran (which is Muslim but not Arab) in an act of Islamic solidarity joined them. During the ensuing days, Arab oil ministers, agreeing that the United States should be punished for its pro-Israel stance, unanimously backed the idea of an oil embargo.

It was a classic game of international chess. President Nixon asked Congress for $2.2 billion in aid to Israel on October 19. The next day, led by Saudi Arabia, Arab oil producers imposed a total embargo on oil shipments to the United States. At the time, few people perceived the cunning behind Washington's move, or the fact that it was driven by a determination to shore up a weakened dollar.

The impact was immense. The selling price of Saudi oil leaped to new records; by January 1, 1974, it had soared to nearly seven times its price four years earlier. The media warned that the U.S. economy was on the verge of collapse. Long lines of cars formed at gas stations across the nation, while economists expressed fears of the possibility of another 1929-style depression. Protecting our oil supplies had been a priority; suddenly, it became an obsession.

We know now that the corporatocracy played an active role in driving oil prices to these record highs. Although business and political leaders, including oil executives, feigned outrage, they were the puppet masters pulling the strings. Nixon and his advisors realized that the $2.2 billion aid package to Israel would force the Arabs into taking drastic actions. By supporting Israel, the administration engineered a situation that generated what was the craftiest and most significant EHM deal of the twentieth century.

The U.S. Treasury Department contacted MAIN and other firms with proven records as corporatocracy henchmen. Our assignment was twofold: to formulate a strategy to ensure that OPEC would funnel the billions of dollars we spent on oil back to U.S. companies and to establish a new "oil standard" that would replace the former "gold standard." We EHMs knew that the key to any such plan was Saudi Arabia; because it possessed more oil than any other country, it controlled OPEC; the Saudi "royal" family was corrupt and highly vulnerable. Like other "kings" in the Middle East, the Sauds understood the politics of colonialism. Royalty had been bestowed on the House of Saud by the British.

Details behind the strategy I helped engineer—the Saudi Arabian Money-laundering Affair (SAMA)—are provided in *Confessions of an Economic Hit Man*. In summary, as far as the media was concerned, the House of Saud agreed to three important conditions; it would: 1) invest a large portion of its petrodollars in U.S. government securities; 2) allow the U.S. Treasury Department to use the trillions of dollars in interest from these securities to hire U.S. corporations to westernize Saudi Arabia; and 3) maintain the price of oil within limits acceptable to the corporatocracy. For its part, the U.S. government promised to keep the Saud family in power.

There was an additional agreement, one that made few headlines but was crucial to the corporatocracy's need to maintain the dollar as the standard global currency. Saudi Arabia committed to trading oil exclusively in U.S. dollars. With the scratch of a pen, the dollar's sovereignty was reestablished. Oil replaced gold as the measure of a currency's value.

As I mentioned in the Prologue, a side benefit—one appreciated only by the most savvy economists—also allowed Washington to continue imposing a hidden tax on every foreign creditor. Because the dollar reigned supreme, we bought their goods and services on credit. By the time they used that credit to purchase oil (or something else) from our companies, the value of their funds had diminished, due to inflation; the difference between these amounts was cash-in-the-pocket for the corporatocracy—a tax without the need for tax collectors.

Jake Dauber's prediction that the dollar's value would be determined by oil proved correct. When Tel Aviv and Washington drove the Arab world into a corner, Arabs had little choice but to strike back, in the Yom Kippur War and through the OPEC embargo. This propelled the U.S. Treasury Department into action. EHMs were enlisted to forge a deal with Saudi Arabia that wed the dollar to oil. The dollar was crowned king, and has reigned supreme ever since.

SAMA changed geopolitics. It helped bring down the U.S.S.R., established the United States as an unchallenged superpower, and angered Osama bin Laden, the Saudi millionaire who would mastermind 9/11.

As I look back at it, I am amazed by the gall we had in those days. I often think about the role fate plays in our lives—fate and the way we react to it. I personally could never have taken on an assignment as complex as SAMA without the training I had received a few years earlier in Lebanon.

31

Manipulating Governments

During my first assignment in Indonesia, I showed my bosses that I was willing to create the inflated economic forecasts they desired. As a reward, they promoted me to chief economist (even though I held only a B.S. in Business Administration and at the time was the company's sole economist), gave me a raise, and sent me to the Middle East.

I had already written reports on Iran, Kuwait, and Saudi Arabia, but my research had been conducted at libraries and through interviews with people from those countries working for us in Boston. This first trip was a short one to get to know Iran and prepare a more in-depth analysis of its energy sector. Charlie Illingworth, who had been my project manager in Indonesia, suggested that I stop over for a couple of days in Beirut. At that time, the city's reputation as a playground was still intact. It would be, he told me, an ideal place to relax, catch up on the time zone changes, and familiarize myself with Middle Eastern culture. He knew someone at the embassy there who would show me around.

Lebanon had enjoyed a golden age following the end of World War II. Agriculture and small-scale industry flourished. Beirut developed into a wealthy, cosmopolitan city, the center of Middle Eastern banking and trade. As I read about the country prior to my departure date, I was intrigued to find frequent comparisons to both Switzerland and Paris. I was amazed to learn that ski resorts dotted the mountains outside Beirut, a Mediterranean city I had visualized as sitting on the edge of a desert. And that the cabarets and art galleries rivaled those of Paris.

I also read about Lebanon's shadow side; it stretched back into history and seemed to turn darker with each passing moment. Tensions between religious factions had smoldered for centuries. The coastal regions were ruled by Maronite Christians. The Druze sect of Islam dominated the southern mountains, while orthodox Sunnis governed the fertile Bekaa Valley. Most of the Maronites were Syrian, a fact that created additional tensions among Arab Muslims. Despite these specific characteristics, I discovered that Lebanon was a sort of microcosm for the Middle East.

Europe had coveted Lebanon since the time of the Crusades. Attempts to colonize it continued through the centuries. Claiming a mandate to protect Christian communities, French troops invaded in the late 1700s. Paris assumed the patronizing role characteristic of imperial powers and dispatched its soldiers several times during the 1800s. In 1926, France formed the Lebanese Republic, which was administered under the French Mandate of Syria. In 1940 the French rulers in Beirut declared allegiance to the Nazi-controlled Vichy government. With France soon occupied by Germany, the Vichy authorities in 1941 allowed Germany to move aircraft and supplies through Syria to Iraq, where they were used against British forces. The United Kingdom, fearing that Nazi Germany would gain full control of Lebanon and Syria by pressuring the weak Vichy government, sent its army into Syria and Lebanon.

Nationalistic fervor swept many countries during World War II. Lebanon gained full independence on January 1, 1944. A National Covenant accepted by the two most prominent Christian and Muslim leaders, Bishara al-Khuri and Riyad el Sulh, apportioned political power among the nation's various communities. Drawing on the 1932 census that calculated Christians at 54 percent of the population, it mandated that the president would be a member of the majority, the Maronite Christians, while the less powerful prime minister would come from the Sunni population and the speaker of the legislature would be Shi'a; the commander of the army would be a Maronite. Many Arabs, feeling that the twelve-year-old census was archaic and that Muslims in fact outnumbered Christians, were outraged at this arrangement that tipped the scales in favor of the Christians in Lebanon—and the West in general.

Arabs also suspected that newly created Israel was not all that it appeared to be. The only country ever mandated by the U.N. and a place that Jews called their "promised land," Israel was offered as a sanctuary after the horrors of Hitler. The Arabs, like Americans and Europeans, were told that the atrocities committed against the Jews necessitated the creation of such a state. The suffering of the Jewish people, the traumas of their lives under fascism, were indisputable. There could be no question that the world owed them something better. But in order for this to happen, millions of Palestinians were told they had to give up their homes. Turned overnight into refugees, they flooded into Lebanon and every other Middle Eastern country.

The Palestinian influx confirmed that the 1932 census was irrelevant; there could be no doubt that Muslims now outnumbered Christians in Lebanon. The realization that the National Covenant was being used as a political weapon was further proof for Muslims that there was a second, more sinister purpose behind the creation of Israel, that it was a servant of empire, an armed outpost for the victors of World War II, designed to control Middle Eastern oil. Lebanon, they suspected, was being groomed to support Israel and its allies; the Christian leadership established by the National Covenant was part of a sinister plot.

Lebanese Arab resentment erupted into a Muslim rebellion in 1958. U.S. politicians blamed "communist terrorists." Washington accused Moscow of fomenting this uprising, although it was backed by Syria more than the U.S.S.R. President Eisenhower sent in the marines. U.S. forces occupied Lebanon for only a brief period, from May until October, but their presence confirmed Arab suspicions that Washington was determined to keep the Christians in power. The U.S. president's willingness to interfere militarily had a profound long-term impact on Muslims throughout the region.

Lebanon was also incensed by Washington's aggressive interference in nearby Iraq. During the late 1950s and early 1960s the popular Iraqi president Abdul Karim Qasim grew increasingly defiant toward the United States and the United Kingdom. He demanded that foreign oil companies share the profits they reaped from Iraqi oil with his people and threatened to nationalize them if they did not comply. When EHM efforts failed to bring Qasim around, the CIA hired an assassination team that included a young man who had not yet completed his schooling: Saddam Hussein. The team opened fire on Qasim's car. They riddled it with bullets, but only managed to wound him. Saddam was shot in the leg and fled to Syria. In 1963, President Kennedy made a fateful decision; he ordered the CIA to join MI6 (British intelligence) on a mission to accomplish what the assassins had failed to do. They executed Qasim by firing squad on Iraqi television. After that, an estimated five thousand people were rounded up, accused of communism, and executed. Within a few years Saddam was brought back and installed as head of national security; his second cousin became president.[34]

During this same period the demographics in Lebanon were changing radically. Muslim populations expanded faster than the Christian. In the late 1960s, they demanded revisions in the National Covenant. However, Maronites refused, continuing to dominate the government. The threat that Washington would send in troops once again to support the Christians was underscored when the United States reinstated the military draft and built up its armed forces around the world.

Geopolitics also changed. In the 1967 Six-Day War, Israel seized parts of Jerusalem, Syria, and Egypt. The Arab world was outraged. Support for Palestinian militants grew. The PLO (Palestine Liberation Organization) used refugee camps in southern Lebanon to stage attacks on Israel.

By the time I headed for Beirut in 1973, the last semblance of stability was unraveling. Yet, like most Americans who did not speak Arabic and therefore communicated only with or through men educated in American or British schools and whose success depended on our continued presence in their country, I was extremely naïve. I could read about the dark history of places like Lebanon; I understood that there were deep-seated antagonisms between Arabs, Christians, and Jews; but I had been trained to believe that capitalism would work miracles. I had recently been promoted. I was flying first class, staying in the best hotels, and dining at the finest restaurants—frequently accompanied by beautiful women. Along with all the other U.S. businessmen, consultants, and government officials, and the "experts" at the World Bank and the IMF, I was confident that we were making great strides toward democracy and progress throughout the Middle East.

Lebanon would open my eyes to a different reality.

32

Lebanon: "Stark Raving Mad"

A chauffeur drove me from the Beirut airport to the luxurious Phoenician Intercontinental. A young bellman greeted me enthusiastically, took my bag, and ushered me into the lobby. As I turned from the reservation desk, I crashed into another man. I stepped back and apologized, shocked by a familiar face that gave me a leering smile and the unforgettable voice that muttered, "It's OK."

The bellman grabbed my arm and hustled me away, then stopped. "Yes, Marlon Brando is your neighbor tonight," he said. He shook his head and added. "He's got a terrible temper. Please don't ask for his autograph."

I could not help gawking as we headed for the elevator. Brando looked older than the last time I had seen him in a movie, but there was no doubt that he was indeed the actor I had long admired for his performances in *On the Waterfront* and *A Streetcar Named Desire*. I had read about his most recent film, *Burn!*—a performance he claimed was his best yet. I took it as a good omen that I had encountered—literally—the great actor and infamous rebel on this, my first trip to the Middle East. Years later when I finally saw *Burn!* I was deeply amused by the irony: Brando played the precursor of an EHM in this groundbreaking film about empire building.

The next morning, Charlie Illingworth's friend picked me up in his car. He introduced himself as "Smiley," although I could never quite figure out why since he was not by nature a jovial person and seldom exhibited the expression for which he apparently was named. As it turned out, he did not work for the embassy, but rather for the United States Agency for International Development. He had spent

his entire professional life with USAID and now, approaching retirement, had requested Lebanon as his final assignment; he had
grown up there, the son of missionaries, and had wanted to retire to
the land of his youth. Now, however, he had changed his mind.

"Too much turmoil," he told me as we drove along a spectacular
stretch of the Mediterranean. "These damn Muslims are getting
out of hand. Simply can't be trusted. No matter what the deal we
strike with them, they never keep their end of it."

I asked him to show me some of the Palestinian refugee camps
I had heard so much about. At first reluctant, he eventually agreed
to drive me by one of them. Despite my recent experiences in Indonesia, I was shocked by the poverty and degradation. The camp
consisted of a mass of hovels crowded together and surrounded by
fences. I wondered aloud how the people living there maintained
their sanity.

"They don't," Smiley assured me. "They're stark raving mad.
The lot of them."

I asked him about water, sewage, and other basic services.

He guffawed. "All you have to do is open the window and take
a whiff to know that 'sanitation' ain't in their vocabulary." He gave
me the closest thing I had seen to a grin, and pointed. "Another
planet from where you and I live." His eyes returned to the road
ahead. "These people are pigs. Consider this: A little over a year
ago the Lebanese government and the PLO signed something called
the Cairo Agreement. It grants residency, labor rights, and auton-
omy to Palestinians. Since then the Lebanese government's been
trying to clean things up." He sighed. "But typical of Arab Muslims, these Palestinians just can't accept a good thing. The PLO
stepped up its attacks and is striking deals with the Lebanese
Communists. Really pissing off the government here, as well as
yours truly, us guys from the good ole US of A. There's going to be
retaliation. No question about it. These A-rabs are about to pay the
price for their insanity."

That day disturbed me deeply. As a Peace Corps volunteer in the

Ecuadorian jungle, I had lived like a campesino and had been disgusted by the elegant lives of U.S. embassy and USAID people—by
their houses, cars, clothes, and the obvious gap between them and
the majority of Ecuadorians. But I had never heard any of them talk
like Smiley. I was stunned by his bitterness and overt prejudices
and by his willingness to share them with a stranger like me. He
derided Islam, contrasting what he referred to as "a sword-wielding
prophet" with Christianity's "prince of peace." I was tempted to
mention the role the Catholic Church has played in fomenting
wars, to compare the Arab Saladin's compassion for captured Cru-
saders with the slaughter of Muslim prisoners by European knights.
However, I was intimidated by him; I was the new guy on the block.
I held my tongue. I tried to write his diatribes off as acrimony. I
supposed that at this point in his life he did not care what I or anyone else thought about him. Retirement was just around the corner.
The place he had dreamed about living in had disappointed him.
Like many bitter people, he was taking his frustrations out on the
nearest, most defenseless target, the Palestinians.

Smiley dropped me off at my hotel. I offered to buy him dinner,
but he said he had other commitments. When we shook hands, he
held onto mine. "I hope," he said, "that you won't take me wrong.
I'm not a pessimist. I know in the end we will win. We have to. Islam is a false religion. Lacks a conscience, a soul. Imagine if your
equivalent to Christ lopped peoples' heads off! What kind of a religion is that?"

Over dinner alone at the Phoenician, I thought about that last
comment. My time in Beirut convinced me that a clash in cultures—
especially around religion—was the overt cause of many of the
problems in the Middle East, although not necessarily the root
cause. I knew that the Crusades had been organized by the Church
as a war against what it called "the Satanic forces of Islam"; however, I had also read that Europe, suffering from strife, high unemployment, and the Plague, was ripe for rebellion and that the
aristocracy used the Crusades to refocus that anger and conquer

new lands. I was struck by the contrast between Smiley's view of Islam and what I had heard in Indonesia just a few months earlier.

Living in the West Javanese mountain city of Bandung I be-friended a young man whose mother managed the guesthouse where I and the rest of the MAIN team were staying. As described in *Confessions*, Rasy introduced me to a number of his university friends. One night they accompanied me to a *dalang*, a traditional Javanese puppet show. A puppet of Richard Nixon and another I took to be Henry Kissinger stood next to a map of the Middle and Far East; each of the countries hung from a hook over its respective position. Nixon lifted countries off their hooks and thrust them into his mouth. Every time he picked up a Middle Eastern country, he tasted it and shouted something that was translated as, "Bitter! Rubbish. We don't need any more of this!" then he tossed it into a bucket held by Henry Kissinger.

After the show, the students and I retired to a local coffeehouse. They explained to me that in the opinion of many Indonesians the United States was waging an anti-Islamic war. They informed me that back in the fifties the British historian Arnold Toynbee had predicted that the real war in the next century would not be be-tween Communists and capitalists, but between Christians and Muslims.

A young English major at the university patiently described their view. "The West," she said, "especially its leader, the U.S., is deter-mined to take control of all the world, to become the greatest em-pire in history. It has already gotten very close to succeeding. The Soviet Union currently stands in its way, but the Soviets will not endure. They have no religion, no faith, no substance behind their ideology. History demonstrates that faith—soul, a belief in higher powers—is essential. We Muslims have it. We have it more than anyone else in the world, even more than the Christians. So we wait. We grow strong."

She looked me in the eyes. "Stop being so greedy, and so selfish. Realize that there is more to the world than your big houses and fancy stores. People are starving and you worry about oil for your cars. Babies are dying of thirst and you search the fashion pages for the latest styles. Nations like ours are drowning in poverty, but your people don't even hear our cries for help. You shut your ears to the voices of those who try to tell you these things. You label them radicals or Communists. You must open your hearts to the poor and downtrodden, instead of driving them further into poverty and servitude. There's not much time left. If you don't change, you're doomed."

Recalling that evening and my more recent day with Smiley, I wondered if there was any hope for a world where religion had become the basis for exploitation. How could so many people be taught to look at religion so differently? How could the messages of Muhammad and Christ both be used to justify war?

The implications of those questions continued to haunt me. That first visit to the Middle East gave me a new perspective on religion's importance in international politics. It was in Egypt, however, that I personally experienced the power of religion as an agent of hatred.

33

USAID Speaks

"The pyramids of Egypt symbolize the role that country must play if we're to win the hearts and minds of the Arabs," MAIN's enigmatic, octogenarian chairman and CEO Mac Hall told a group of us who had assembled for lunch at the posh Engineers Club on the top floor of the Prudential Tower, Boston's tallest building and the home of MAIN's executive offices. "Egypt will form the base, large and firm. Then we will pile them up, one country after the next."

It was 1974, a pivotal moment in Egypt's long history. MAIN and our corporatocracy clients were determined to take advantage of this opportunity. A door opened when we won a contract to complete a major study in Alexandria. A USAID officer had flown up from Washington for a luncheon briefing on the country's struggles and the goals of our work there.

His cropped hair, immaculately trimmed mustache, starched shirt, gray suit, blue necktie accentuated with a slash of red, and two lapel pins—one of the U.S. flag, the other, a black hand clasping a white one—accentuated his role as a government representative, one of the new breed of colonizer-posing-as-altruist. He sat very stiffly at the table and, as he talked, frequently shot deferential glances at Mac Hall. I realized that he came to us in several guises: that of an expert on Egypt, the man who would evaluate our study and approve payment of our fees, and also as a potential employee, a Washington bureaucrat always on the lookout for a better job or lucrative retirement consultancy.

While he described his experiences in the Middle East, he wove Egypt's history into his monologue, emphasizing that centuries of foreign domination had laid the foundation for post–World War II events. "The Muslim Brotherhood," he said, spitting out the words as though they stung his tongue, "became very influential. They demanded that Egypt break off ties with Europe. The Brethren joined forces with the Society of Free Officers, a revolutionary group of Egyptian army brass, to oppose King Farouk—hated because he was an Albanian whose family gained prominence in Egypt under the Ottoman Empire and was later supported by the British—and us. This coalition toppled Farouk, much to our chagrin. Well, you know who came next. Lieutenant Colonel Gamal Abdel Nasser was sworn in as premier in 1954 and then president in 1956."

In what the USAID man described as "a reckless gamble," Nasser declared his independence from the Western powers. "He negotiated deals to buy Soviet weapons. Of course we and the Brits withdrew our offers to build a dam at Aswan. It infuriated Nasser. So he nationalized the Suez Canal. Israel responded in 1956 by invading the Sinai Peninsula. You can bet we had something to do with that, but not officially. England and France both claimed the canal as essential to their security. They bombed Egyptian positions and sent in their armies. The canal was shut down."

The USAID man frowned. "We simply couldn't tolerate that. The world clamored for U.S. goods and Middle Eastern oil. The long haul around Africa was way too costly. A bunch of corporate executives visited the White House. Ike heard them. The general took command." He grinned at Hall. "A cease-fire was proclaimed in November 1956, and a U.N. peacekeeping force arrived to patrol the borders between Egypt and Israel." He paused to take a sip of water and, I supposed, allow the rest of us to ponder the levity of his words. "In essence," he continued, "Uncle Sam forced Israel, Britain, and France to pull out. Only a little over a year earlier, we'd returned sanity to Iran by deposing that Commie Mossadegh and reinstating our friend the shah. Now, we showed the Arabs we would stand behind them in Egypt. Washington became the undisputed dominant power in the region."

The review that afternoon in a private club atop the Prudential

Tower strengthened my growing cynicism as well as my desire to enjoy the fruits accruing to this dominant power I called home. As I listened, it seemed evident that the "triumphs" in Iran and Egypt had established the supremacy of the corporatocracy and that this government employee was paid to brag about it. Those corporate executives, who just happened to control the defense industry along with most of the rest of the American economy, had forced the president of the United States to acquiesce to their demands. Now, less than two decades later, a government agency was spinning its revised view of history into its official talks. I was amazed at the cunning of these people and I felt both privileged and guilty to be included in this scheme for building what I was coming to understand was nothing less than the world's first secret empire.

I glanced out the window at the Charles River far below; across it in the distance, the sun reflected off the ivy-laced buildings of Harvard, which had undoubtedly educated at least several of those executives who visited the White House that day. I recalled Eisenhower's speech about the military-industrial complex. It seemed extremely ironic that a career military officer and supreme commander of Allied forces during World War II was the first to publicly expose the existence of what today we refer to as the corporatocracy. He had watched those executives gain influence over U.S. foreign policy during the Korean War. He had witnessed how they manipulated the press and Congress and employed the communist threat as a justification for whittling away at civil liberties. He had stood by as they sold technologies to the military for delivering missile-guided nuclear warheads to distant lands. But in Egypt, during the Suez crisis, he must have begun to truly fear the pact between the government, military, and corporations. He had acquiesced, yes. But deep inside, he must have seethed. A man trained to discipline himself, he had, I guessed, bided his time, waiting until his term as president was over. Then he dropped his own bomb. Like many good anti–Vietnam War protesters in the late 1960s I had hung a framed copy of Ike's January 17, 1961, address—his farewell speech—over my desk.

Eisenhower described his country as one whose economy had been built on peaceful endeavors. "Until the latest of our world conflicts," he said, "the United States had no armaments industry. American makers of plowshares could, with time and as required, make swords as well." Then he issued a warning:

> In the councils of government, we must guard against the acquisition of unwarranted influence, whether sought or unsought, by the military-industrial complex. The potential for the disastrous rise of misplaced power exists and will persist.
>
> We must never let the weight of this combination endanger our liberties or democratic processes. We should take nothing for granted. Only an alert and knowledgeable citizenry can compel the proper meshing of the huge industrial and military machinery of defense with our peaceful methods and goals, so that security and liberty may prosper together.

"Nasser was a hothead." The USAID officer's voice brought my attention back to the Engineers Club. "He was a hothead who thought he could outsmart us. So he foolishly continued to court the Soviet Union. He got them to build the Aswan High Dam. You can only imagine how your friend"—he turned to Mac Hall—"Mr. Bechtel felt about that."

Hall chortled. "Not just Bechtel—the whole lot of us, everyone in the engineering business."

"Right."

"But Bechtel had the connections, the president's ear." Hall glanced around the table. "Very good at kissing ass."

This brought laughter.

The USAID man took another sip of water before continuing. "Meanwhile the Muslim Brotherhood was back in play. They felt betrayed by Nasser's partnership with atheistic Communists and his refusal to create an Islamic government. They claimed all this ran counter to an agreement they made when they joined forces with the Society of Free Officers to overthrow Farouk. They wanted their president to adopt the Koran as the basis for their constitution. When he refused, they sent in one of their hit teams to assassinate him. But they botched the job and it backfired. Nasser's popularity grew. He banned the Brotherhood, sentenced four thousand of its members to prison camps, and had the ringleaders executed. Those who escaped went underground. Some attempted to infiltrate labor unions, schools, and even the military. Many left the country, heading for Jordan, Saudi Arabia, Sudan, Syria, and—as you know—Kuwait, where you guys have a major electrification project. Right?" He nodded at Hall. "Well, over the years they've evolved into one of the most influential pro-Islamic forces in the world. Their goal is to drive us—everyone from the West, all the Christian cultures—out of the Middle East, overthrow secular leaders, like those in Egypt and Iran, and replace them with mullahs."

I was tempted to ask him about the rumors I had heard that, despite their stated goals and because they opposed communism, the Brethren received CIA funding and training. But I knew that he could only answer such a question one way and that asking it might cost me dearly, especially under these circumstances.

"Any questions?" He glanced around. "Just about done. The sixties were tumultuous for Egypt. Nasser instituted economic reforms, Marxism, including a mandate that the government own at least 51 percent of all Egyptian businesses. What a disaster. All it did was manage to piss us off more. The U.N. peacekeeping force remained until 1967, sporadic fighting occurred between Egyptian and Israeli forces until 1970, and the canal continues to be closed to shipping to this day. Nasser died less than four years ago, in 1970. Vice President Anwar Sadat took over.

"We worked diligently to bring Sadat around to our side. Believe me, I was there. At first he resisted. He made a big deal out of concluding a treaty with the Soviets that Nasser began. He seemed to enjoy thumbing his nose at us. But we ignored the insults and hung in there. It worked. Sadat did an about-face. He expelled the Soviets in seventy-two." He sighed. "Then he blew it again. He sent troops across the Suez Canal and attacked Israeli positions in the Sinai. Simultaneously, Syria invaded Israel along the Golan Heights. Israel drove back their attackers, and you know the rest: The Yom Kippur War ended in a cease-fire on October 24, 1973. Now, Sadat's feverishly courting us again, trying to make amends—negotiating disengagement accords with Israel, actively encouraging foreign investment, and requesting U.S. and World Bank aid. The window of opportunity has opened . . ."

He drained his water. "Mr. Hall, I very much agree with your statement." He glanced down at a paper on the table next to his plate. " 'The pyramids of Egypt symbolize the role that country must play if we're to win the hearts and minds of the Arabs. Egypt will form the base, large and firm. Then we will pile them up, one country after the next.' " He leaned toward Hall, a subtle but obvious bow of respect. "Sir, I'd like to commend you for that. A brilliant evaluation. It totally reflects the reality of where we stand today."

After lunch, we milled around and shook each other's hands. At one point I wandered over to the window to take another look at Harvard. I felt a tap on my shoulder. When I turned I was shocked to see George Rich's ancient and weather-beaten face smiling kindly at me; next to Hall, he was considered the most powerful man at MAIN. "Presidents come and go," my boss Bruno Zambotti had once told me, "but Hall and Rich are always there, pulling the strings."

George Rich had been sitting at a nearby table with a couple of other men. "Quite a view," he said. "Got a moment? Can you come to my office?"

34

Egypt: Controlling Africa

I could not believe my good fortune. First, lunch with Mac Hall and a group of top executives; now, an invitation from a man who was truly a living legend in the engineering profession. I had heard many stories about George Rich's exploits in Africa and the Middle East. He was one of the first to venture into remote areas and develop hydroelectric sites for rural towns. He had traveled down the Congo River back in the days when it was still Joseph Conrad's *Heart of Darkness*. Rumor had it that he had trudged across deserts with Lawrence of Arabia. Now, late in life (I had been informed that he was eighty-four), he was held in the highest esteem by engineers from around the globe. I had discovered that mentioning his name to the heads of companies in Bogotá and Tehran would win invitations to home-cooked meals in their homes (something practically unheard of among Iranians). He was also one of the founding partners of Uhl, Hall, and Rich, an engineering firm that had been created by MAIN's CEO and his two closest associates to do work that, for reasons no one ever satisfactorily explained to me, could not be accomplished by MAIN itself. I had been told that the laws of New York state required such a company. But my hunch—and it was just a hunch—was that it had been set up to conduct more clandestine activities, or perhaps to help its three principals launder money— their own and that of wealthy clients and government organizations.

I followed George Rich out of the restaurant. However, we did not go to his office. Instead, after taking the elevator down to the floor where MAIN's executive offices were located, we headed along the corridor to the boardroom. He produced a key and ushered me inside. "Changed my mind," he said, motioning for me to sit in one of the plush chairs. "I think this place is a bit more private than my office."

He turned his back and strolled over to a display on the wall. It centered around a lighted map of the world with a parabolic shadow that moved across it indicating where day became night. I had been admitted to this room once before to study this map. Mac Hall's private secretary had unlocked the door and stood discreetly to the side as I determined what time I would have to rouse myself that night to make a telephone call to Bangkok.

Rich pointed at the top of the African continent. "Egypt." He turned to face me. "I know you just got the cheerleader version from that A-I-D guy. Now, I want to make sure you know the real story. I understand you're pretty sharp, got the true picture of what we do. You'll be going to Egypt soon and then to Kuwait, Iraq, and Saudi Arabia." He let this sink in, fully aware, I was certain, of the thrill the names of these countries—and the knowledge that I would visit them—inspired in me. "You know, of course, that our job is much bigger than what it appears, what the contracts state." He leaned forward and stared at me. "Right?"

"Yes, sir. I fully understand."

"Good. I've never been knighted. I'm no 'sir.' My name's George."

I could only smile, wondering whether I would ever be able to call him that, to his face.

"OK," I said.

He tapped the map with his knuckles. "You've been informed about the Muslim Brotherhood."

"Yes."

"Well, they're very dangerous, must be won over, compromised, bought out, destroyed, whatever, because they can't be stopped. Sadat proved that. You go after them and they just gain more support. Like throwing kerosene on a fire." He pulled a chair up in front of mine and stood behind it, facing me. "But that's not your job, not now at least." He sat down, so close our knees nearly touched. "Look at that map." He pointed. "What do you see?"

I was confused. "Egypt, you mean?"

"Of course, Egypt. But where is it? Where's Egypt?" He patted my knee. "Get up there and take a good look."

I did. "On the Mediterranean and Red Seas, next door to Israel."

He gave a sigh. "What continent?"

"Africa."

"Yes, the light flashes on!" He reached above his head and made the motions of a man pulling a string. "Yes indeed, Africa. Take another look at that map. Contrary to what most Americans seem to think, Egypt's an African country. Is it part of the Middle East? Sure. The Middle East isn't a continent. Middle country. A rope that ties Europe and Asia. And, contrary to public opinion, Egypt ties both of them to Africa. Now, let me ask you a really tough one. Does Egypt have a river?"

"The Nile."

"Right. And what can you tell me, from that map, about the Nile River?"

"It runs through Sudan . . ."

"Which until 1956 was part of Egypt. It was granted independence by the British, of all things, by the Brits and the Egyptians. However, many Egyptians are still pissed off about that, they consider that huge piece of real estate theirs. Where else does the Nile go?"

"Well, if you include both branches of the Nile, Lake Tanganyika, and those other smaller lakes, it covers a good share of the continent."

"Aha. Welcome to the land of Dr. Livingston I presume. One more question. If you get this one right, you can come back here and sit down again. What direction does the Nile flow?"

"North."

"Bravo. So, what you're saying is that a great deal of the African continent drains into the Nile and the Nile flows into Egypt, right? Good. Then can we surmise that the fertile flood plain where the pharaohs built their pyramids contains the silt—the topsoil, the heart and soul if you will—of a great portion of Africa? That Cairo is built on African soil, not just because it sits on the African continent but because it sits on soil that originates in the lands south of it? Right you are. Come, rest yourself here again."

I took my seat and waited for him to continue. He just sat there staring at me. I tried to choose my words carefully, aware that this man could make or break my career. "I understand what you're saying. Egypt may play an important role in the Arab world, but it also has an impact on Africa." I glanced back at the map. "It's a bridge, from both a geographic and a social perspective. Also economically and ethnically." He continued to stare. I had missed something. "And, of course, religion too."

"Very good." He stood up, clasped his hands behind his back and wandered over to the map again. "Egypt, Sudan, Ethiopia, Somalia, Kenya . . . these are all ancient lands, interconnected through the threads of history, not to be taken lightly. The Greek historian Herodotus sang their praises in the fifth century B.C. Legend has it that the Ethiopian monarchy—today's Emperor Haile Selassie— was founded by the son of Israel's King Solomon and the Queen of Sheba. This entire region is an amazing place. Not to be taken lightly." He shook his head solemnly. "No, sir, not to be taken lightly at all." He stared at the map for another long moment. Then he came back to me. "You know there's one hell of a lot of oil in that region too. I'm certain of it. I've spent a lifetime studying geology and I can tell you that during your life Africa will become a battleground over oil." He sat down. "So go ahead and mind the words of Mr. U-S-A-I-D, go off to Egypt and use it as a staging ground for subjugating the Middle East. And also, recognize what few people are talking about today . . ."

"It's the staging ground for Africa too."

"And if you ever intend to have children, and want them to live prosperous lives, you damn well better make sure that we control the African continent. We need the Middle East. Yes. But we must have Africa too."

Walking out of that boardroom I felt elated. During a few short hours I had attended a meeting with MAIN's CEO and a senior USAID officer and I had been singled out by George Rich. I had never before thought about the fact that Egypt was part of Africa as well as the Middle East or that it performed such a significant function in geopolitics. I was certain that few Americans were privy to this perspective. I felt like a man on a mission, who had been initiated into an exclusive club.

I rode the elevator to the ground floor and began to walk across the Prudential Center toward the building that housed my office, the Southeast Tower, 101 Huntington Avenue. Perhaps, I thought, Rich's last comment was the key. Someday I would raise a family. I peered through the window of an upscale clothing store at a male mannequin wearing a pinstripe suit. I promised to return later in the week and purchase that suit. The decision to do so liberated me. I told myself that George Rich, the venerable engineer, was right; we had to take control of countries with resources our corporations wanted, for the sake of future generations.

I bought that suit. And within weeks, I stepped onto a plane, headed for Egypt.

35

Infidel Dog

During my times in Cairo and Alexandria, I grew increasingly frustrated by the lack of cooperation from local officials. I had been hired by USAID to develop economic forecasts that would be used by the Egyptian government to procure World Bank financing. To do my job properly I needed detailed population statistics for specific regions of the country. Although I knew they existed, I was told by one bureaucrat after another that the information was not available for public consumption. I kept pointing out that I was not the public, that I was working for them, in the strictest confidence, and that I had to obtain those statistics if they expected me to compile a report that would ultimately bring billions of dollars into their country. This sort of appeal-cum-threat had worked for me in Asia and Latin America; however, it seemed to have no impact in Egypt.

The officials in Cairo and Alexandria who were assigned as my counterparts, and therefore were supposed to expedite my work, showed me around their cities. We visited spice markets and smoky cafes where turban-wrapped men played dominoes and puffed on bubbling hookahs, strolled along the Nile and the Mediterranean, gawked at precious jewels and priceless antiquities in ancient palaces, and consumed gallons of tea. But whenever I reminded them that I was waiting for the population statistics, they reiterated the difficulties while soliciting my patience. "Things take a great deal of time here," they would say. Or "This is not like America, we are a very old country, camels walk slowly." When I offered to bribe them—legally, of course, by paying excessive amounts for people to work overtime, with the officials pocketing the difference—they merely shook their heads and offered me another cup of tea.

Finally, in utter frustration, I decided to go above my counterparts' heads. It was a drastic step—one I had always avoided before because of the risk of antagonizing people I relied on—but this was a situation that had turned desperate.

I arranged a meeting with a man at the top of the government, someone who had served in several ministries and now was a personal adviser to President Sadat. He had a long formal name, but I was told to simply refer to him as Dr. Asim. He had graduated from Harvard Business School, was intimately familiar with organizations like the World Bank and USAID, and had a reputation for getting things done. For my part, I understood that his assistance would not be cheap; I was prepared to bribe him generously.

I was delivered to a modern high-rise office building and then escorted by a burly security officer into an elevator and to the top floor. A dour-faced, tall, thin Egyptian man in a black suit showed us into a tiny room with a couple of couches and in perfect British-accented English informed us that there would be a very short wait. The security officer, who spoke no English, sat down across from me. We waited. I read an old copy of TIME from a pile of magazines on the table between our couches. The security officer dozed. I read a *National Geographic*. We waited for nearly two hours. Tea was never offered. There was no doubt in my mind that Dr. Asim was serving notice of his importance—and, judging from the lack of tea, his displeasure that I would try to bypass the normal channels; although seething, I prepared myself to offer an even bigger bribe.

At last, the tall, thin Egyptian reappeared. Without apologies, he ushered me down a long corridor to a massive wooden door that would have suited King Tut's tomb far better than this contemporary building. He opened it. I was shocked by the vastness of the room; it was opulent enough to please the most egotistic pharaoh, decorated in a combination of ancient Egyptian and modern Park Avenue. Antique papyrus scrolls vied with Picasso vases. Modern designer furniture rested on Persian carpets.

Dr. Asim was hunched over a colossal desk, dressed in a dark blue suit and gold tie. His face was pudgy and soft, like a melon. He wore wire-rimmed spectacles, the kind I associate with Benjamin Franklin. He did not bother to look up when I walked in. The tall, thin man bowed out. I stood near the doorway waiting as the Dr. apparently finished some paperwork. Finally he raised his eyes. "Sit," he said indicating a chair in front of his desk and then returned to his work.

I felt confused and slighted. I might have transgressed, but this was overkill. Had he forgotten that I represented a prestigious consulting firm hired to help his country?

After what felt to me like a very long time, he straightened and peered at me over the tops of his glasses. He seemed to measure me as one might an insect caught scurrying across the dinner table. Then, in an effort that appeared to summon all his energy, he reached across his desk and held out his hand. I had to stand to shake it.

My confusion turned to anger. I suppressed it and forced a smile. Trying to adhere to local etiquette, I thanked him profusely for agreeing to meet with me.

He ignored my niceties and, without the exchange of greetings that are customary in Egypt, bluntly asked me what I wanted.

There could be no doubt that a polished diplomat was insulting me. Openly, flagrantly. I was tempted to walk out. Instead, I took myself back to the Engineers Club atop Boston's Prudential Tower and then to George Rich in MAIN's boardroom. Suddenly I felt vindicated. My revenge for his insolence was the knowledge that I was an EHM on assignment to exploit him and his country. I could suffer his little victories knowing that my side would win the Big One; this battle might be his, but the war would be mine. I relaxed into my chair and my smile turned genuine. "Population data."

"I beg your pardon."

"I need population data." I explained my dilemma in the briefest language. "So, you see," I ended, "unless your people cooperate with me, your country won't get all that money your president is requesting."

He slammed his fist down on his desk and stood up. His girth reflected that of his office. His chair rolled back across the floor until it bumped against the wall. "I don't give a damn about your billions," he said, his voice surprisingly low and controlled, given the histrionics of his actions. "Young man—for you can't be as old as my youngest son—what gives you the right to march in here and make demands?" He waved a spongy hand to forestall my answer. "Let me tell you a thing or two. I've lived in your country. I know all about your fancy cities, cars, and homes. I know what you think of us." Placing his hands on his desk, he leaned across it and glared at me. "Do you know how many people at Harvard asked me if I rode a camel? At Harvard! Amazing, your stupidity. The myopia of your country. We Egyptians have been around thousands of years, tens of thousands. We will be around when all of you are dust." He retrieved his chair and sat back down, emitting a loud sigh as he did so, and turned his attention once again to the papers on his desk.

I sat there staring at him, forcing myself to recall those moments in the boardroom. I also journeyed back to meetings in Indonesia where—because I spoke their language and my hosts did not realize it—I overheard government officials denigrating me, while smiling politely and offering me their finest teas. I steeled myself. I would beat him at his game.

Eventually he looked at me across the tops of those spectacles. He waved me away. "Go."

"But . . ."

He slammed his fist down once again. This time he remained seated. "Always remember," he said with that disorienting calm, "you are an infidel dog." His eyes held mine, unflinching, a trait from Harvard I supposed. "Infidel dog." He spoke the words excruciatingly slowly. "Now, go. You'll get your population data if Sadat and Allah will it."

Several days later the information was delivered. It arrived unceremoniously, in a soiled manila folder, handed to me by a courier who had ridden through the dust and gas fumes on a motorbike. There was no note attached, nothing to explain where it had come from or why, but it was all there, everything I needed. And I never paid anyone for it.

As I pored over the dozens of pages of boring numbers, I wondered why it had been such a big deal. Was there a logical reason for withholding these statistics? The only explanation that came to mind was the Egyptian fear of an Israeli air strike. But I could not see how population projections could help Israel. They already possessed, I was certain, all the information they needed to guide their planes and missiles; bombs did not care whether a specific suburb would increase by an additional 100,000 or 110,000 people during the next twenty years. Then I recalled Dr. Asim's words.

I was an infidel dog. The Egyptians knew something that only a few of my countrymen comprehended: We used data like the projections Dr. Asim had provided to me for empire building. EHM economic reports were far better weapons than Crusader swords had ever been. Israeli bombs served their purpose, delivering havoc, raining down fear, and compelling government officials to capitulate. But people like me were the real danger. We were the ones who took advantage of the havoc, channeled the fear, and made sure that those who capitulated honored their articles of surrender—and hopefully learned their lessons well enough to avoid future bombings. Ultimately we had to be pampered because we sat at the top of the heap. Men like Dr. Asim had no choice but to give in or loose their jobs. And he detested me for it.

36

Iran: Highways and Fortresses

I hopped around the globe a great deal in those days. Dr. Asim's words accompanied me. My emotions turned from defensive to angry and then I arrived at the realization that he was a proud man who hailed from a proud culture and hated the knowledge that, like Cleopatra's courtiers, he had to bow to Caesar. I understood that in his place I might have been even ruder.

I was struck by the irony that my country might be Rome to modern Egypt, but at home we experienced our own tumult. I had grown up during an era of national self-examination. We had lived through a series of events that deeply impacted my generation: the Watts and Detroit riots, the standoff at Wounded Knee, marches by César Chávez and his United Farm Workers, and multitudes of other, less publicized acts of rebellion by minorities in the United States. I equated these events with those of my ancestors who had experienced similar oppression at the hands of English masters. Impassioned indignation had led all of them to take up arms. Blacks, Indians, and Hispanics had been labeled as subversives by the corporatocracy, and my ancestors had been "traitors" to the British empire builders; yet, now young people looked up to the minority leaders as heroes and those men and women who had defended their rights against foreign masters were our founders.

And here I was: a man caught between worlds, on the one hand sympathizing with the freedom fighters, on the other serving the captains of Empire. As if to emphasize my dilemma, I traveled to Iran many times; I worked for the shah.

We EHMs portrayed the shah as a ruler determined to cultivate his country into the flower of civilization it had represented during the reigns of Darius and Alexander the Great—three centuries before Christ—a man who would employ his vast oil reserves, combined with the expertise of companies like MAIN, to materialize dreams of grandeur. Somehow we managed to convince ourselves that from this transformation would rise a democratic, egalitarian society.

Our strategy to offer the shah's government as an alternative to those in Russia, Libya, China, Korea, Cuba, Panama, Nicaragua, and other nations where anti-Americanism was rampant focused on the alleged "facts" that in 1962 the shah broke up large private land holdings and turned them over to peasants; he—and we—then created his White Revolution, a program that appeared to inaugurate extensive socioeconomic reforms. I shudder now, looking back, because I know that in our hearts we understood that all this was really a whitewashed revolution. It was a subterfuge for boosting the shah's power. On the surface, Iran was a model of Christian-Muslim cooporation. However, in actuality it was a proxy for U.S. hegemony in the Middle East. It was exactly what Dr. Asim had feared for Egypt. It was also an outcome of the type George Rich wanted when he advocated controlling the Middle East and Africa for the sake of America's future generations.

MAIN's contractual assignments in Iran increased significantly after 1974. The push for oil had grown frenetic. The word was out: Bring OPEC into our fold, make them servants to the Empire.

My job was critical. The planners and engineers depended on my forecasts of regional development to design electrical systems that would provide the huge amounts of energy needed to fuel the industrial, commercial, and military growth required to assure wealthy Iranians that they would prosper. Their happiness was the key to maintaining the shah's rule—and the steady flow of oil.

"You'll fly from Tehran to Kerman," Bruno Zambotti, my boss at MAIN, told me. "An oasis in the famous Dasht-e Lut, the high plateau desert where Alexander made his historic march. An oasis of secret delights. From there you'll drive through some of the most spectacular desert on this planet, to Bandar-e Abbas. Today it's a sleepy fishing village. Tomorrow it will rival the Riviera." By then I knew Bruno was prone to hyperbole, but I had no idea . . .

I joined two MAIN engineers on a small plane from Tehran to Kerman. It was midsummer; although late afternoon, the heat was stifling. The town appeared neglected by time and, except for a few children and old people loitering in the shadows, vacant. If the dust and squalor were hiding secret delights, they were certainly beyond my reach—or imagination. Sweating profusely, we checked into the town's best hotel. The lobby was small, gloomy, and practically devoid of furniture. The young man behind the receptionist's counter was pleased to inform us that, yes, they served cold beer at the patio bar. Each of us had our own room—amazingly "with bathroom"— and we agreed to meet at the bar in thirty minutes.

The room was typically sparse, but delightfully clean. To my relief, it sported a window AC unit—very noisy, but functioning. Although there was indeed a bathroom, I discovered that the toilet did not flush. Two faucets protruded next to it. The higher one turned on a tiny spigot above my head that I supposed served as a shower; the lower one could be used to fill a rusty bucket that allowed me to flush the toilet.

I stripped down to take a shower standing in the tiny space between the toilet and the wall. There was no shower curtain; when I turned on the faucet a paltry spray missed me but drenched the toilet. If I leaned over the porcelain bowl I could dampen myself enough to work up a lather and rinse off. The only other indication that this contraption was supposed to perform the function of a shower was the hole in the floor at the opposite end of the bathroom through which the water eventually drained. I wondered when Bruno had last visited this "oasis."

Surprisingly refreshed after my shower I made my way to the patio bar, four rust-flecked iron tables and a dozen chairs situated on a terrace that opened to an impressive view of the nearby desert. One of the engineers, Frank, was already seated there, three full beer glasses on the table in front of him.

"Only one brand," he said. "I figured you'd take it."

We waited fifteen minutes. Then we decided that our companion must be napping. We toasted the next day's journey and took a drink. As we set our glasses down, James arrived. He shuffled across the terrace looking bedraggled. He was holding the shirt he had worn on the flight out. It was sopping, dripping wet. He slapped the shirt onto the table, plopped down in the empty seat, and drained his glass of beer.

"What happened?" Frank asked.

"I had to take a crap," James replied. "The toilet wouldn't flush. I saw that damn bucket and turned on the faucet—the wrong one. I got soaked by the shower."

When we finally stopped laughing, Frank pointed out that the desert air would dry the shirt in no time.

"That's what I figured," said James. "Otherwise I'd never have carried it out here to this fancy bar."

The next morning we were picked up by two Iranians—a government engineer/translator and a driver—in a jeep wagon. They took the front seat and the three of us crammed ourselves into the backseat, me—the youngest—in the middle, straddling the mound of the driveshaft. As we drove along the crude road that would transport us from the high central plateau desert down to the shores of the Persian Gulf, the Iranian engineer explained that we were following the route of ancient caravans.

"This desert has always been both a curse and a blessing," he said, craning to look at us. "It protected my ancestors from enemies and made it almost impossible for them to cross their own country. Today it's more important than ever. You see, Dasht-e Lut separates Europe, Africa, and what you call the Middle East from Asia. It also offers a direct route between the Soviet Union and the Persian Gulf. Look at a map. You know that the Russians want to occupy us.

This very road we travel, rough as it is today, would become a super-highway for their military. Right alongside"—he pointed—"they'd build a huge oil pipeline. The little town where we'll sleep tonight, Bandar-e Abbas, would become a communist fortress. Jets, missiles, nuclear subs, aircraft carriers—they'd control the world's most important oil routes."

Frank, James, and I shot looks back and forth. "Guess that sums it up," James observed. "We got quite a job ahead of us. Don't feel pressured though, my friends; all we have to do is save the world from communism."

"The key," the Iranian continued, "is for us—you Americans and us Persians—to do it first. We must build that military highway and we must turn Bandar-e Abbas into our own fortress."

"That's why we're here," said Frank.

"Always keep in mind," the engineer observed, "that Iranians are not Arabs, we're Persians, Arians. We're Muslims, but the Arabs threaten us. We're with you guys 100 percent."

The desert was not the endless waves of sand Peter O'Toole had struggled through in *Lawrence of Arabia*. There was nothing monotonous about the mountains of red, purple, and russet that stretched for as far as the eye could see. To my mind, it was absolutely beautiful, as spectacular as Bruno had promised. And it was foreboding. I could not imagine caravans of hundreds of people and camels crossing it.

Despite the jeep's AC, there was no relief from the oppressive heat. We made a number of stops so the engineers could test the soil and other conditions that would impact the transmission line, pipeline, and highway. When we vacated the car, at first it seemed cooler, but then the sun bore down relentlessly. Once we took a break for tea and dates at a tiny village that truly qualified as a desert oasis, a tranquil island in a hostile sea.

Shortly after leaving the date oasis, the car filled with a terrible odor.

"Something's burning!" Frank yelled.

The driver pulled to the side of the road and slammed on the brake. "Everyone out," the Iranian engineer commanded.

The doors flew open and all the men leapt to the ground, except me. I could not lift my feet from the floor. My legs felt paralyzed.

"Hurry up," James commanded. "What's wrong with you?"

I had no idea. I strained with all my might, but my feet simply would not obey. Panicked, I slipped out of the loosely-tied topsiders I was wearing. Thankfully my feet responded. I pushed myself through the door and tumbled onto the desert floor.

Cautiously Frank peered back inside. Then he began to laugh. "The rubber soles of your shoes," he turned to me, "melted and are welded to the carpet over the drive shaft. I've seen engines overheat before, but this takes the cake!"

It required work, but eventually I was able to separate my topsiders from the burnt carpet and we continued on. We arrived in Bandar-e Abbas just as the sun was beginning to set.

37

Israel: America's Foot Soldier

Located on the Straits of Hormuz, opposite the horn of the Arabian Peninsula where the United Arab Emirates, Oman, Bahrain, and Qatar were created when the British withdrew in 1971, Bandar-e Abbas commands one of the world's most strategic corridors. It was once the headquarters of fierce pirates who marauded ships sailing out to the Arabian Sea. Today, much of the world's petroleum passes close to its shores.

When we arrived it was still a small, impoverished village, with an enormous modern hotel located right on the gulf—a prerequisite to attracting the types of consultants who could transform this town into a state-of-the art military-industrial center. The five of us were some of the hotel's first guests. We assembled for dinner to find that we and three waiters had the spacious restaurant to ourselves.

"Come back in five years," the Iranian engineer said, "and you won't recognize this place. One way or another, it'll change. Either you'll do it or the Russians will."

After we broke up, I grabbed a cigar and went alone into the night. I headed for the water. A newly constructed wharf extended out over the shallow gulf, reaching perhaps a half mile from the shore. There was no moon, but the night sky was bright with stars. I wandered slowly out onto the wharf. A breeze stirred the gulf. Despite the lit cigar, the stench of decaying fish permeated the air. Looking across the dark water, I wondered what was happening on the other side. I realized that I knew little about the countries that rimmed Saudi Arabia.

About three-quarters of the way out, I stopped, halted by a jolt of fear. A strange red glow rose and fell in a slow arc at the end of the wharf. I stood still and watched it, telling myself I should scurry back to the hotel but anchored there by a perverse curiosity. I took another step. As my eyes adjusted, the ghostly image of a man materialized. I raised my cigar; the red glow mirrored my action. He too was smoking. It seemed he was mocking me. I lowered my cigar. His followed. The longer I observed him, the more curious I became. My fear dissipated. Surely a thief would not have picked the end of a wharf to find his victim. Who was he? I immediately thought about the Russians. But what would one of them be doing here, at this time of night?

I continued on, consciously altering my stride. I wanted to convey an impression of determination. And strength. Perhaps fifty feet away from him, it struck me that he might be anxious about my presence too; I slowed down.

He coughed.

I stopped.

Then he spoke. In Farsi or Arabic—I was not sure which.

"I don't understand," I said very slowly.

"American," he responded. "You're American, aren't you? I can tell from the way you walk and your accent. My English is pretty good."

"Yes, I'm American."

"I'm Turkish," he said. "Like you, a visitor, a guest in this hotel. Please come join me."

I walked up to him. We shook hands. His name was Nesim. He smoked a cigarette, not a cigar. "I'm a college history professor," he explained, "researching a book on old trade routes. I've traveled from Istanbul, following some of those routes. They brought me here."

We talked for a while about our impressions of Iran. He made no secret of his loathing for the shah, "the dictator king" as he called him. Up until this point I had not heard anyone in this country criticize the shah. I had of course read of an underground that wanted to overthrow him, but all the Iranians I knew worked for one of the branches of the shah's government. This man was different. Obviously well informed, he was not shy in expressing his beliefs. I suspected that he was pleased to have an audience; an American who was willing to listen to him must have been about the last thing he expected to encounter on the wharf. Perhaps it was the night, the place, or simply exhaustion from the journey; in any case, I found myself listening intently to Nesim's point of view.

"All of you are deceived by the dictator king," he said. "Well, not all. I'm certain your president knows the truth and the other people who run your country know it too. That is, after all, their specialty. Deception. Your leaders hide their imperialism. Or try to anyway. They hide the money they make, the things they do to corrupt people. They brag about helping the downtrodden, while they hide the fact that they protect the rich." He took a long drag on his cigarette. "You are a country behind a mask."

Several times I felt that I should interrupt, that I needed to defend the United States and by doing so justify myself; but instead I listened. Referring to the 1973 Yom Kippur War, he asked, "Why did Egypt and Syria strike at Israel? They felt they had no other options. Your people haven't a clue of the crimes the Israelis commit against Arabs, the threat they pose. Or that it is really an American war, Israel is just your foot soldier. It wasn't enough that you stole Palestine, the land its people call Dar al-Islam, the eternal domain of Muslims, and handed it to the Jews. You had to keep taking more. You used your wealth to make the Jews think you were building them a homeland. You rub Muslim noses into the shit of history. You sing fancy songs about democracy. But we saw what you think of democracy right here in Iran when your CIA overthrew Mossadegh. Oh, Israel isn't about democracy, or protecting a people victimized by Hitler. You torture, lie, and steal for oil."

He placed the hand that held his cigarette—the right one—over his heart. "I feel for the Jews in Israel. Really I do. I'm not Palestinian, so I can do that. I suppose I would kill them if it came to battle, if you try to shove your borders into Turkey, but I also sympathize with them. They're like sheep sent before armies. Shields. You Americans are to blame. You encourage Jews to sacrifice their families while your corporations pump oil. Jews are your watchdogs. You give them nuclear warheads so they can keep us Muslims in our place. You fund their army. The Palestinians have no army, just a few patriots. They have no government, no land to live on.

"For you, Israel is all about domination, about controlling oil. For the Jews, it is a dream—one that will prove illusory. For Palestinians, it is their home—a home they've been forced to vacate. For Arabs it is an enemy fortress built on Arab lands. For Muslims everywhere, it is an insult, a humiliation, a reason for us to hate you."

38

The Iraq-Iran War: Another EHM Victory

Nesim came back to me thirty years later. On a June night in 2004 I was soaring above the Middle East, headed for Qatar, a stop-off point for changing planes on my way to Nepal and Tibet. Located across the Persian Gulf from Bandar-e Abbas, Qatar was a country I had barely heard of during my EHM days. Peering through the window, I watched the sun set over Greece, Turkey, Syria, Iraq, and Iran. I thought about my grandmother, the long winter evenings when she read to me from the *Odyssey*, *The Arabian Nights,* and the Bible. My plane passed over the islands where Homer's adventurer roamed and toward the mountain where Noah had built his ark; we entered the airspace above a magical land that was the home of Babylon's hanging gardens, humanity's first cities and farms, and our earliest written language; below me was where the wheel and modern mathematics were invented. I recalled the stories that had captivated me about the fortresses attacked by Richard the Lion-hearted and defended by Saladin. Then my thoughts focused on Nesim.

It had not taken much time—a blink in history—for his prophecy to become reality. I myself had written a book exposing the deceits he had described. His Iranian dictator-king had fallen, replaced by radical mullahs; Israel had grown even more aggressive, and the United States had supported her every move; the Palestinians suffered and showed others, like bin Laden, about the power of a single person wearing a homemade bomb; the United States had demonstrated its brutality in a hundred unknown places and a few known ones: Panama, Haiti, and Sudan. Then came 9/11, Afghanistan, and Iraq. After so many years on this planet we humans had failed to wean ourselves of the compulsion to subjugate and slaughter our brothers and sisters. Gory crusades were not relegated to the past.

I felt exhausted, overcome by a profound sense of discouragement. The whole world had watched the United States launch what Muslims called a New Crusade when Stealth bombers invaded Iraq for the second time in little more than a decade. Yet, although shock and awe elevated military violence to new levels of horror, from my point of view it was simply the next predictable step in Washington's plan to dominate Middle Eastern guardians of the world's largest oil repository. Controlling, or destroying, Saddam had seemed an inevitable consequence of my own EHM successes in Saudi Arabia.

Throughout the 1980s, Washington supported Saddam's war on Iran. Not only was he our vehicle for revenge against the ayatollahs who had deposed the shah, stormed our embassy, humiliated American hostages, and expelled our oil companies, but also he sat atop the world's second-largest oil reserves. The EHMs went to work on him. We gave him billions of dollars. Bechtel built him chemical plants that we knew would produce sarin and mustard gas for killing Iranians, Kurds, and Shi'a rebels. We provided him with fighter jets, tanks, and missiles and trained his military to operate them. We pressured the Saudis and Kuwaitis to lend him $50 billion.

Watching events unfold in Iraq, I often thought back to the words of that Iranian engineer who escorted me and the other two MAIN employees from Kerman to Bandar-e Abbas. "Iranians are not Arabs, we're Persians, Arians," he had said. "The Arabs threaten us. We're with you guys 100 percent." Suddenly the tables had turned. The Iranians had become the bad guys and an Arab named Saddam was our ally.

The eight-year Iraq-Iran war was one of the longest, costliest, and bloodiest in modern history. By the time it ended in 1988, more than a million people were dead. Villages, farms, and the economies of both countries were devastated. But the corporatocracy had enjoyed another victory. Military suppliers and contractors profited handsomely. Oil prices were up. Throughout, the EHMs tried to convince Saddam to accept a deal similar to SAMA, the one I had helped forge with the House of Saud. They wanted him to join the empire.

But Saddam kept refusing. If he had complied, like the Saudis, he would have received our guarantees of protection as well as more U.S.-supplied chemical plants and weapons. When it became obvious that he was entrenched in his independent ways, Washington sent in the jackals. Assassinations of men like Saddam usually have to involve collusion by bodyguards. In the cases I knew personally—Ecuador's Roldós and Panama's Torrijos—I was certain that bodyguards trained at the United States' School of the Americas were bribed to sabotage the airplanes. Saddam understood jackals and their techniques. He had been hired by the CIA in the sixties to assassinate Qasim and had learned from us, his ally, during the eighties. He screened his men rigorously. He also hired look-alike doubles. His bodyguards were never sure if they were protecting him or an actor.

The jackals failed. So in 1991, Washington chose the option of last resort. The first President Bush sent in the U.S. military. At this point the White House did not want to take Saddam out. He was their type of leader: a strongman who could control his people and act as a deterrent against Iran. The Pentagon assumed that by destroying his army, they had chastised him; now he would come around. EHMs went back to work on him during the nineties. He did not buy their package. Once again the jackals failed. A second President Bush deployed the military. Saddam was deposed and executed.

Our second invasion of Iraq sent the strongest possible signal to Islamic militants. They knew that 9/11 was simply a justification, that the highjackers were not connected to Saddam or Iraq. They also understood that the Christian Right strongly influenced U.S. politics, had aligned itself with the Israeli lobby, and was determined to subjugate the Middle East and control world oil supplies and transportation routes.

The Arab response was predictable. From the days of lionhearted

King Richard of England to President Bush, Arabs have made two things very clear. They want: 1) Europeans (and now Americans) to stay away and 2) their own forms of government, for the most part based on Islamic law, rather than our concepts of secular democracy.

Middle Easterners never forgave Europe for arbitrarily imposing borders on tribal lands and crowning "kings" friendly to their distant regimes. Resentments that began in the Middle Ages grew over the centuries. Many Arabs believed that the new post–World War II empire led by the United States had designs similar to those of the Crusades. The more savvy among them, like Nesim, suspected from the beginning that Israel was more than a haven for a suffering people. When Prime Minister David Ben-Gurion proclaimed the birth of the new state on May 14, 1948, Egypt, Syria, Jordan, Iraq, and Lebanon immediately attacked. During the ensuing years, Muslim distrust seemed justified by the United States' uncompromising support of a country that, through a succession of wars, grabbed more and more territory from them. They were incensed by the deal we EHMs cut with Saudi Arabia and by the subsequent Westernization of that country, home to Islam's most sacred sites. The 1991 invasion of Iraq and the United States' high-profile military presence following it supported the theory that the West was continuing a tradition introduced by medieval European zealots. The second invasion was, for Middle Eastern Muslims, an intolerable affront; it conferred on Arab militants a new legitimacy; in the eyes of many around the world, they were transformed overnight from "terrorists" to "freedom fighters," and those who saw them in this new light were not restricted to the Muslim world.

My despair mounted as I thought about the escalation in weapons and its implications for the Middle East. Ours is a world bristling with arms like never before. The corporatocracy thrives on an economy that depends on manufacturing military equipment. Our arms companies rank among the world's most profitable businesses. Combined with those of the U.K., France, Russia, and Brazil, their sales approach $900 billion annually. Today's chemical, nuclear, and biological arsenals, along with the more traditional ones, may boost economies; however, they also threaten mass murder. Arms consumption has reached global addiction levels; a country's political status is often measured by the size of its armory. The corporatocracy has managed to link the business of selling death with international diplomacy. Example: Israel and Egypt each receive billions of dollars every year from Washington because they participated in the 1978 Camp David Peace Accords; as part of this "peace" deal, they must earmark a large portion of the money they are given for purchasing U.S. military equipment.

Darkness enveloped my plane and I thought about the change in geopolitics since the time of that trip with Frank and James from Kerman to Bandar-e Abbas. We traveled down that ancient desert caravan route as the Vietnam War was ending. After that, the Middle East became the arms industry's primary testing ground and market. And later, when the Cold War ceased, Islamic revolutionaries replaced communists as justification for escalating the War Machine. A rudimentary knowledge of history made all this—and the commercial motivations behind it—seem extremely obvious. I wondered how so many "educated" people could be deceived into believing that the current struggles were about defending noble ideals. The EHMs and media moguls excelled at providing disinformation that translated *greed* and *domination* into *liberty* and *democracy*. They served the corporatocracy magnificently.

By the time my plane landed in Qatar, I had been flying for nearly twenty-four hours. I was exhausted and jet-lagged. I certainly was not prepared for the man I was about to encounter.

39

Qatar and Dubai: Las Vegas in the Land of Mullahs

I disembarked into the Qatar terminal, disoriented. Glancing around, I was stunned to discover that the place resembled a modern shopping mall more than the Middle Eastern airports from my EHM days. The people themselves provided the only link to that past—at least a few of them did, the groups of men in their long traditional robes and *kaffiyehs* and the women in their *hijabs*.

Waiting in line to buy an ice cream, I struck up a conversation with a man in blue jeans, a polo shirt, and sports coat. He turned out to be a real estate developer from Los Angeles. Responding to my amazement about the airport, he said, "Most people focus on the violence in the Middle East. However, there's another side. You see it right here in this building, although it's nothing compared to what you'll find in Dubai. The financing for much of that violence comes out of the countries on this side of the Persian Gulf, the Billionaires' Club. Pure capitalist materialism. Pure gluttony." He grinned broadly. "My kind of people. Turns out Muslims are pretty much like everyone else. They love diamonds and gold, and Rolexes and Mercedes. These Arabs may talk a big story about living ascetically, following Allah's commands, not charging interest on loans, keeping their women veiled, and so forth, but just look around. They sure as hell aren't practicing it."

We arrived at the counter. He insisted on paying for my ice cream. We wandered through a sea of tables that could have been a food court in an upscale mall anywhere in the United States and sat down. He was eager to talk. "Dubai is *it*, the big enchilada among all these other tacos," he said, trimming the ice cream at the edges of his cone with his tongue. "Nothing like it in the world. The Arabs are playing Allah, bringing in hundreds of thousands of workers and humongous bulldozers to excavate, drain, dam, and dredge the sea. Dubai's expanding faster, higher, and bigger than any other country on earth. It's got an eighty-meter indoor ski slope, the world's tallest hotel, and soon it will have the world's highest building." He was now attacking his cone, as though his words drove him into a feeding frenzy. "Fancy this: Dubai is home to the World itself—hundreds of man-made islands, each representing a country or region, the whole thing extending five miles wide and five miles long out into what was once the Persian Gulf. A real estate developer's wet dream!" He finished off his cone and wiped his hands along his jeans. "You think Allah's boys don't like their booze and women? Think again. In Dubai anything goes: the best Scotch, gambling, women, drugs, prostitution. You got money, you buy anything you want. Anything."

As our plane took off from Qatar, the stars illuminated the Persian Gulf. It was a night like the one I had experienced in Bandar-e Abbas; I wondered whether that long wharf where I had met Nesim was still there, somewhere below my plane. Peering into the darkness I saw nothing. I recalled that at the end of my time as an EHM, President Carter's political future had revolved around Iran. The shah—the man Nesim detested—had fallen, the U.S. embassy was occupied, the fifty-two hostages were at center stage, and the president had tried to boost his waning polls by declaring that any attempt by militants to gain control of the Persian Gulf would be interpreted as an assault on the United States. Such an attempt, he declared, would be repelled by military force, if necessary.

Carter's threat had not been idle. He sent Delta Force to extricate the hostages. The maneuver ended in tragic failure, but now I understood that the United States' overall Middle Eastern policy—especially its support of Israel and the deals it had struck with the critical Arab governments in Saudi Arabia, Kuwait, and Egypt—had accomplished something even more vital to the corporatocracy's interests. Although our overt policies in Iran and Iraq seemed a shambles, in a more subtle way we had co-opted the Arab world once again. In Dubai, we had sold them "the world." Like China, the Middle East had bought our form of materialism.

The plane suddenly banked. A flurry of lights appeared beneath my window. Bandar-e Abbas! I looked for that wharf. Then I realized that this cluster of lights clung to the southern edge of the dark Gulf, not where Bandar-e Abbas was located at all. I was looking at Dubai, at a place that could not have been detected from a plane at night the last time I visited this area. It too had been a sleepy village. Now it was the world's most grandiose shopping mall, ski resort, casino, and entertainment center.

I craned to take it in, to try to comprehend this paradox, the brainchild of Arabs who espouse traditional Islamic beliefs and have built a new type of Mecca that mocks the original. Below me: a monument to excess that Cleopatra and King Tut might appreciate. But Osama bin Laden?

I recalled the comment MAIN's president, Jack Dauber, had made to me that night he and his wife invited me to dinner at the Hotel Intercontinental Indonesia regarding oil as the new standard for establishing the dollar's sovereignty. He had been right. Then he had turned to his wife and remarked that "the U.S. is launching a new period in world history . . ." He had been right about that too. But now a quarter century later, that period was already fading; something entirely different was emerging.

40

Into the Abyss

For many years corporatocracy policies appeared successful to businessmen like MAIN's Jack Dauber. However, events that later unfolded in Asia and Latin America have exposed those policies as failures. They propelled Asia into the 1997 economic crisis, elevated China to a global leadership role while opening it to an orgy of materialistic gluttony modeled after our own, and drastically expanded the gap between Asia's rich and poor. In Latin America, our actions relegated millions of people to destitute lives, undermined an aspiring middle class, and finally empowered indigenous and nationalistic uprisings that brought a new wave of anti corporatocracy leaders to power.

Yet Washington denied culpability for its failures. The newspapers, magazines, and airwaves were flooded with reports that blamed corrupt foreign government officials, religious fanaticism, and left-wing dictators for all the problems. The corporatocracy and its agents were painted as the good guys, intent on promoting democracy. Seldom was it mentioned that we were the ones who corrupted those officials, that our repressive policies empowered the fanatics, or that many of the Third World's leaders we classified as "dictators" were actually democratically elected, often by greater majorities of voters than U.S. presidents. Through the concerted efforts of politicians, corporate executives, and a collaborating press, the breakdown in U.S. foreign policy—at least in Asia and Latin America—was hidden from most citizens.

The failures, however, were obvious in the Middle East. Even before the invasion of Iraq, it was apparent that the corporatocracy had lost control and that EHM strategies had backfired. Violence was rampant, anti-Americanism transparent. Kermit Roosevelt's scheme led to "blowback" when, in 1979, militant nationalists dethroned the shah. U.S. support for Israel rendered millions of Palestinians homeless, generated endless warfare, and angered Muslims on every continent. Transforming Saudi Arabia into a miniature of Western culture enraged conservative Muslims. Arabs educated at Oxford and Harvard saw through the schemes for plundering their oil.

On September 11, 2001, the corporatocracy's dream of oil acquired through the collusion of Islamic surrogates and a proxy army stationed in Israel exploded into a fiery nightmare.

Washington's reaction followed a familiar route, one that put the country into greater jeopardy. U.S. military intervention in Afghanistan turned a sympathetic world against us. The invasion of Iraq sent a message that Washington was more interested in securing oil supplies than ferreting out Osama bin Laden. In the longer term, it inflamed already-furious Muslim populations, inspired millions to join terrorist cells, highlighted the vulnerability of the U.S. military, and sank the United States into what amounted to bankruptcy. The post–9/11 policies in fact were just the last and most obvious in a series of blunders. For every action the corporatocracy claimed as a success—establishing the shah of Iran, the House of Saud, ruling families in Kuwait and Jordan, and a friendly dictator in Egypt, and supporting Israeli militarism—there had been counterbalancing losses, such as the rise of the mullahs, popularity of al-Qaeda, replacement of moderate governments by radical ones, hero worship of martyred suicide bombers, and an escalation in fanaticism.

Then Lebanon again was plunged into war, much as it had been shortly after my first visit there. The turmoil began in February 2005, when former prime minister Rafik Hariri was killed in a car bombing in Beirut. His death prompted hysteria and massive street protests. The new government, voted in during democratic elections, appeared powerless to control the strongest faction in the country, Hezbollah, a Shi'a Islamist organization whose leaders were classified by Washington as terrorists.

In the summer of 2006, Israel launched massive air strikes against Lebanon, destroying parts of Beirut, killing innocent civilians, and cutting the main highway to Syria. Although many world leaders condemned this invasion as an irresponsible attempt to wipe out the Lebanese government, Washington defended Israel's actions. The United States was criticized for once again placing its oil and commercial interests above those of world peace and Middle Eastern stability.

Political scientists today marvel at the intransigence of U.S. policy makers, especially in light of similar mistakes during the Vietnam War. The North Vietnamese had proven that the most technically advanced, well-financed military in the world was not invincible. Why, a quarter century later, was it so difficult for the White House, Congress, and Pentagon to comprehend this? Why did so many experienced leaders blunder so terribly?

Perhaps the answer revolves around the fact that the corporatocracy reaped immense profits, regardless of all the miscalculations— or, some would say, because of them. The War Machine was a financial success even when it failed militarily; U.S. contractors reaped windfall profits in Vietnam, Afghanistan, and Iraq, as well as in dozens of other places suffering from armed conflicts. For the families of those who died and for the United States as whole, the cost of these wars was outrageously high. For the scorporatocracy, the payoff was huge.

The consequences of mistakes in Iraq are far more serious for the future of our country than those in Vietnam. Despite Washington's attempts to convince us that the domino effect was a global threat, Vietnam was essentially a regional conflict. By contrast, the war in Iraq, combined with antagonism throughout the entire area, is a clash of ideologies. It not only pits Christianity and Judaism against Islam, it also is a referendum on the very meaning of consumptive materialism.

It may appear that the corporatocracy is winning that referendum in places like Dubai. But all we have to do is flip the television channel to news reports from Iran, Iraq, Egypt, Lebanon, Israel, and Syria to know that Dubai is an anomaly, the illusion of an oasis in the desert. As we approach the end of the first decade of the 2000s, we can only conclude that the corporatocracy has led us into an abyss of historic proportions.

Nowhere is this abyss deeper than in Africa.

Part 4: Africa

41

Modern Conquistadors

"If you ever intend to have children, and want them to live prosperous lives, you damn well better make sure that we control the African continent."

George Rich's admonition helped me live with myself and tolerate the other U.S. consultants I shared a mansion with in Alexandria in the summer of 1974. His shadow had followed me from Cairo to the pyramids at Gaza; now it hovered behind the Egyptian government official who stood at the head of the massive cedar table that appeared almost too large for the elegant dining room in the house we rented. A colossal residence that harkened back to a bygone era, it had been built by a British merchant who amassed fortunes shipping African ivory, mummies, and jewels snatched from ancient tombs to European museums.

"History proves that Egypt is the head of the dog whose body is Africa," the official said with a smug grin. His eyes roved around the table, taking each of us in—ten men, U.S. citizens, there to develop water, sewage, and other infrastructure systems. He thumped the table with his fist. "Make it easy for our president, the honorable Anwar Sadat, to embrace America, and Africa will follow. Capitalism for the world!" He paused and motioned for the waiters to start serving dinner.

"We're the cavalry," a civil engineer from Colorado muttered, "arriving just in time to save the fort."

"Let's hope we're not Custer," someone mused. It brought a round of laughter.

Convincing ourselves that Egypt was the spearhead for development on the rest of the African continent had become a nightly exercise. We American consultants prided ourselves on our sophistication and on our abilities to quantify, to reduce complex problems to statistics that we could summarize in tables, graphs, and charts. Several held Ph.D.s, the rest a variety of advanced degrees—except for me, a lowly B.S. wise enough to keep quiet on the subject. Typical of development experts, we were head-people who spent an inordinate amount of time assuring ourselves that our work in Alexandria would generate a new epoch throughout the continent and that by the beginning of the third millennium Africa's most serious problems would be relics of the past.

For most of the team, like the majority of Americans, it seemed an easy sell. Following the examples of preceding empires, these modern-day conquistadors had signed up to transform wayward societies into shadow replicas of their own. The heathens could be saved, if only they would convert to Catholicism, or, in contemporary terms, democracy, if only they would bend to the enlightened leadership of a Caesar or a king—or to a U.S. president.

Although I tried to conform, increasingly I grew more cynical. Whether I heard these arguments in Indonesia, Iran, Colombia, or Egypt, they seemed to carry the religious overtones of my Calvinistic upbringing; in them, I heard the Puritanical preachings of early New England's Cotton Mather. But could I really believe that hell's fires would devour anyone siding with the Soviet Union? Did Saint Peter stand smiling at the gates of heaven with open arms for capitalists? And even if someone could convince me to answer "yes," could we exclude ourselves from those fires? By what stretch of the imagination would the American Way appear as free-market capitalism? Everything I saw indicated that the small-town entrepreneur was headed for extinction, replaced by the predators at the top of the food chain, the big corporations. We seemed determined to return to the monopolistic trusts of the late 1800s. And this time around it was happening on a global scale.

So what was I doing? I asked myself this question every single night. I thought about my first trip to the Middle East, those brief days in Beirut, Marlon Brando, Smiley's tour of the refugee camps, the sights, smells, textures, tastes, and sounds. It had been less than four years and yet seemed a lifetime. After dinner, I often wandered down to the Mediterranean, just a few blocks away from our mansion. The dark waves crashing against the seawall took me back to earlier times, to Anthony and Cleopatra, the pharaohs, the kings and queens who erected the pyramids, Moses . . . I peered across the waters toward Italy and east to Greece, and then farther east to the land of the Phoenicians—now Lebanon.

These thoughts of ancient empires brought an odd sort of comfort. History was a tapestry of conquest and brutality that we humans had muddled through. The sound of the waves soothed my tormented soul. George Rich stood before me pointing at the lighted map in MAIN's boardroom; the only thing that mattered was the future for the child that someday would issue from my loins. For his or her sake we had to control Africa and the Middle East. It was the knowledge that my progeny depended on it that kept me going. That and of course the fact that I was living an adventure, seeing parts of the world I previously had only dreamed about, and doing all of it on a very generous expense account.

Sometimes on those nights down by the Mediterranean I would turn and look back toward the lights of Alexandria and I would see beyond them the great expanse of Africa. I imagined it as the nightmare land depicted in Conrad's *Heart of Darkness*, a sinister, foreboding place where human beings treated each other in unspeakable ways. The violence of Africa was, in my eyes, more ghastly than the violence of other continents, the horrors more horrific.

Although I had lived in the Amazon, I felt the Congo was something different and this difference defined Africa as a whole. In my youth I had loved the Tarzan books; his jungle had been my paradise. Later, as I traveled in EHM circles and began to comprehend the truth of modern history, Tarzan's home deteriorated in my mind. Where had Edgar Rice Burroughs's hero been when the slavers arrived? The Amazon came to signify a vibrant rainforest, the Congo a malevolent swamp.

I had visited the slums of Latin America, Asia, and the Middle East, had recoiled in shock at the Museum of the Inquisition in Lima and photos of Apache warriors shackled to U.S. Army dungeon walls; I knew about the violence of Suharto's military and the shah's secret police, the SAVAK; yet, in my opinion, nothing compared to Africa. What I had not seen I visualized and my visions included innocent men, women, and children snared in nets, hauled screaming aboard slave ships, piled one on top of another, puking, shitting, rotting, trundled off to auction blocks, sweating, bleeding, dying, while back home in Africa their lands, their people, animals, and jungles were ravaged by "civilized" Europeans. All of it so my ancestors could strut in their cotton gowns.

I thought about these things often. Then one afternoon I met a young man and woman who had fled from their home in Sudan. Hearing their shocking story forced me to admit that I was repeating the sins of those slavers.

42

Sitting in America's Lap

I was leaning against the seawall, watching fishermen unload their boat when they came up and stood beside me. We exchanged smiles. One said, "Hello. How are you? Do you speak English?" This was not an uncommon experience in those days. People would often strike up casual conversations with me, out of curiosity and to practice their English.

"Yes," I replied. "I'm from the United States. My name is John. Yours?"

"My English name is Sammy. This is my sister, Samantha."

I invited them to a café where we chatted for several hours. They told me they came from southern Sudan.

"The north is Muslim," Sammy explained. "Where we live, in the south, is very different." He refused to go into detail, but I knew that those were tribal lands.

"Are you Muslims?" I asked.

"We practice it," he said.

Although I did not press him at the time, during ensuing days when they escorted me around the sights of Alexandria, they confided that their people worshipped "the spirits of the land." They had come to Alexandria after their father was murdered and their mother dragged off by northerners to be sold in the sex slave markets.

"We had gone to carry water," Sammy explained. "We heard our mother screaming and hid in the rocks."

"I was so scared," Samatha said, silently burying her face in her hands.

They found the small cache of money their parents had hidden, and made their way to Alexandria, which they said was safer for them than Cairo and where distant relatives offered them shelter. They converted to Islam, although they admitted that they continued to pray to the nature gods of their ancestors. Through their uncle, they met a British couple who ran a small school for orphans and gave them room, board, and an education in exchange for the menial tasks they performed around the school.

Following that first encounter, we spent a lot of time together. We met late in the afternoon, when they had completed their work. I would treat them to coffee and sometimes dinner. They showed me the markets, museums, and galleries listed in the guidebooks, as well as introduced me to Sudanese restaurants and sections of the city few foreigners ever visit. Despite the hardships they had endured, they were warm and open.

For me, Sammy and Samantha provided a welcome relief from the self-serving banter of my fellow consultants. Given the nature of my work, I could always justify time with them on the basis that I was gathering information to use in the report I would eventually have to write. After a while, I became convinced that I was falling in love with Samantha. I fantasized marrying this beautiful African and taking the two of them back to the States with me. I enjoyed imagining the reactions of my parents on the day I showed up with a young black Sudanese woman on my arm. When I mentioned the idea of living in the United States to Sammy, I expected him to react with appreciative enthusiasm. Instead he gave me a distressed look.

"We're African," he said. "We must return to Sudan and help our people."

"How? What will you do?"

"Fight for independence."

"But Sudan won independence in 1956."

"There is no Sudan. We're two countries, not the one the British and Egyptians created."

"The Muslim north and the south?"

"Yes. The north is part of the Middle East. The south is Africa."

This gave me a new perspective, even different from George Rich's. Egypt was one thing; Sudan quite another. I was amazed that I had never considered it before. "What about Egypt?" I asked. "Is it Middle Eastern or African?"

"Neither."

"What then?"

"Do you realize that this country never had an Egyptian-born leader after the death of Pharoah Nectanebo around three hundred years before the time of your Christ—until now, this century?"

I confessed to shock. "So where does Egypt sit?"

"Egypt used to sit with Europe."

"And now?"

"She sits in America's lap."

43

A Jackal Is Born

Jack Corbin was a teenager living in Beirut when I first visited that city in 1971. By the time I arrived in Alexandria about four years later, he had grown restless; at nineteen he contemplated leaving his family and home. He had dreamed of Africa most of his life. His decision to follow that dream would change his life forever. It would turn him into a jackal. Among his many assignments: assassinate the president of one of that continent's most strategic countries. It would also create a friendship between Jack and me that endured for years.

The son of an American corporate executive, Jack grew up with violence. He and his buddies passed many an afternoon sitting on a fence in a suburb overlooking a section of Beirut, observing the scenes of life playing out far below. Unlike the daily occurences in other boys' lives, these were sometimes deadly. One afternoon, through powerful binoculars they watched three men beat a fourth and heave his limp body into the back of a pickup truck. Another time, they witnessed the rape of a mother in front of her infant son. Afterward, a lone man crept out of the bushes and helped the two to a nearby house.

A cease-fire came. Jack and one of his friends ventured down to the city to take in a movie. As they left the theater, gunfire erupted. The cease-fire had ended. A black Mercedes raced past, stopped, reversed, stopped again. Three men leapt out, brandishing AK-47s.

They prodded Jack and his friend with their guns and shouted Arabic insults. They pushed them into the backseat of the big black sedan, accused them of spying for Israel, pistol-whipped them, and

promised to kill them before sunset. The Mercedes sped down back
alleys, through Arab slums, parts of the city that were off-limits to
people like Jack, and then delivered them to a man sitting calmly
behind a desk.

"Thank God he was PLO, not one of the radical militias," Jack told
me. "I showed him the ticket stubs from the movie. I don't know why
but I'd stuck them in my pocket. He reprimanded his men, said
they'd made fools of themselves, and ordered them to escort us out."

That experience convinced Jack to leave his city. However, he
headed into war, not away from it. "I learned that I could handle violence," he confided. "Those kidnappers didn't scare me; they pissed
me off; they stirred my adrenaline." He took off for Africa.

"The continent was a powder keg, the sort of place where a guy
like me could make real money—and have some fun." Jack and I
were sitting on the patio of a South Florida Irish restaurant. It was
2005. Although those times and places seemed distant, the fact
that Jack had just returned from Iraq, where he had completed an
assignment the U.S. military was prohibited from carrying out itself, gave our discussion a contemporary perspective. "I'd kept informed, talked with mercenaries who came through Beirut, read
my dad's *TIME* magazines. I knew what was going on. Back in
seventy-four Portugal did something that altered African history.
It opened a big door and I walked through."

I had traveled to neighboring Spain shortly after the insurrection
in Portugal overthrew a United States–friendly dictatorship. The
economic and military loses that accompanied the wars for independence in Portugal's African colonies, the debilitating illness of long-
time dictator and corporatocracy collaborator António Salazar, and
the coup staged by dissidents within the armed forces that deposed
Salazar's successor, Marcelo Caetano, had turned a former ally onto
the path of socialism. It was an EHM failure that aroused grave
concerns and sent me on a fact-finding expedition.

"After the 'Carnation Revolution,'" Jack said, grimacing, "Lisbon
immediately freed her African colonies. All of them. Suddenly and

without warning. Brought the troops home. Hundreds of thousands of Portuguese citizens who'd lived in those colonies for generations lost their lands, businesses, everything. They had to flee for their lives, mostly to South Africa, Rhodesia, Brazil, or back to Portugal. The old colonies had gained what they wanted—independence—but now were left floundering. Of course the Soviets stepped in to fill the gap. It was only a matter of days before vital oil and gas resources fell to the communist camp. After that, the liberation war against Ian Smith's Rhodesia took off big-time."

Like Jack, I had seen that time as an opportunity to advance in my profession. For him: the jackal route; for me: the EHM one. I recalled how the march to empire was double-stepping forward in places like Indonesia, Iran, and most of Latin America, but faced serious obstacles in Vietnam, where U.S. and South Vietnamese forces were in retreat, and Cambodia and Laos, where the Khmer Rouge and Pathet Lao were gaining control. Until 1974, Africa had been the great unknown. Independence movements were on the rise; however, they were often split over where to turn for help. Many of their leaders were reluctant to embrace communism and antagonize the West. We EHMs were assessing our options and jockeying for positions. MAIN had established footholds in Zaire, Liberia, Chad, Egypt, and South Africa (although in the latter we maintained a low profile due to growing anti-Apartheid sentiments). Our agents were working diligently on Nigeria and Kenya. I had recently completed a study that established the viability of erecting a huge dam across the Congo and using it to produce electricity to power mining operations and industrial parks throughout central Africa.

Lisbon's precipitous decision to free her colonies changed everything. It shifted the balance of power and threw the Pentagon and Defense and State Departments into turmoil. Heated debates over courses of action resulted in conflict among their leaders, especially the Cabinet secretaries: William Rogers (1969–73) and Henry Kissinger (1974–77) at State and Melvin Laird (1969–73),

A JACKAL IS BORN

Elliot Richardson (1973), James Schlesinger (1973–75), and Donald Rumsfeld (1975–77) at Defense. The weakened presidencies of Nixon, mired in the Watergate scandal, and Ford, who received the job by default rather than election, added to the chaos. Washington was incapable of reaching consensus on how to respond.

For the Africans the situation was unprecedented and absolutely chaotic. Centuries of European struggles for domination had left them with fabricated countries, borders that suited foreign powers rather than cultural differences. Their colonial rulers had done nothing to help them institutionalize governmental and commercial sectors. They were ill-prepared to accept the responsibilities of independence and ripe for exploitation by anyone who could move swiftly to fill the vacuums.

"We allowed the Soviets to come in like gangbusters." Jack shot me a disgusted look. "Even China outmaneuvered us. Moscow-sponsored Mozambique, a hotbed of Marxist terrorism, trained thousands of Zimbabwe African National Liberation Army recruits and sent them in packs to murder Rhodesian farmers—blacks as well as whites. Zambia jumped aboard Mao's bandwagon and set itself up as a staging site for raids into Rhodesia. To me that little country was an underdog that needed help. I landed in Rhodesia and joined its army."

Jack had always maintained that Rhodesia, unlike South Africa, "wasn't a propagator of blockheaded Apartheid." The war he joined was not, he argued, about whites versus blacks; it was a battle of survival, pitting Rhodesia against neighbors who had fallen under the Soviet spell.

Once there, the conclusions he had reached about himself after his kidnapping by the PLO in Beirut were confirmed. "I discovered I had a natural talent for soldiering. I joined the Rhodesian Light Infantry Commandos, and later passed the selection into the Special Air Service, SAS, an elite force. The training was rigorous; the jobs even more so. One time, after blowing up some bridges, we had to run for our lives for three weeks, evading thousands of enemy troops.

We were making twenty miles a day through the mountains, ambushing them, and moving on again. We had no backup that whole time and nearly died of thirst."

He remembered his first kill. "A gook rushed from a clump of trees shooting at me. I fired one shot—blew out his face. That night I worried about his family. But the next time, I simply saw an enemy, a man who wanted to kill me. Like anything else, killing gets easier the more you do it."

After his time was up in the Rhodesian army, Jack became a mercenary. "Opportunities were everywhere. By 1979 at least six African countries were embroiled in 'liberation struggles': South Africa, Angola, South-West Africa, Zambia, Mozambique, and Rhodesia."

He headed for South Africa and was recruited by a fellow jackal for one of the most dangerous operations of his life: an assignment that exposed a great deal about the illicit activities of a U.S. government few of its citizens understand. He was sent to assassinate a president who had antagonized powerful men in Washington and London.

44

The "Non-Peoples" of Diego Garcia

The determination to control African resources took on a new urgency following the OPEC oil embargoes of the early 1970s and the military debacles in Southeast Asia. Corporate executives and their lobbyists flocked to Washington. They took advantage of the confusion in the Nixon and Ford administrations and Carter's preoccupation with Iran to demand international laws guaranteeing them the right to what amounted to unfettered exploitation of African resources, especially petroleum. The executives also insisted on an extremely strong military presence—one that would establish American hegemony and protect shipping lanes, and could be used to bolster African leaders who collaborated with the corporatocracy against the wishes of their people.

Soviet and Chinese successes in Africa strengthened arguments for a strong, militarized U.S. response. The press inflamed the public with articles about the dire consequences of communist incursions in Africa and of plans in Moscow and Beijing for amassing secret forces to invade countries allied to Washington. Television networks flashed images of jungle-hardened Cuban guerrillas training African "terrorists." Rumors spread that Castro had dispatched the infamous Che Guevara to mount massive attacks against U.S. mining operations.

The pressure on Washington was immense. The closure of the Suez Canal and the introduction of supertankers buttressed the case for a "fortress" to protect the shipping lanes that ran out of Middle Eastern ports, through the Red Sea, Persian Gulf, and the Arabian Sea, into the Indian Ocean, south along the length of Africa, around the Cape of Good Hope, and into the Atlantic. Politicians jumped on the bandwagon. Social programs were sidetracked, money diverted to the Pentagon. The decision was made to build a fortress—a nuclear warhead–equipped airbase—on Aldabra Island, off Africa's east coast.

"It would reinforce Simon's Town, the South African naval installation near the Cape, of Good Hope," Jack explained. "American nuclear subs used Simon's, far away from prying eyes, to refit before returning to their long, lonely patrols in the South Atlantic and Indian oceans. An air base north of Madagascar was the perfect complement to Simon's."

However, once the project began to take form, planners discovered that Aldabra was the breeding ground for rare giant tortoises. Fearing adverse publicity from a growing ecological movement, Washington redirected its efforts to nearby Diego Garcia, the largest atoll in the Chagos chain, part of Mauritius, then a British territory. Although there were no endangered turtles on Diego Garcia, 1,800 people lived there, mostly descendents of African slaves.

"It was unacceptable," Jack told me, "to have any people inhabiting an atoll slated to become a state-of-the-art U.S. military base."

In a 1970 deal brokered by EHMs and involving U.S. and British intelligence agents, London forced Diego Garcia's residents to abandon their homes. Every attempt was made to maintain secrecy. According to the BBC:

> British politicians, diplomats and civil servants began a campaign—
> in their own words—"to maintain the pretence there were no permanent inhabitants" on the islands. This was vital, because proper residents would have to be recognized as people "whose democratic rights have to be safeguarded" . . . The inhabitants therefore became non-people.[35]

Many of the islanders were hustled across the water to neighboring Seychelles. England then leased an "uninhabited" Diego Garcia to the U.S. government. In exchange, Washington offered the British an $11 million subsidy on Polaris submarine technology. The lives of island inhabitants and their homes had been valued at about $600 a person.

The Pentagon rushed ahead to build its military base. Developed to house B-52s and, later, the radar-evading B-2 (Stealth) heavy bombers, it would play a key role in U.S. empire building, serving as a staging site for forays into the Middle East, India, and Afghanistan, as well as Africa.

Despite its strategic importance, Diego Garcia remained low-profile, a relatively unknown U.S. presence off the coast of Africa. Few people are aware that protecting it was justification for one of the most blatant assassination attempts ever undertaken by CIA-sponsored jackals.

James Mancham had been elected the Seychelles' first president after independence was declared on June 29, 1976. His primary contact with Washington and London was by way of South Africa, a staunch corporatocracy ally. Through the South Africans, Mancham made it clear that he supported the Diego Garcia deal; he offered to quietly absorb displaced islanders and understood that he and his cronies would enjoy personal benefits from the nearby military base. In the process, he also infuriated many of his countrymen.

Seychelles citizens placed a high value on their newfound nationalism. This sense of pride caused a backlash against Mancham. In addition to resenting his deference to the United States and the United Kingdom, the islanders abhorred the role their government had played in forcing their neighbors off their lands, and resented the influx of people who threatened to take their jobs and disrupt established social patterns. While Mancham was visiting London, Prime Minister France-Albert Rene decided to act. In a bloodless 1977 coup, he overthrew the president. He then embarked on a program the BBC hailed as "aimed at giving poorer people a greater share of the country's wealth."[36] He also proclaimed that Diego Garcia islanders should be allowed to return to their homeland and voiced his objections to a U.S. military base in Africa's backyard.

Washington flew into a frenzy, one that was kept invisible from the voting public. While Jack Corbin was honing his skills in Rhodesia, the corporatocracy plotted against Rene.

I was brought into the planning as Jack's EHM equivalent, ready to take action once our leaders decided which route to follow: subterfuge or assassination. Though in the end I was never asked, as Jack was, to act against Rene, I was privy to conversations that illuminate the depths to which the U.S. government will sink to maintain its power base.

45

Assassinating a President

Jack Corbin was watching the turmoil in Seychelles from Rhodesia. Gen. Chuck Noble and his friends in what Eisenhower had defined as the military-industrial complex were watching from Washington.

"Rene's chatter about helping the destitute is BS," Chuck said. The former commanding general of the U.S. Army Engineer Command in Vietnam had enjoyed a meteoric rise at MAIN—from project manager to vice president to heir apparent to CEO Mac Hall—in a dizzying couple of years. Despite my history of avoiding the draft by joining the Peace Corps, he had taken me under his wing. I was certain he had seen my National Security Agency recruitment files; he valued me as a loyal EHM. Whenever we traveled together to Washington, he invited me to stay at the exclusive Army and Navy Club. This was one of those times. We were sharing dinner in the formal dining room with two other retired generals and one retired admiral—all working for firms that did the corporatocracy's bidding.

"Rene's a Soviet puppet," Chuck continued. "He's got one mission. Throw us the hell out of Diego Garcia and turn it over to the Russians. Then he'll invite the Cubans to join the Muscovites and pretty soon the whole damn continent turns red."

The four military men questioned me extensively about my nonviolent successes in places like Indonesia and Saudi Arabia. I was impressed by the pragmatism of generals and admirals. Unlike many politicians, they seemed to want to avoid warfare if at all possible. Although the late seventies were a time when political coups and assassinations against leftist leaders were accepted Cold War weapons, high-ranking members of the armed forces seemed more dedicated to the rule of law than their counterparts in Congress and the White House. Perhaps they had learned from experience that violence begets more violence; possibly they feared that condoning such actions in other countries might lead to similar strategies in their own that could backfire against them; or maybe somewhere deep in their conscience they recalled the oaths they had taken to defend democracy.

The admiral observed that Rene seemed "determined to follow in Allende and Prat's footsteps."*[37]

All three generals immediately gave him stern glances. "Let's not go there," one of them murmured. The conversation returned to approaches that might be employed to bring Rene around to our side. I was told to be prepared to fly to Seychelles at a moment's notice.

One of the generals assigned a handsome young protégé the job of developing a relationship with the wife of a top Seychelles' diplomat. The general had observed during the course of several cocktail parties that she—in her mid-thirties—seemed bored by a husband who was nearly twice her age. Sex as a tool of espionage is not limited to professionals like the geishas I had met in Jakarta. In my experience it is used with stunning results by a variety of men and women in the service of building empire. Confidences are betrayed during the heat of passion. A common ploy for an EHM is to invoke love (or sex) as an excuse to plead for inside information in order to help his or her "official" career. "I just need a little information in order to get that promotion," goes the argument, or the more desperate, "I'm afraid I'll lose my job if I can't find a way to help my boss learn something, just a tidbit of news about . . ." When all else fails, blackmail usually brings results; while spouses may lack access to the amounts of cash perceived necessary to pay off an extortionist, they almost always can provide information.

---

* The assassination of Gen. Carlos Prat, commander of the Chilean army, shortly after that of President Allende, foreshadowed Operation Condor, a coordinated effort by six South American military governments and U.S. jackals to hunt down and kill opponents of the extreme right.

My initial meeting with the generals and admiral was followed by others in Washington and Boston. Although the individuals sometimes changed, the profiles of those attending remained the same: influential members of the military retired into high corporate positions or their understudies. Chuck attended several but, always one to delegate, often left me to move forward on my own.

The general with the handsome young protégé had a long association with Diego Garcia and initiated many of the meetings. He reported back that his protégé was making progress, although not as quickly as had been expected. "He says she's horny as a cat in heat, but wants to be assured that he *loves* her." The general smirked at me. "I think your female counterparts have it easier than you guys. At least they did in my case. I never demanded love, just wanted to get inside the lady's panties. The difference between men and women I guess. Hell, I'd hand over the keys to the Pentagon for the right piece of ass."

Finally the protégé had what the general referred to as "the breakthrough we've been waiting for." The woman began to confide in him. Eventually he reported back the opposite of what we wanted to hear: Rene would not be bought off. Still worse, he was planning to go public with the clandestine removal of the inhabitants from Diego Garcia. "The lady says he's a very determined man, maybe even an idealist." The general sighed. "Rene's talking about a 'conspiracy'—apparently that's the word he uses: *conspiracy*—going to spill the beans about the little game played by London and Washington to make it look as though that place was never occupied by those couple thousand ex-slaves. He's pushing us to the limit."

I never knew how far up the chain of command this information went or how many other people were involved in attempting to corrupt the Seychelles' president. At that time, besides being considered for the Seychelles case, I was bogged down in my own efforts to bring Torrijos of Panama and Roldós of Ecuador around. Because they refused to comply, these two Latin leaders died in plane crashes,

CIA-orchestrated assassinations, before midyear 1981. In November of that same year, the EHMs were pulled off the Seychelles case. The order none of us wanted to hear was given. Jack Corbin and a group of elite mercenaries were sent in to assassinate President Rene.

46

The Highjacking of an Air India 707

"We assembled a team of about forty top-notch jackals in Durban, South Africa." Jack said. "Our cover was the 'Ancient Order of the Froth Blowers,' a rugby-playing, beer-quaffing charity that brought Christmas toys to the children of the Seychelles, which happens to be predominantly Catholic. The plan was pretty straightforward. We would split up and then re-assemble in Swaziland, fly in a Royal Swazi jet to Victoria, the capital city on the island of Mahe, and proceed to our hotels where we would meet up with the advance team, including a few women who had been hand-selected to cull out vital information from higher-ups.

"Our weapons and gear were cached on the island, so we didn't have to worry about being caught at customs, either in Swaziland or Mahe. This was really important to the guys. We were told there was a Seychellois movement, mostly local cops, ready to help out and act as our guides. But all the fighting would be up to us.

"The main opposition would come from several hundred Tanzanian soldiers brought in by Rene and stationed near the airport. Rhodesian experience taught us that the Tanzoons were serious fighters, tough and tenacious, real threats, especially since they outnumbered us five or six to one. On the appointed night, early in the morning, four of us would creep into their barracks while they slept and machine-gun the lot of them. This would signal the uprising. We'd then take the radio station and the presidential palace simultaneously, and blast a prerecorded message from Mancham across the airwaves announcing his return to power. He'd call on his people to stay inside and remain calm.

"The Kenyan Army would have an aircraft loaded with paratroopers standing by in Nairobi. Once the radio station call went
out, they'd go airborne, arriving shortly after first light to put an
African face on the coup, take the credit for all the mischief. Before
the press arrived, we'd quietly disappear, flying commercial airlin-
ers back to South Africa."

The jackal team never got within sight of the presidential palace.
The plan fell apart at the Mahe airport when a security guard spotted an assault rifle that one of the team members had stowed in his
luggage. At the last moment, some of them had been told to bring
weapons, but why he had been so careless in packing would be a
matter of intense speculation for years to come.

A furious gun battle ensued. Jack described it as one of the rare
experiences in his career when he felt he might not escape with his
life—and had time to think about it. "We were surrounded there in
the airport. We had only a few magazines for our weapons, from
the accomplices who'd been waiting for us and one or two grabbed
from airport security. We captured more weapons and ammo from
the troops we ambushed who were rushing back to their barracks
on the other side of the airport. Some of the guys attacked the Tanzanian barracks, but that attempt failed. There was a lot of fighting
throughout the night. It was getting pretty desperate, as more Tanzoons were moving in."

Then one of his team up in the control tower heard an Air India
commercial jetliner requesting permission to land, while asking
why the runway lights were off. The mercenaries immediately
turned on the lights and granted the pilot permission to land, explaining that the lights had been out due to "technical problems,
now resolved."

"There was a telephone discussion between us and the Seychellois authorities. They agreed to a cease-fire if we would board the
aircraft and leave the island. Most of us favored climbing on that
damn plane; with daylight only an hour away, surrounded, and
hearing that Russian warships had arrived in the harbor or were on

the way, I didn't see any other option. The decision was made to go. We refueled the plane, a Boeing 707, loading the body of one of our men who had been killed earlier, along with most of the personal gear into the cargo bay. Several guys decided to stay behind rather than face the possibility of being sitting ducks in an airplane. The rest of us boarded; as we took off the Tanzanians and Seychellois did their best to shoot us down, filling the sky with tracers in a wild send-off. Next stop was Durban, South Africa. When the dust settled, we had one dead, seven of us missing, captured, and taken prisoner, including one of the women accomplices."

On landing in Durban, the Air India plane was surrounded by South African security forces. Radio contact was made and the head of security soon discovered that the plane had been commandeered by his buddies. Jack surrendered, along with the rest of the team. After a brief prison stay, he was quietly released. The Seychelles government arrested the seven they had captured at the airport. Charges against the woman were dropped. Four of the men were sentenced to death; the other two to prison terms of ten and twenty years. The South African government immediately opened negotiations for their release. In the end, it was reported that Pretoria paid the Seychelles $3 million to set them free, or $500,000 each.

Although ostensibly a failure, the Seychelles Case amounted to a corporatocracy success. Despite extensive media coverage of the highjacking and subsequent trials, the United States and Britain managed to avoid most of the controversy; South Africa took the heat. Rene, who had posed such a threat, became more cooperative, tempering his policies toward Diego Garcia, Washington, London, and Pretoria; he remained in power for another three decades, until 2004 when his former vice president, James Michel, won a five-year term in national elections The U.S. military base continues to play a significant role in Africa, Asia, and the Middle East.

It is a standing joke among jackals that their value is clearly defined: about ten times that of the average Diego Garcia islander.

47

An Environmentalist Is Executed

The Seychelles story is a dramatic case of an attempted assassination of a head of state—particularly remarkable because it involved a massive force of mercenaries and resulted in the highjacking of a commercial airliner. It also underscores the fact that such tactics generally are undertaken only when EHMs have failed.

In Africa, the EHM failures are many; therefore, assassinations have played a major role in the politics of that continent. Although most have been conducted in secret, some have taken the guise of legal executions. Perhaps the most famous in this category is that of Ken Saro-Wiwa.

Saro-Wiwa was a Nigerian environmentalist and member of the Ogoni tribe who led the movement against the exploitation of his homeland by oil companies. In 1994 he was interviewed by Amy Goodman on Pacifica radio station WBAI, New York:

Ken Saro-Wiwa: [Shell Oil Company] decided they should keep an eye on me, and watch wherever I go to. Follow me constantly to ensure that I do not embarrass Shell. So as far as I'm concerned, I'm a marked man . . . Early this year, on the second of January to be precise, I was placed under house arrest with my entire family for three days. In order to stop a planned protest against Shell—300,000 Ogoni people were going to move to protest the devastation of the environment by Shell and the other multinational oil companies. . . . All they did was simply send the military authorities to my house. They disconnected my telephones, confiscated the handsets, and I was held for three days, without food.

Ken Saro-Wiwa was arrested again later that year and tried by the government of Sani Abacha—a pro-corporatocracy dictator—in what many observers described as a "kangaroo court." On November 10, 1995, Ken Saro-Wiwa and eight of his fellow environmentalists were hanged.

The executed leader's son, Ken Wiwa, appeared on Amy Goodman's *Democracy Now!* in 2005:

Ken Wiwa: My father didn't bear grudges, it's not in the nature of my family or my community to bear grudges. We believe that Shell was part of the problem and must be part of the solution. We still feel that with some kind of dignity and a commitment to social justice that the situation could still be salvaged. But it's been almost ten years since my father was executed . . . Not a single member of the Nigerian military, which invaded Ogoni, conducted extrajudicial murders, raped young girls, women, all in the name of trying to suppress the protest of our organization so that oil could resume, not one member of the military has been arrested . . .[38]

Assassinations, whether carried out by jackals like Jack Corbin or in the courts of dictatorial governments, have an enormous negative impact on social and environmental movements. The fear of arrest, torture, and death—and its effect on families and communities—has convinced many reformers to abandon their campaigns. That fact is certainly not lost on the corporatocracy.

Today, as I write this sentence, Jack and other members of the Seychelles team are plying their trade in Iraq. Under the pretense of "defending democracy," they conduct operations designed to protect the facilities of U.S. corporations that are reaping windfall profits. Similar to EHMs, they work for private firms hired by the State Department, Pentagon, or through one of the accounts hidden among the "black lists" of the intelligence community. According to their contracts, they provide "security services" and "management consulting."[39]

The sad story of the displaced people of Diego Garcia continues.

In the last years of the twentieth century, the exiled islanders launched a campaign to return to their homes. Claiming physical and emotional suffering for the thirty years of poverty, dispossession, and exile, they sought compensation as well as titles to their lands.

One of their barristers, Sir Sydney Kentridge QC, referred to the original deal as "a very sad and by no means creditable episode in British history." The BBC decried it as a scandal that "involves 'bribes' from the United States, racism among senior civil servants, and the UK Government deceiving parliament and the United Nations."[40]

In 2000, a London court "ruled that the deportation was illegal . . . But the government does not want the islanders back on Diego Garcia which could be used as a base for a U.S. attack on Iraq."[41]

The stories of the attempted coup in Seychelles and the plundering of Diego Garcia are extremely disturbing, especially considering that they were carried out under the pretext of defending democracy. Tragic as they were, however, they pale beside the crimes that were perpetrated throughout so much of the rest of the continent—and continue today.

48

The Least Understood Continent

Jack was one of many jackals and EHMs I spent time with following the publication of *Confessions*. Given the abuses carried out for the corporatocracy on every continent, I often wondered why my conversations with them turned so frequently to Africa.

The men and women who have been so intimately involved in shaping the last four decades of world history seem absorbed by activities on that continent: the United States' role in the assassination of Patrice Lumumba in the Congo, our support of dictators like Jonas Savimbi in Angola, Mobutu Sese Seko and Laurent Kabila in the Congo, Abacha and Olusegun Obasanjo in Nigeria, and Samuel Doe in Liberia, as well as recent atrocities in Rwanda, the Sudan, and Liberia. Some were distressed by the failure of the Clinton administration's "African Renaissance," which most agreed was a not-so-subtle ploy to support one ruthless strongman after another. They talked at length about more recent attempts to forgive debt in many countries, of the Bush administration's determination to craft this seemingly generous act into the latest and most subtle EHM trick to promote the rule of the corporatocracy.

They came to me after reading my book because they too had been sucked in, taught at business and law schools that progress demands approaches that sometimes seem inconsistent with democracy but are required as a means to the end, and because they were skilled warriors in need of employment. They had bought the company line, were either lulled into believing it or accepted that it served their best interests, or both. And now, like me, they were haunted, racked with guilt. They wanted to talk, to confess, to share their stories with a sympathetic listener and perhaps to do something to redeem themselves.

These men and women knew only too well that the people of the United States have been deceived and that they themselves were the instruments of deception. Despite political rhetoric, the African continent is poorer today than it was when I lived in Alexandria, Jack headed for Rhodesia, and many of the others were starting their careers thirty years ago. Forty-three of the fifty-three African nations suffer from chronic hunger and low income levels; famine and drought periodically plague large areas; mineral resources are exploited by foreign industries that take advantage of lax regulations and corrupt officials to avoid investing their profits locally, thus perpetuating weak economies and incompetent governments; people are driven to violence, ethnic conflict, and Civil War; three million children die each year from hunger and hunger-related diseases; the average life expectancy for the continent is forty-six, approximately that of the United States in 1900; and 45 percent of the population is under the age of fifteen but will never realize their productive potentials because of hunger, cholera, yellow fever, malaria, tuberculosis, polio, HIV/AIDS, and war. Nearly thirty million Africans suffer from HIV, and millions of children have been orphaned by AIDS.

The problems that confront Africa are by no means new; their roots stretch back to the colonialism that began with the Age of Exploration and continued through the first half of the twentieth century.

"I've got no idea where I come from," James, a man holding a middle-management position at the World Bank, told me in 2005, summing up a dilemma that he suggested symbolizes the plight of the entire continent. "My great-great-grandparents were dragged out of their homes and brought here as slaves. Unlike the Latinos, Asians, and Middle Easterners living in the States, I find it hard to relate to my own background. I don't even know what language my forefathers spoke."

The slave trade was arguably the most horrific and destructive act by men against men in a long history of human brutality. Add to it the ruthless repression of indigenous cultures, the influence of literature, art, and film that frequently portrayed the native peoples as less-than-human savages, the diversity of the colonial powers that swarmed Africa, and the outright attempts to divide, conquer, and exploit and it becomes tempting to conclude that Africa is the most thoroughly abused and the least understood region on the planet today.

Countries in Asia, Latin America, and the Middle East are interwoven with common threads. Africa is a tangled knot. Its history, geography, cultures, religions, politics, crops, and natural resources are discordant. This engenders a sense of separateness—even isolation—that in turn facilitates exploitation from within as well as from the outside. In many countries the colonial masters of the past, the European elites, have simply been replaced by native African elites. They follow patterns established by their predecessors and openly collaborate with foreign executives who wantonly ravage the land and its people.

While identifying historical trends may help define future options, faulting past eras for current inequities merely postpones attempts at reaching solutions. The EHM and jackal men and women I met with know beyond any doubt that responsibility for the current endemic poverty lies at the feet of the post–World War II empire builders. They also understand the importance of talking and writing about Africa. They accept that we now must take on the tasks of spreading the word and insisting on change.

Since Africa is the least understood continent, it is also the one most easily ignored and therefore vulnerable to plunder. A majority of participants at my speaking engagements raise their hands when I ask if they know something about Bolivia, Venezuela, Vietnam, Indonesia, or any country I name in the Middle East. But I see few hands when I ask about Angola, Gabon, or Nigeria. This is not because the African countries are unimportant to us. Nigeria is the fifth-largest supplier of U.S. oil, Angola is sixth, and Gabon tenth. Nigeria has the ninth-largest population in the world—just before Japan (tenth) and Mexico (eleventh).

U.S. ignorance about Africa is ingrained in our educational systems, including the mainstream media. It is calculated. Because we do not know, we do not care. Because we do not care, these countries are open territory for mistreatment, even more than those that fall within our radar. We have read about Bolivia; so it takes an effort to convince us that Evo Morales is a radical cocaine-growing socialist instead of the nationalistic farmer Bolivians overwhelmingly voted into office. However, no one has to convince us of anything about African leaders; they are essentially invisible to us, non-persons like the Diego Garcia islanders. Invisible people can be driven off their lands, imprisoned, and executed.

"I'm ashamed to be an American whenever I travel to Africa," James confessed. "Africans ask if my people in the States know about them. Did we hear about the millions of children who have died in the wars? The orphans and amputees? The locust invasion? The floods and droughts? I can't bear to admit the truth. We don't know. Most Americans simply don't care. Even African Americans." He rubbed his hands over his eyes. "And you know what's one of the worst aspects of this? The agencies that are supposed to be the good guys are part of the game. I'm not just talking about the World Bank either. The deception includes some of the nonprofits, the NGOs."

49

NGOs: A Stake in Keeping Africa Poor

"Are we being used?" Jenny Williams asked, referring to her work with NGOs in Africa. "Are the concepts of aid and development simply tools in the arsenal of the West, wielded not for the sake of charity but for the sake of control?"

I had become acquainted with Jenny during the editing of *Confessions*. An intern at Berrett-Koehler, my hardcover publisher, she offered brilliant insights—and then headed off to travel across Africa and work for a nonprofit that runs both emergency relief and development projects in Uganda and Sudan.

"I was fed up with the hypocrisy of the West and tired of being an armchair critic," she said. "I wanted to actually get on the ground and do something, see for myself what was happening with all that aid money."

I found her perspective especially interesting because growing up in San Diego, graduating from UC Berkeley in 2004, she had been subjected all her life to the media hype that promotes habituated consumerism and the idea that foreign aid helps the poor. She, like my daughter, Jessica, represents the generation that will lead us into the future.

The e-mail she sent from Uganda in September 2006 continued:

The signs of Westernization in Africa are constant and clear: "Coca-Cola" plastered across kiosks in drought-ridden Northern Kenya; the proliferation of American rap and hip-hop paraphernalia among impoverished African youth; people drinking imported instant coffee instead of locally grown beans because "it tastes better" when, in fact, it's because their own products are more expensive due to corporatocracy-imposed tariffs and taxes.

I'm sure corporations would have seen Africa as ripe for consuming regardless, but NGOs are part of the machine that sustains Westernization. From leadership styles to ex-pat salaries, NGOs enforce Western cultural, social, and economic standards that create a gap between aid workers and the people they're trying to serve—a gap that Africans are constantly striving to narrow by emulating the foreigners. Western values overturn cultural beliefs and send local economic systems into upheaval.

Another dilemma: in Northern Uganda, a region ravaged by twenty years of rebel warfare that has left thousands of people killed and nearly two million displaced, NGOs have been accused of prolonging the conflict simply by being there. As long as the situation is considered an "emergency," donors will continue funding activities and NGOs will continue flocking to the scene to care for people living in horrifying conditions in squalid camps. (One Ugandan radio station joked that "there are more NGOs than boda-bodas"—motorcycle taxis that crowd the streets of every city.)

There's no question that the Ugandans living in these camps—some for ten years or more—would be dying in even greater numbers without the provision of boreholes for wells, sanitation, educational facilities, and food relief by NGOs. But because of the NGO presence, both the Ugandan government and the West have been able to shirk responsibility for ending the fighting that has stalled the development of an entire region. The peace talks happening now, in the summer of 2006, are long overdue.

"We're like a fig leaf that Western governments hide behind when they don't have—or want—a diplomatic or political solution," one co-worker told me. "In any conflict, any crisis, who goes in first? Aid organizations of course, so the West can say 'look, we're doing something,' even if they don't really want to solve the real problems in the end."

Ultimately, it's not just that the West is apathetic or has no motivation to solve conflicts, it's that the West has a real stake in keeping Africa poor. People in Western countries have sincere feelings of charity and they have faith that aid works—but Western governments and multi-national corporations reap enormous benefits from the continued instability and destitution of African countries. The successful manipulation of cheap labor and agricultural products, smuggled resources, and arms trading relies on corrupt politicians, prolonged warfare, and an underdeveloped civil society that lacks the capacity to stand up for its rights. If there were peace and transparency in the Congo, it would be much more difficult—if not impossible—for foreign corporations to exploit the mineral resources; if there were no rebel groups or tribal conflicts, there would be no market for small arms.

Not all causes of poverty or violence are directly linked to Western motives. Corruption among African leaders and latent tribal tensions play a big role in poor governance and the disunity of African people. But I believe if the West truly wanted to see a stable, developed Africa, the continent would be well on its way. Instead, the situation is worse after decades of Western involvement and billions of dollars of aid money.

I fully believe that most aid workers are honest, hard-working people who want to help vulnerable and marginalized people in developing countries. They—we—are up against a system that is difficult to comprehend and still harder to fight. Yet, that is exactly the point. We must change this system.

Jenny is not alone in her commitment to understanding the situation and working to change it. University students and recent graduates around the United States seem to understand the problems confronting their generation better than their parents did. When they travel abroad, they often shun the old destinations—Paris, Rome, Athens—and head instead for Africa, Asia, and Latin America. They attend rallies and conferences, like the World Social Forums, and they mix with the local people. They play music, dance, drink beer, and fall in love. But, above all, they discuss world politics, compare ideas, and plan.

Something that even the most environmentally and socially aware members of that generation might not realize, however, is that another widely accepted trait of their generation—dependence on cellular and computer technology—is destroying the lives of millions of people.

50

Laptops, Cell Phones, and Cars

Four million people have been killed in what is euphemistically called the Democratic Republic of the Congo (formerly Zaire) since 1998. They have died so that wealthier people can buy inexpensive computers and cell phones. Although the country won its independence from Belgium in 1960, it soon fell under Washington's influence. *TIME* magazine, in a 2006 cover story entitled "The Deadliest War In The World," stated bluntly that Congo's "first elected Prime Minister (Lumumba) had been killed by Belgian- and U.S.-backed opponents because of his growing ties to the Soviet Union."[42]

After Lumumba's assassination, army general Mobutu Sese Seko eventually took control. In *TIME*'s words, "A U.S. favorite during the cold war, Mobutu presided over one of the most corrupt regimes in African history."

Mobutu's long rule was ruthless, as well as corrupt, and deeply disturbing to neighboring countries. In 1996 and 1997, Rwanda and Uganda sent soldiers into Congo, overthrew Mobutu, and installed the rebel leader, Laurant Kabila, as its new president. However, social and economic conditions deteriorated rapidly under Kabila's administration. Uganda and Rwanda invaded again in 1998. Six other countries, seeing this as an opportunity to take advantage of Congo's rich resources, joined what became known as Africa's first world war.

Ethnic, cultural, and tribal conflicts played a role in the war; however, mostly it is a struggle over resources. According to *TIME*: Congo's "soils are packed with diamonds, gold, copper, tantalum (known locally as coltan and used in electronic devices such as cell phones and laptop computers) and uranium." The country is vast—about one and a half times the size of Alaska—and is covered in many places with lush tropical forests and fertile agricultural lands. As I had discovered in conducting my studies of this region, the waters of the Congo River have the potential of providing hydroelectric power to much of the continent.[43]

Without Congo's tantalum, we would not have many of our computer-based products (for example, a tantalum shortage resulted in the scarcity of the Sony PlayStation 2 during the 2000 Christmas season). Militias from Rwanda and Uganda may justify invasions on the grounds that they are defending their people against rebels, but they earn billions of dollars from the tantalum they collect and smuggle across borders during these raids.

EHMs, jackals, and government agents from the United States, the United Kingdom, and South Africa constantly flame the fires of conflict. Fortunes are made from arms sales to all sides. War enables corporations to dodge the scrutiny of human rights and environmental groups and avoid paying taxes and tariffs.

Congo is but one of many places where similar things are happening. U.S. congresswoman Cynthia McKinney (D-Georgia) exposed many aspects of this "Anglophone conspiracy" during a hearing she chaired on April 16, 2001. Her opening statement included the following indictment:

> Much of what you will hear today has not been widely reported in the public media. Powerful forces have fought to suppress these stories from entering the public domain.
>
> The investigations into the activities of Western governments and Western businessmen in post-colonial Africa provide clear evidence of the West's long-standing propensity for cruelty, avarice, and treachery. The misconduct of Western nations in Africa is not due to momentary lapses, individual defects, or errors of common human frailty. Instead, they form part of long-term policy designed to access and plunder Africa's wealth at the expense of its people.

... at the heart of Africa's suffering is the West's, and most notably the United States', desire to access Africa's diamonds, oil, natural gas, and other precious resources ... the West, and most notably the United States, has set in motion a policy of oppression, destabilization and tempered, not by moral principle, but by a ruthless desire to enrich itself on Africa's fabulous wealth ... Western countries have incited rebellion against stable African governments ... have even actively participated in the assassination of duly elected and legitimate African Heads of State and replaced them with corrupted and malleable officials.[44]

Although the United Nations has committed to halting the bloodshed in Congo (in the summer of 2006, the largest U.N. force in the world was stationed there), the United States and other G8 countries have not cooperated. In *TIME*'s words:

... the world has been willing to let Congo bleed. Since 2000, the U.N. spent billions on its peacekeeping mission in Congo ... In February the U.N. and aid groups working in Congo asked for $682 million in humanitarian funds. So far, they have received just $94 million—or $9.40 for every person in need.[45]

The violence is not contained within borders. Congo's neighbor, the Darfur region of Sudan, is experiencing a similar nightmare. Two million people have died in a war that has raged for twenty years. This one is fed in part by that most coveted of resources, oil. Although the conflict is rooted in old religious and ethnic antagonisms that reached new levels in the 1980s and 1990s, the violence has been used and exacerbated by EHMs and jackals to mask activities aimed at seizing control of the oil fields. The fighting and social turmoil also facilitate the trafficking of human beings. In recent years roughly a quarter of a million Sudanese have been kidnapped as slaves, many, like the mother of my Alexandria friends Sammy and Samantha, sold into the sex trade. Most people in the "civilized" world believe that such practices ended in the nineteenth century; they did not.

One justification for doing so little to help the Sudanese is the country's reputation as a training ground for terrorists. Sudan was the refuge of Osama bin Laden after he was expelled from Saudi Arabia in 1992 and is considered the birthplace of al-Qaeda. It is easy for the media to write it off as an ally of the "axis of evil."

Congo and Sudan are examples of countries caught up in classic resource grabs. War and poverty facilitate the perpetuation of systems that exploit natural resources and cheap labor while corrupting local politicians.

Another African country offers an example of the more subtle empire-building approach witnessed in Kenya and Uganda by Jenny Williams: the role of NGOs. In some respects the story of two young Americans who joined the Peace Corps because they were determined to help Africans is even more shocking than Jenny's. It uncovers what some consider a conspiracy between U.S. policy makers, foreign governments, NGOs, and the huge agribusiness industry.

51

Ex–Peace Corps Volunteers Offer Hope

Mali, a landlocked country in northwest Africa, at first appears benign, one of those places no one cares about, neglected even by empire builders. That appearance is deceptive; in the deception lies a key to corporatocracy strategies on the African continent.

Mali won its independence from France in 1960 and is now a republic; about a third of its people (twelve million) live in the capital city of Bamako; 80 percent of the workforce is employed by the agricultural sector; 90 percent are classified as Muslim, 9 percent indigenous/animist, 1 percent Christian; it has deposits of gold, uranium, bauxite, and other minerals. Its former president, Alpha Konaré, bought the World Bank plan and implemented measures that revived the economy, primarily through cotton and gold production. He also honored a constitutional provision barring third terms. Amadou Touré was elected president with 65 percent of the votes in 2002.

If I ask how many people in my audiences know about Mali, I almost never see a hand. However, when I spoke at a fund-raiser for a public library in Dover, Vermont, a town near my New England home, I met a young couple who had lived in Mali and who love the land and her people deeply. We corresponded after that and spent time together chatting on a terrace at my house, overlooking the Berkshire mountains. The story Greg and Cindy told me was not merely moving, it represented so much that is beautiful, tragic, and encouraging about modern-day Africa. They bring an American voice to a country and continent that for most Americans is a blur of confusing images. Their commitment to the future—their own and their Malian friends'—is inspirational.

Greg Flatt was stationed in Mali as a Peace Corps volunteer from 1997 to 1999. He returned on his own in 2000 to record an album with Malian musicians. Songs from that album *Zou et Moctar "La Sauce"* hit Number 1 on Mali's charts and Greg became a celebrity throughout the country. Cindy Hellmann was a Peace Corps volunteer from 1999 to 2001. She met Greg while he was there recording the album.

"How could I miss him?" she asked, laughing. "People recognized him everywhere. They stopped him on the streets, broke into dance, and played air guitar. Children followed him like the Pied Piper." She and Greg married three years later.

They had joined the Peace Corps at different times, but for similar reasons. Before entering careers in the United States, they wanted to learn about other countries and cultures. They aspired to the ideal of making a contribution to the world, an ideal expressed by John F. Kennedy when he created the Peace Corps before either of them was born. They each held a vision of a better future for the family they hoped to raise one day, and they recognized that such a future had to embrace the world.

Both also had long-standing interests in agriculture. Cindy grew up on a large family farm in Indiana and Greg loved tending his mother's garden. They told me that the Peace Corps made it sound appropriate for them to accept assignments teaching Malians about farming. "We were naïve enough to believe them." Greg scowled.

I felt an immediate kinship with this young couple. Through their eyes it was easy to see why the modern empire has spread so quickly and so surreptitiously. Cindy and Greg had joined the Peace Corps with the best of motives. They figured they had skills to offer and that by working with U.S. government agencies and international organizations like the World Bank they could help bring prosperity to Africa. Instead, they discovered they were playing a very different role; they were being used to pave the way for a new type of empire, to lay the foundations for another wave of exploitation. The first inklings of the deception hit them when they saw that their assignment was to teach people things that those people knew more about than they did.

"The Malians we worked with were farmers," Greg said. "Can you imagine the gall it takes for a U.S. agency like the Peace Corps to send a bunch of kids to tell experienced farmers how to farm their own land? How does that look to the Malians?"

Despite feelings of guilt and confusion, both admitted that they had benefited immensely from their Peace Corps tours. They learned about customs, languages, and music, and about the subject they had gone there to teach: farming.

"Cindy and I decided to return to Mali in 2005 with another development organization, Opportunities Industrialization Centers International [OICI], as consultants in their Farm Serve Africa program. This USAID-funded organization sends American farmers who volunteer their time and skills to teach rural farmers in Africa improved agricultural techniques."

"I thought," Cindy said, "that this would be different from Peace Corps because by that time I now had been a farmer. I had expertise. And I knew Mali. But to my dismay I found that I was still participating in a top-down approach. I felt like I had stolen money from Malians, who could have earned decent wages teaching the same things more effectively. Who am I? They know the market, they know so much. Farm Serve spent a lot of money to get us there: airfare, transportation, medical insurance, and some living expenses. We were supposed to be agricultural experts, consultants. But I sat in the village where I had been sent, frustrated, asking myself what I was doing. The amount of money spent on my being there in this role would support a rural Malian family for years."

Their suspicions increased as they became aware of the harm caused by Genetically Modified Organisms (GMOs) and of the collusion between U.S. agencies and the big businesses that produce and market GMOs. Farm families that had lived off the land for hundreds of years, saving seeds to replant their crops, were now becoming dependent on fertilizers, pesticides, and seeds they had to purchase from foreign companies.

"One evening, a large group of locals invited Greg and me to join them as they gathered around the one TV in the village. An advertisement for an anti-GMO conference showed images of Malian farmers taking to the streets in protest over the introduction of GMO crops, mainly cotton. We looked at each other and knew that we had to participate in this conference. We left the very next day. It was amazing: a weeklong conference on GMO crops, cotton subsidies, and African agricultural heritage. It was attended by farmers representing Mali, Guinea, Burkina Faso, Togo, Benin, and Gambia, as well as academics, scientists, activists, and politicians. There were countless testimonials of disenfranchised farmers suffering the consequences of unfair trade policies. There was also a great deal of education about the economic, environmental, cultural, and political dangers posed by GMO crops.[46] And many discussions around the fact that USAID and Monsanto were working together to rewrite Malian legislation. We learned directly from someone inside USAID-Mali that the U.S. government agency is working with Monsanto to write into the Malian constitution language that will allow the introduction, sale, and patent rights of GMO crops.

"At the conference," Cindy continued, "we also discovered more about the ravaging effects of U.S. cotton subsidies on Malian farmers. By allowing American farmers to sell their cotton at artificially low prices, our government undercuts African producers in world markets. African farmers often have to store their cotton for a year or more and then may be forced to sell at rock-bottom prices, or not at all. To make matters worse, our 'experts' are persuading farmers to shift from food crops to cotton, as a cash crop. In an attempt to boost production, farmers acquire seeds, pesticides, herbicides, newer plows, and fertilizer on credit, and this sends them deeper into debt to the CMDT [Compagnie Malienne pour le Development des Textiles], which has a virtual monopoly on cotton production and marketing in Mali. The CMDT is a 'partnership' between the Malian government and a French company, CFDT [Compagnie Français pour le Development des Textiles]. The French partners own sixty percent of the company."

"So Americans aren't alone." Greg gave the hint of a smile. "After all, the French got into this business while we were still part of England. But today, I'm ashamed to say, our country is the leader. Participants in the conference passionately expressed their anger toward the U.S. government and transnational corporations with their manipulative policies. Fierce, heart-wrenching pain and anger. You could almost feel it in the air. It made my hair stand on end.

"Cindy and I concluded that economic development in Mali is driven by corporate interests. The faces of the development organizations appear benevolent. They depict themselves as aid organizations that work to improve the lives of these folks. However, the publicity campaigns serve to mask their true intentions, the control of natural and human resources and the domination of markets. Because economic development in Mali is corporate driven, the process is not democratic. The great majority of programs are not requested, initiated, managed, or governed by Malians. The results are often devastating, leaving Mali in worse economic and social situations than before. Furthermore, the development industry has created a large sector of highly paid foreigners who live luxurious lives and who are out of touch with the very people they are supposed to serve."

"On the other hand," Cindy added, "the myth of development is alive and well in the U.S.A. This myth paints a picture of people in Africa and other 'Third World' countries as ignorant, backward, helpless, stupid, and incapable of managing their own lives. That belief creates a sense of superiority and power. It generates feelings of otherness, of us versus them."

Greg and Cindy told me that they intend to create a foundation dedicated to truly participatory, democratic, and sustainable development in Mali, with a focus on organic agriculture, cooperatives, and fair trade. But they will do so only if they are certain that it will be a partnership that honors Malian knowledge and wisdom.

"Such an organization," Cindy emphasized, "would pay Africans to teach their own people. A Malian's average annual income is about $400. We figure that for the cost of a single Peace Corps volunteer to receive training, travel expenses, health coverage, and a stipend, we could pay dozens of locals a very good wage, by their standards. And they would do a better job."

We talked about the importance of distinguishing between NGOs that perpetuate the existing system and those that are genuinely committed to changing it. "In general," Greg said, "the good ones work directly with local people—the little guys. Their employees speak the language and live like their constituents."

I pointed out that the best NGOs—including those discussed in the next section of this book—are often dedicated to turning corporations into good citizens through changing by-laws and operating policies. They also help the rest of us understand the implications of our lifestyles and the responsibility we have to take positive actions.

We agreed that while "bad" NGOs are servants of the empire, "good" NGOs offer the promise of a better world for future generations.

52

Resolved: To Turn Things Around

Every story about Africa hinges on deception. From Egypt to Mali to Diego Garcia, subterfuge and denial are the keys to the American Empire's policies. It is as ruthless as any in history. It has enslaved more people and its policies and actions have resulted in more deaths than those under the imperial regimes of Rome, Spain, Portugal, France, England, and Holland or at the hands of Joseph Stalin and Adolf Hitler, and yet its crimes go almost unnoticed, disguised in the robes of eloquent rhetoric. Our educational systems and media actively participate in this conspiracy of lies. So, while Asia teaches us about the pitfalls of IMF and World Bank policies, Latin America lights the way toward democracy, and the Middle East exposes the extent to which neocolonialism has failed, Africa serves up what may turn out to be the most important lesson of all. Facing west toward America, Africa cups her hands around her mouth—where the Niger Delta joins the Bay of Guinea—and shouts out: Be Aware! Be alert and diligent. Take action.

Africa is a fitting topic to close out the parts of this book that deal with the history of the modern empire and to launch ourselves into a plan for turning it all around. More than anywhere else, Africa highlights the urgency. She is the dead canary in the mine.

The mine is a deathtrap. We need to save ourselves and we need to pave a way for our children to survive in a sustainable and stable world. To do so, we must listen to Africa. It is imperative that we open our ears to that voice screaming at us from across the Atlantic. *You live on a small planet*, it says, *in a tiny community. To save your kids, you must also help me save mine; they are one and the same; we are family.*

Africa tells us that enriching Indiana farmers while impoverishing those in Mali will no longer work. It may have once—for those in Indiana. But not anymore. The same can be said for so many things that seem to make our lives convenient. The days of "national interest" are gone. The success of future generations rests on "global interests"—for the entire human community—in fact the community of all living things. We are one people and we are one planet. There is no room in this family for an Idi Amin, "the Butcher of Uganda," or for Savimbi of Angola, Mobutu and Kabila of the Congo, Abacha and Obasanjo of Nigeria, or Doe of Liberia, any more than there is for Hitler of Germany. And there can be no tolerance for oil spills in Nigeria any more than in California. Or slaves in Sudan any more than on Virginia plantations. This message is slowly reaching across the world. In New York, during the fall of 2006, this poster appeared in the subway system throughout the city:

Milton Glaser,
*Darfur: What Happens in Darfur
Happens to Us*, 2006.

Africa brings all the issues together. It is, in a way, the last frontier of unabashed exploitation and it receives that dubious honor because we have allowed ourselves to be drugged into a stupor of self-deception. We succumb to television ads hawking cheap diamonds and gold. We brag about declining prices for laptops and cell phones. We waste gasoline and complain when the prices rise. We sweep the faces of diamond and gold miners and children poisoned by oil spills under the rug of materialistic greed.

We forget that our own children will inherit that rug. They will be called upon to replace it. They will have to clean up the terrible messes we leave behind.

Africa cups her hands and shouts to us. It is indeed time to change. Fortunately, we have all the tools we need to transform this world we created. Together we can lift up that carpet, remove the messes, and quite literally clean out the house we are about to hand over to our children.

Part 5: Changing the World

53

Four Essential Questions

On October 17, 2006, my alarm clock woke me up very early at my home in western Massachusetts. I had to catch a morning flight to San Francisco where I was scheduled to speak at a fund-raising event for Rainforest Action Network (RAN), a nonprofit organization that has convinced some of the world's most powerful corporations to change their policies toward cutting trees. I rolled out of bed, stumbled down the stairs, and filled the kettle with water for coffee. I glanced through the small window above the sink at the sun as it rose over the distant mountains, the dawning of a magnificent New England autumn day, one of the most brilliant I had ever witnessed. I set the kettle on the stove and, shaking off my drowsiness, ambled into the dining room and peered through the larger window there across the rolling fields at those vibrant mountains, the crimson sun, and the fiery foliage. A movement on a frost-covered knoll caught my eye. A flock of wild turkeys picked their way along the ridge. There must have been a hundred of them. Their silhouettes jerked forward, slowly, oddly, almost unnaturally, like cartoon parodies of prehistoric birds.

I checked the clock on the bookcase and, aware that I had dallied too long, headed for the shower. As I passed the radio I flicked it on to the local NPR station. Adjusting the water temperature, I thought about the speech I would give at the RAN event. I wanted to emphasize a point the organization's chairman, Jim Gollin, often makes—that we must work with the corporations, not against them, that the goal is not to end capitalism but to hold it to a higher standard. Then suddenly the words of the radio announcer caught my attention.

"Within less than a hundred years," she said, "all the maple trees—and the fall foliage—will be gone from Massachusetts. According to a recent scientific study, global warming will make our climate here similar to North Carolina's. So," she sighed, "enjoy this year's display. We may not have many more like it."

I stood there for a moment staring through the bathroom window. Outside, the old red maple next to the house bowed in the wind, its branches scrapping against the wall. The familiar sound now seemed foreboding, a death rattle. I felt absolutely devastated.

Later that day, while flying across the country, I kept thinking about the possibility that the New England fall would be relegated to history. I realized that the demise of autumnal foliage was not a "possibility"; it was a scientifically predictable occurrence. For the first time I could truly empathize with Eskimos as they silently watch the Arctic ice melting. And those Himalayan nomads I had met in Tibet who bemoaned the retreat of their glaciers. For years I had accepted the concept of global warming intellectually. But the idea that fall foliage, something I had grown up with, a symbol of my favorite time of year, was on the extinction list hit me hard.

Then I had another thought: Scientifically predictable occurrences do not need to happen. At least not the ones that are caused by us humans. We can stop them. Something I had said many times during my speeches came back to me: that to change the world we need to change the corporatocracy; we must stop allowing those few men to continue shaping our planet's destiny. We must halt their attack on the ice caps, glaciers, autumn spectacles—on our progeny.

Looking down through an airplane window at the United States of America, a land that generations of my ancestors toiled and fought for, I was struck by the fact that all the stories of EHMs and jackals in Asia, Latin America, the Middle East, and Africa are just that. Stories. They may evoke pride, anger, joy or sadness, but in the end they are simply stories about our past. Unless we choose to turn them into something more important. Unless they become lessons that motivate us to take action.

That day was pivotal for me. I had committed to writing a book that would inspire people to change the world. This book. I had completed drafts of all the sections except this final one, the crucial part. Up until that moment, my efforts had been impeded by doubt. I had a good idea of what I wanted to say, but not of the manner for expressing it. How, I asked myself, do you convince men and women who live comfortably to change a system that provides their comforts—even when they know about EHMs and jackals, when they understand that attached to their comforts are terrible price tags? Where do you find words to empower them to stand up to a force like the corporatocracy? How do you inspire them to take actions that will bend the corporations to the will of the people?

That day, as I flew from the East to the West Coast, reading articles and manuscripts I had brought with me, I realized that these are not new questions. Similar ones have been asked throughout history by everyone who has stood against oppression and for justice. Over the next few days, meeting with old friends and making new ones among the people who support RAN and its sister organizations, I came to understand that the key to answering those questions can be provided by the answers to four others.

The first question we must address deals with optimism, the possibility of achieving our goal. Are we in a position where we can actually hope to effect change? Assuming we become convinced that there are reasons for optimism, we move to the next question. Are we certain that we want change? The stories about EHMs, jackals, and suffering around the globe strike raw nerves, but now we demand absolute proof that our grievances justify the efforts change will demand. Third: Is there a unifying principle that will validate our efforts? We look to ascertain that we are not merely seeking to impose our moral, religious, or philosophical values on others but instead are intent on creating something of true and lasting universal benefit. And finally: What can we each do? You and I personally need to evaluate our talents and passions. What are our individual options and desires? How do they fit into the bigger picture?

In the following chapters, we will explore these questions in depth. We will rely on real-world responses—both historic and current—to answer them. We will talk with today's pioneers, men and women who themselves have asked these same questions, arrived at answers, and now are taking actions that will help each of us make our own decisions. We will examine approaches that have worked in the past and ones that are successful today. At times like these, it is important to be philosophical and to investigate the ethical implications of what we do; however, it is essential that we also apply ourselves in down-to-earth ways, ones that will result in concrete and lasting change.

54

Change Is Possible

We have to be convinced that change is possible in order to make commitments to taking action and risks. Do we have grounds for optimism?

I have mentioned the American Revolution a number of times in these pages. It is not a casual comparison. There are many parallels between the situation we find ourselves in today, living under the misguided hand of the corporatocracy, and the challenges faced by those early settlers. Just as then, now there is a gathering storm of conviction toward changing the corporatocracy. Yet the American Revolution could not happen until the colonists persuaded themselves that victory was possible.

British subjects first saw that the Empire was vulnerable in 1755, during the French and Indian War, at the Battle of the Monongahela ("Battle of the Wilderness"). George Washington, serving under British General Edward Braddock, personally witnessed one of the worst defeats in English history; its impact on him was enormous. Braddock was killed, Washington emerged a hero, and the colonies had a new respect for their homegrown leaders, as well as a diminished regard for an army that until then had been considered invincible. However, in addition to Tories loyal to England, large numbers of Americans deferred from making any decision.

Then, during the Revolution, at the Battle of Bunker Hill in 1775, American forces outfought the British in a ferocious pitched battle. Although the Americans ran out of powder and the British claimed victory, nearly half the English forces lay dead or wounded. The colonists were elevated to new levels of confidence. General Washington's crossing of the Delaware on Christmas night, 1776, and his spectacular defeat of the feared Hessian mercenaries at Trenton the following day convinced approximately eight thousand new recruits to join the Continental Army. Less than a year later, the colonial victory at Saratoga established American superiority on a battlefield and persuaded the British that their own self-interests might best be served by accepting change; it was a decisive turning point that swayed the French into becoming American allies.

My personal equivalent of Monongahela happened during the last years of the nineties and the beginning ones of the new millennium when I led a number of Dream Change trips deep into the Amazon. Every time I flew across the jungle I witnessed more devastation. I was constantly reminded by the Shuar that this was a sign of failure, of a lack of long-term awareness, and an indication that the corporatocracy was fallible—like the British during the French and Indian War. I came to understand that a change of course was not merely something to be desired; it is a prerequisite for the survival of our species.

We learn from history that a collapsed empire leads to chaos, wars, and a new empire. In the modern context, the chaos and wars are likely to cause the annihilation of life as we know it. For me, it took the South American jungles to bring this home. I came away knowing that we simply have to find an alternative. *But*, I asked myself, *is it possible?* I needed proof.

In addition to the Amazon trips, I was also teaching workshops to help executives find creative approaches for solving problems. My "students" represented a cross-section of the world's most powerful companies—Exxon, General Motors, Ford, Harley-Davidson, Shell, Nike, Hewlett-Packard, even the World Bank.

Several books and films popular at that time pointed out that the corporation enjoys the same rights as a living person under the Fourteenth Amendment to the Constitution. This concept was upheld in 1886 by the Supreme Court in *Santa Clara County v. Southern Pacific Railroad Company* and has been a fact of law ever since.[47] I emphasized to those executives that the corporation should also be required to accept the same responsibilities as those expected of a person; it too should be a good citizen, an honorable, ethical member of the community. In the case of international corporations, that community has to be defined as the world.

In actual practice, corporations are the opposite of good citizens. They bribe politicians to write laws that cheat society on a mammoth scale, most significantly by allowing them to avoid paying many of the very real costs incurred in conducting their businesses. What economists refer to as "externalities" are left out of pricing calculations. These include the social and environmental costs of destruction of valuable resources, pollution, the burdens on society of workers who become injured or ill and receive little or no health care, the indirect funding received when companies are permitted to market hazardous products, dump wastes into oceans and rivers, pay employees less than a living wage, provide substandard working conditions, and extract natural resources from public lands at less-than market prices. Furthermore, most corporations are dependent on public subsidies, exemptions, massive advertising and lobbying campaigns, and complex transportation and communications systems that are underwritten by taxpayers; their executives receive inflated salaries, perks, and "golden retirement parachutes," which are written off as tax deductions.

Under proper accounting all these "externalities" would be factored into the costs of products. Those goods and services that are inherently "clean" would also be the cheapest. Consumers would pay a premium for products that strain the environment and society; the price would include funds for correcting the damage. In a truly "free" market economy, these very real costs would be "internalized"—included. But they are not. Why? Because accounting firms are not obligated to enforce sound accounting principles; they only need to adhere to those required by the laws—which are written by politicians who are dependent on the corporatocracy.

Modern corporations have all the rights of individuals but none of the responsibilities. In fact, they are licensed to steal. From an economic standpoint, there is simply no other word for it. They plunder the poor and future generations in order to further enrich the wealthy.

As I conducted workshops and thought more on these matters, I realized that it is one thing to understand that we must insist on fundamental changes in our corporations and it is quite another thing to convince people that we can make it happen. What are the contemporary equivalents of Bunker Hill, Trenton, and Saratoga? Where are the leverage points that give us hope?

I found the answer in a packet of magazine articles I took with me to read on the flight to San Francisco that October day when I learned that New England's fall foliage is threatened with extinction. It was a pivotal day for many reasons.

55

Modern Minutemen

"Environmental warriors."

"Minutemen at Concord Bridge."

"Green guerrillas."

These phrases referred to Rainforest Action Network, the nonprofit where I was about to speak. Although RAN is famous for saving endangered forests, the articles I read on that flight reminded me of something I had thought about a half decade earlier and then pretty much forgot. They suggested that RAN can serve as a model for something bigger. These articles, in magazines ranging from the corporate bible, *Fortune,* to *Tricycle: The Buddhist Review,* discussed in detail how volunteers practice freedom of speech through civil disobedience, street theater, and nonviolent protests. RAN's people march outside the headquarters of corporations, wave placards, and even scale buildings to drape them with banners that highlight the companies' most blatant violations. They buy full-page newspaper ads and write letters to editors. However, they are careful never to harm people or property. And they offer to help executives fashion win-win approaches that benefit all parties. Those successes illustrated that "we the people" can motivate corporations to change. RAN proves that we can bend the will of the mightiest of the mighty. Change can serve corporate self-interests, as well as those of the community at large.

Those articles jarred my recollections of RAN's campaign in the mid-1990s to convince members of the Mitsubishi corporate family, at the time considered the world's most destructive logger of tropical forests, to change their policies. When Mitsubishi's managers rejected RAN's initial overtures and instead refused to negotiate, the endeavor took on a personal element. Mitsubishi officials faced off against RAN's founder and executive director. The exchanges were heated and sometimes personal.

In the end, RAN emerged victorious. On November 12, 1997, Mitsubishi Motor Sales of America and Mitsubishi Electric America signed a historic agreement with RAN that committed the companies to "ecological sustainability and social responsibility"; in addition, they pledged to implement fourteen specific steps aimed at fulfilling this commitment.

Several months after this agreement was reached, I attended a conference on the California coast. I had heard that RAN's founder and executive director, Randy Hayes, would be among the conference's three dozen or so participants. I looked forward to meeting this man who had taken on a monumental challenge and was winning. In my opinion, he was a modern hero whose feet filled tracks put down by Tom Paine, Harriet Tubman, Martin Luther King Jr., César Chávez, Rachel Carson, and others who aroused us to change the way we view ourselves and behave toward the world.

The conference center was located high in the hills above the Pacific. I had decided to make a tent my home for the extended weekend, rather than accepting one of the rooms reserved for participants. I pitched my tent in a small field on a steep slope just above a clump of fir trees that hugged the top of the cliff overlooking the ocean. Although I would have to sleep on an incline, I could open the flap and look down on spectacular views of the rugged coast. Since the day was clear and mild, I did not worry too much about fine-tuning. The tent went up quickly and I lay back to watch the sun creep toward the horizon. The scent of fir mingling with that of the ocean was intoxicating . . .

Suddenly I sat up and looked at my watch. I had dozed off for nearly half an hour. I roused myself and headed down to the reception cocktail party, my reluctance to leave this idyllic setting offset by an eagerness to meet RAN's executive director.

I had no idea that Randy's archrival, an executive from Mitsubishi, was at that very moment on his way to the same cocktail party.

———

I recognized Randy immediately from the press photos. I introduced myself, expressed my appreciation for his work, and congratulated him on his recent victory. We chatted about my experiences in the Amazon. Then he glanced at the door; a look of surprise crossed his face; he excused himself and strolled over to the man who had just entered. They shook hands, exchanged a few words, and then we all were asked to be seated so the conference could officially begin. The woman sitting at my side whispered that the newcomer was a Mitsubishi executive. After that first greeting, he and Randy seemed to avoid each other.

The next day was intense with group meetings. During dinner I invited Randy to join me for a beer at the hot tub where we could continue the discussion begun the day before. We arrived at the top of the cliff above the Pacific Ocean and headed along a narrow trail. As we approached the tub, we noticed that someone was already in it. The Mitsubishi executive seemed equally shocked to see us. But he recovered quickly, smiled up from the bubbles, and raised his own beer can. "Beautiful sunset," he observed. "Please join me."

I felt rather anxious as we stripped down and stepped into the hot water. Here I was, alone on this mountain, the only person between these two men who until recently had been archrivals. We talked about the events of the afternoon, reviewed conference matters, and discussed other participants who were mutual friends. We studiously shunned any reference to the recent conflict.

The sun dropped into the ocean. The sky went from pink to magenta to purple. We opened another round of beers and clicked our cans together. Randy and I sipped from ours, but our companion continued to hold his high. "I have something important to say to you, Randy."

Randy looked directly at him. I sensed that he, like me, had no idea of what to expect.

"I need to thank you," the other continued. "I and a number of Mitsubishi managers wanted to change our policies long before RAN came calling. But we didn't dare confront our board. We were afraid we'd get fired. Your protesters and ads forced the issue. It was tough. You made us all pretty uncomfortable. But, ultimately, you brought us together. Someone pointed out that our responsibilities shouldn't stop with today's stockholders; they should include the stockholders' kids, our kids. RAN gave us an opportunity. We convinced ourselves, our company, to do the right thing." He leaned toward Randy; their cans clicked again; mine joined theirs. "Thank you," he said.

Later that night, a storm moved in off the Pacific. I woke up, listening to the rain hammer my tent and thinking about the evening. The Mitsubishi man's words offered hope. Like me during my days as an EHM, he and his fellow executives had understood what needed to be done to make the world better but they felt trapped in a system that demanded they not listen to their conscience.

I recalled how in my heart I had known that many of my actions were wrong, but things conspired to convince me otherwise. Business schools, international organizations, and revered economists taught that building huge infrastructure projects was essential to development, the solution to poverty. I was praised for following the formula; I was promoted, given raises, larger staffs, power, sex, corporate stock, a partnership, insurance . . . all the things that define success in our society. I was invited to lecture at the world's most prestigious colleges and wined and dined by heads of state.

The Mitsubishi executive had experienced something similar— he and all those other men and women who surrounded him. Their careers were devoted to the bottom line: short-term dollar profits. Promotions, benefits, their children's health care depended on the quarterly income statement. They had been trained to see the world through wine-colored boardroom glasses. Then RAN entered the picture . . .

The wind picked up. Howling at my tent, it seemed to proclaim nature's determination to set things right. The words of an Andean shaman returned to me. "The world doesn't need to be saved," she said. "The world is not in danger. We are. We humans. If we don't change our ways, Mother Earth will shake us off like so many fleas." Now the shaking had begun. This night seemed symbolic of the larger shaking expressed through floods, droughts, rampant epidemics, and melting glaciers.

Suddenly, there was a wrenching sound. Water cascaded through the top of my tent. The rainfly flap had torn loose! I cursed myself for not paying more attention to details when I set it up, then quickly gathered my belongings, flicked on my flashlight, and made a mad dash through the torrential rain into the house where our meetings were conducted.

To my relief I found a couch with a blanket and cushion, as though someone had left it there for me. I removed my sopping clothes, settled in, and fell asleep to the sound of the storm battering against the cliffs below.

56

Changing the Myth

I woke up early and peered through the window. The sun was just rising. Not a cloud visible anywhere. Despite the glorious weather, I had a nagging feeling, embarrassed at the thought that the Amazon adventurer had done such a sloppy job of securing his tent. I slipped into my soggy clothes and crept out the door.

A breeze cooled the air, the sole remnant of the night's storm, as I picked my way back to the small field. When I got there, I froze. The tent had disappeared.

I stood gawking, wondering if somehow I had taken a wrong turn. The circle of yellow grass in a storm-flattened sea of green told me otherwise. Perhaps someone had already been there and dismantled it. But who? Why? My eyes were drawn to the shoreline far below. The storm had kicked up giant waves. A couple of ambitious surfers bobbed in the breakers. Then I spotted something in the fir trees near the edge of the cliff. A globe of nylon the color of my tent.

I hurried to it. Amazingly it was intact, on its side but still fastened to its frame. Cautiously I hauled it out and up the slope. Other than a slightly bent aluminum rod and a lot of mud, the tent seemed none the worse for its wanderings. I went about resetting it. This time much more carefully, giving extra attention to the rainfly flap. I returned to the house and found a bucket. Grateful not to encounter other participants, I filled it with water, lugged it to my tent, and scrubbed away the mud.

After finishing, I took a stroll along the clifftop path. The rain had brought out the scent of fir trees. I came to a wooden bench. The sun at my back, I sat down, faced the ocean, and thought about frailty. First, my own. I had ignored a key tenet of camping: Always anticipate the worst, expect a storm. As an EHM I had found it equally as easy to ignore the facts behind the myth of my job. I was creating an empire rather than making the world a saner, safer, more compassionate place, serving the corporatocracy instead of solving the problems of poverty.

Then I thought about the frailty of the Mitsubishi executive. Like so many others, he had refused to expect a storm, to anticipate that raping rainforests would ultimately destroy his children's futures. I guessed that he had convinced himself that some inventive mind would discover a way to postpone the long-term suffering—solar and wind power, hybrid autos, hydroponics farming. He, like most of us, could find excuses.

Watching the waves crash against the beach in the distance below, I thought about how most of the people who attend Dream Change workshops or join our trips to the Amazon seem to take for granted that corporate executives are amoral at best, and evil at worst, and that the corporations are so powerful that no one can possibly turn them around. This too was a distortion, a type of denial that shifted responsibility away from us, the people; if corporations are omnipotent and their leaders evil, then there is nothing the rest of us can do other than accept their advertising and convince ourselves that we need more of their products.

RAN and its volunteers were changing the myth. They were telling corporate executives to use their inventive minds wisely and at the same time demonstrating to the rest of us that those executives are neither amoral nor evil, that corporations are not omnipotent, and that we are not impotent. They were telling us—executives and everyone else—that we must accept responsibility for our lives and the world we will pass on to our progeny.

When I rose from that bench, I felt inspired. The hot-tub meeting had opened my eyes to new possibilities. That day and the next I concentrated on talking with the attendees who worked for big corporations. As an EHM I had known such people—I had been one of them—and had taught workshops for them and had mixed with them at seminars and cocktail parties. The fact that they were at this conference indicated that they were open to alternative ways of doing business, but I had an even more specific set of questions in mind. I wanted to study them in a new way, to test a hypothesis. If the hypothesis was true, that most are decent people who desire to pass a better world on to their offspring and who welcome "interference" from organizations like RAN, then the implications were staggering.

I continued to test my hypothesis. In addition to talking with corporate managers, I also read studies conducted by others. I concluded that although among executives there are pathological personalities—people who have no regard for the life and well-being of anyone other than themselves—their numbers are small, probably reflecting those in society at large. Most executives care passionately about the consequences of their actions and about the world they will leave to their children and grandchildren. While it may be part of their corporate culture to fear the Randy Hayeses of the world, deep in their hearts, they welcome them. When an organization like RAN hangs banners on their headquarters, those executives give a very quiet sigh of relief.

Shortly after reaching these conclusions, I was hit with a number of personal crises: family illnesses and my father's death. I reduced my activities to the essentials—trips to the Amazon and workshops that had been scheduled far in advance—and set all other projects aside. Then 9/11 struck. After my visit to Ground Zero, I focused on writing *Confessions* and, following its success, on speaking tours. It was not until I took that 2006 flight to RAN's fund-raiser that I once again pondered the deeper implications of its campaigns against Mitsubishi and so many other bastions of the corporatocracy.

I realized during that flight that if we are to change a world ruled by the corporatocracy, we must change the corporations. The more

I thought about this, the more convinced I became that Randy and his staff and their volunteers had hit on something huge. Those picket lines and banners were the contemporary equivalent of the crates of tea tossed into Boston Harbor. And you had to throw the tea before you could win at Saratoga.

57

The New Capitalism

RAN does not fit the profile of the type of organization that intimidates the world's most powerful corporations. In 2006 its staff and budget were less than forty people and $4 million, amazingly small considering the job they do. I traveled several times to San Francisco and met with many of those people after that initial speaking engagement.

"Susceptible to pressure," RAN's chairman of the board, Jim Gollin, responded when I asked him about the weak spot of the corporatocracy. "We see time and again that they can be persuaded to make major policy changes." Fluent in Japanese, Jim had been one of the first Westerners to work in the Tokyo headquarters of what was at the time the largest securities firm in the world, Nomura, then traveled around the globe for Morgan Stanley, and started his own investment company. He understands the corporate world.

"To persuade them to change, you have to be flexible, adjust to the situation." Jim described Home Depot as an example. "They were the world's largest retailer of lumber and not interested in dealing with us. So, we gradually turned up the heat with demonstrations at stores and shareholders' meetings. A friend on the inside leaked us the security code for the intercom system in his store and it turned out that every store had the same code. One day, our volunteers punched in the code and announced: 'Attention, Home Depot shoppers! A sale on wood in Aisle 10. This wood was ripped from the Amazon. There may be blood spilled on the floor; please be careful. Cutting this wood is leading to the dislocation of indigenous communities, soil degradation, and the destruction of the Earth.' Once we got our student allies organized, we could hit up to

162 stores in a single day. As you can imagine, the phones rang off the hook at the Home Depot headquarters in Atlanta. Then they wanted to talk. When they agreed to stop selling old-growth timber and wood from endangered forests, the other major lumber retailers, such as Lowe's, decided to join them.

"I'm a capitalist," Jim admitted. "Corporations are the most dynamic forces in the world today. They've got the power, the energy to create change. It's up to us to make it happen. I believe in activism."

Fortune magazine referred to RAN as "a mosquito in the tent" because the organization has never allowed itself to be intimidated by the size of its targets. Among other corporations that have capitulated to RAN's demands are Kinko's, Staples, Boise Cascade, Citigroup, Bank of America, JP Morgan Chase, McDonald's, and Goldman Sachs.

Randy Hayes turned the day-to-day management of RAN over to Mike Brune in 2003, although the founder himself continued to serve as a very active board president. The new executive director had previously been campaign director and had demonstrated his prowess at shaping strategy. He explained to me that people cannot understand how a $4 million organization is able to convince $100 billion corporations to change their policies. "We're part of a larger global justice movement," Mike said, "the nonviolent shock troops for a loosely organized network of environmental organizations, socially responsible investors, enlightened philanthropists, and sympathetic insiders. Organizations we 'partner' with include Forest Ethics, BankTrack, World Wildlife Fund, Friends of the Earth, Amazon Watch, The Pachamama Alliance, the Ruckus Society, Greenpeace, Global Exchange, the Sierra Student Coalition, the Student Environmental Action Coalition, Rainforest Action Group, and others. We have great hope that we actually *can* change corporate America." He smiled.

I asked him why he was so confident.

"Four reasons. The first is that we have the truth on our side. Our global economy and indeed the quality of all life, depends on a stable climate, flourishing biodiversity, clean air and water. These are all basic human rights, really. As the bumper sticker says: THERE ARE NO JOBS ON A DEAD PLANET. Second, corporate executives and CEOs accept this as true. Many of them are beginning to realize—slowly—that they can be part of the solution, not part of the problem. Third, we see these corporations as potential allies; we work with them, identifying win-wins; we advise them on policy solutions and celebrate responsible leadership. Finally, we won't give up. The vast majority of the public supports environmental protection, and groups like RAN will hold these companies accountable.

A key is understanding the mind-sets of executives. Ilyse Hogue, director of RAN's Global Finance Campaign, was raised by a stockbroker father. "People forget," she told me, "that corporations consist of human beings, many with children. They're very concerned about the future."

RAN's approach took on new significance with a 2006 program called Jumpstart Ford; its goal is to change a corporation that is not generally associated with forest destruction. As campaign director Jennifer Krill points out, "Cars use oil. A lot of oil comes from rainforests. Besides, oil is the single biggest contributor to climate change, which impacts forests and all of us." This campaign sends a signal that RAN's goal is broader than its name suggests.

Krill has no doubts about the outcome of Project Jumpstart Ford. Every RAN campaign has produced tangible results. "The question is not whether we will succeed," she says. "The question is will we do it in time."

Not if the corporatocracy gets its way. The House Ways and Means Committee subpoenaed RAN to hand over information on every protest it has conducted since 1993. In a move that typifies the cozy relationship between big business and the U.S. Congress, the investigation aims at revoking RAN's tax-exempt status. According to Mike Brune, his organization is complying fully; on May 31, 2005, it handed over hundreds of documents and video footage. "It's costing us time and money," Mike confirmed, shaking his head sadly. "We're determined to protect our donors from a possible witch hunt; so we removed every name and face from the material we gave them. What a job. But we want to demonstrate that we believe in the system and we also don't intend to be bullied."

I asked him how he felt about the Ways and Means Committee's action.

He paused. "How do I feel? On the one hand, it pisses me off— they should be going after the companies that abuse their power, not groups like ours who are trying to protect our kids' heritage. On the other hand, I hope it will alert the American public to the power we all have, especially when we come together and organize ourselves. Congress doesn't go after a small nonprofit unless very important people feel terribly threatened."

In the days and weeks following those meetings in San Francisco, I became aware that a lot of very important people are feeling threatened by many NGOs. The corporatocracy is still officially in control, but they are beginning to realize that their days are numbered.

58

A List of Grievances

RAN is just one of many organizations demonstrating that corporations are vulnerable, that they can and will change. Subsequent chapters will describe the successful methods of a number of these NGOs. They have forced the giants of industry to clean up polluted rivers, outlaw ozone-layer-destroying aerosol sprays, protect endangered species, open their doors to minorities, ban gender discrimination, and implement a wide range of other policies that address social, environmental, civil rights, and humanitarian issues. Similar approaches can be applied to changing the fundamental goals of corporations, to transforming them into good planetary citizens who serve the interests of societies and environments rather than those of a tiny global aristocracy.

Following extensive discussions and research, I concluded that change is possible; it is happening in very significant ways. Corporations are bending to our will. We have the power to achieve monumental changes in the way our society is structured.

Now the second question: Are we certain that we want change? In Asia, Latin America, the Middle East, and Africa, we have seen the terrible consequences of the EHMs, jackals, and the "final solution" of the military, even as the colonists witnessed the inequities and suffering caused by British policies. We ask ourselves whether these are enough to motivate us to take the necessary actions.

Prior to the Revolution, journalists like Benjamin Franklin, orators like Patrick Henry, and pamphleteers like Tom Paine understood the importance of succinctly defining the injustices perpetrated by the Crown. There was simply no substitute for the presentation of ironclad reasons, data, and statistics. Their arguments resulted in a long list of grievances against the British monarchy that ultimately was summarized in the Declaration of Independence. It served as a motivator—as well as rationale—for taking action. Today we have an even longer list of grievances against the corporatocracy. It is presented to us regularly by the press (often inadvertently), over the Internet, and in films and books. A summary of salient points:

Because of corporatocray policies and actions . . .

• More than half the world's population survives on less than $2 a day—about the same real income as they had thirty years ago.

• More than two billion people lack access to basic amenities, including electricity, clean water, sanitation, land titles, phones, police, and fire protection.

• There is a 55–60 percent failure rate for all World Bank–sponsored projects (according to a study by the Joint Economic Committee of U.S. Congress).

• The cost of servicing Third World debt is greater than all Third World spending on health or education and nearly two times the amount those countries receive each year in foreign aid. Despite current lip service to forgiving it, Third World debt grows every year, currently approaching $3 trillion. The record is not encouraging. During the 1996 round of "debt forgiveness," the G7 countries, IMF, and World Bank announced a cancellation of up to 80 percent in HIPC (Heavily Indebted Poor Countries) debt, but between 1996 and 1999 the overall amount of debt-servicing payments from HIPC actually increased by 25 percent, from $88.6 billion to $114.4 billion.

• A trade surplus of $1 billion for developing countries in the 1970s turned into an $11 billion deficit at the beginning of the new millennium and continues to grow.

• Ownership of Third World wealth is more concentrated than it was before the 1970s era of massive infrastructure development and the 1990s privatization wave. In many countries, the top 1 percent of households now accounts for more than 90 percent of all private wealth.

• Transnational corporations have taken control over much of the production and commerce in developing countries. For example 40 percent of the world's coffee is traded by just four companies while thirty supermarket chains account for almost one-third of worldwide grocery sales. A handful of oil and other resource-extractive companies control not only the markets but also the governments of countries that possess the resources.

• Corporate greed was highlighted when ExxonMobil announced another record-breaking profit, $10.4 billion, in the second quarter of 2006—the second biggest profit ever reported by a U.S. company, surpassed only by Exxon's $10.7 billion in the fourth quarter of 2005; both were years when rising oil prices caused intense suffering among the world's poor. Oil companies are highly subsidized through tax breaks, trade agreements, and international environmental and labor laws that favor them.

• The overall share of federal taxes paid by U.S. corporations is now less than 10 percent, down from 21 percent in 2001, and more than 50 percent during World War II. One-third of America's largest and most profitable corporations paid zero taxes in at least one of the first three years in the new millennium. In 2002 U.S. corporations booked $149 billion in tax-haven countries such as Ireland, Bermuda, Luxembourg, and Singapore.

• Of the one hundred largest economies in the world, fifty-one are corporations. Of these, forty-seven are U.S.-based.

• At least thirty-four thousand children under five years old die every day from hunger or preventable diseases.

• The United States and many of the countries Washington touts as democracies exhibit the following undemocratic characteristics: the media is manipulated by huge corporations and the government; politicians are beholden to wealthy campaign contributors; and policies made "behind closed doors" ensure that voters are not informed about key issues.

• When the international treaty to ban land mines was passed by the U.N. in 1997 by a vote of 142–0, the United States abstained;

the United States refused to ratify the 1989 Convention on the Rights of the Child, the International Biological Weapons Convention, the Kyoto Protocol, and an International Criminal Court.

• Global military spending reached a new record high of $1.1 trillion in 2006, with the United States accounting for nearly half of that (averaging $1,600 for every U.S. man, woman, and child).

• The United States was ranked #53 on the World Press Freedom list in 2006 (compared to #17 in 2002) and has been severely criticized by Reporters Without Borders and other NGOs for jailing and intimidating journalists.

• The U.S. national debt (amount of money owed by the U.S. federal government to creditors who hold U.S. debt instruments), the largest in the world, reached $8.5 trillion in August 2006 or $28,500 for every U.S. citizen; it was increasing by $1.7 billion a day. A large percentage of this debt is held by the central banks of Japan and China and by members of the EU, rendering us extremely vulnerable to them.

• U.S. external debt (total public and private debt owed to nonresidents repayable in foreign currency, goods, or services) is also the largest in the world, estimated at $9 trillion in 2005. (It is noteworthy that Washington uses the National and External Debts of other countries as weapons, forcing their governments to comply with corporatocracy demands or face bankruptcy, economic sanctions, and severe IMF-imposed "conditionalities"; yet the United States is the largest debtor nation in the world.)

This partial list leaves no doubt that we must use the tools at our disposal to effect change. These grievances serve as our motivator— as well as our rationale—for altering the abominable reality of the world the corporatocracy has created. At the heart of every one of the inequities are corporations. By changing them we will change the world.

We must insist that corporations become democratic and transparent. No longer will we accept imperialistic capitalism, where a very few rich men make all the decisions and most of the money and do so largely in secret. We will demand that they abide by those principles we hold to be self-evident, as stated in our most sacred documents, principles of justice, equality, compassion, and governance with an eye toward providing peace and stability for future generations. We will recognize that we live in a tiny global community and that corporations must set new goals that reflect this reality. Rather than accumulating wealth for the few, they must take care of their employees, even after retirement; serve their customers; look after those who supply the resources they use—who mine, plant, pick, weave, smelt, process, fashion, shape, and assemble— and they must protect the communities and environments where all these people live.

This process also requires that we honor the nurturing aspects of ourselves, those associated with the feminine, and reject the idea that this is a "man's world" where might is right. Riane Eisler, author of the national best seller *The Chalice and the Blade*, joined a number of researchers in analyzing measures that compared the status of women with those relating to the quality of life. Relying on statistics gathered by eighty-nine nations, their study concluded that the status of women is a better predictor of the general quality of life than is Gross Domestic Product.

In her new book *The Real Wealth of Nations,* Dr. Eisler reports: "in societies where women have higher status and are almost half the government, such as the Nordic nations, more fiscal priority is given to caring policies such as universal health care, high quality child care, parenting education, and generous paid parental leave. . . . When the status and power of women is higher, so also is a nation's general quality of life, and when it's lower, so is the quality of life for all."[48] We must understand that our very survival depends upon our ability to be compassionate. We must nurture. We must embrace and love.

Our tiny planet is, like the *Titanic*, sinking rapidly. Unlike the *Titanic*, it does not have too few lifeboats; it has no lifeboats. Our most powerful institutions, our corporations, need to operate the pumps. They ran the boat into the iceberg; now they have to bail it out and set a new course.

And we the people must do the right thing, the rational and pragmatic thing. We must make ourselves heard. We must demand that the corporations become democratic and transparent.

Before addressing the issues dealing with unifying principles and what we each can do, the actions we can take individually and communally, it is important to address an obstacle that halts many of us from ever asking those questions. I came face-to-face with this obstacle while attending a conference on an island in the Atlantic. I discovered just how effective the corporatocracy has been in silencing its opposition, at striking fear into some of the very organizations that are in the best positions to change it.

59

Facing Our Fears

During that period in 2006 when I was exploring the impacts of NGOs on corporations, I joined a group of twenty-three men and women on the island of Martha's Vineyard for several days of meetings. The discussions were echoes, I believe, of debates that raged in the colonies during the years leading up to the Revolution. Many colonists were terrified of the British; along with the "loyalists" or "Tories" they opposed taking action. "The British empire is just too big, too powerful," they warned. "We'll lose and be persecuted for defying it." The setting for those 2006 meetings, off the coast of Massachusetts, was auspicious, a sort of microcosm for today's larger world.

The Vineyard was once home to a large whaling fleet and became the eighteenth century's equivalent to the current Middle East and Amazon—a primary source of oil for American industries and homes. Like deserts and rainforests today, whale populations back then were devastated. The discovery of petroleum in nearby Pennsylvania offered a cheaper alternative and led to the collapse of the whale oil industry. In more recent years, this island gained a reputation as a playground for the famous: the Kennedy and Clinton families, actors, writers, and musicians. It served as location filming for the movie *Jaws*. By the time I arrived in 2006, it also reflected the ecological imbalance so common in our world. Overpopulated by deer, it became overrun by the dreaded Lyme disease–carrying deer ticks. I was told that many residents had contracted the illness. As a result, we were warned not to stroll through the lush grasslands or enchanted forests. "Best to view them from the safety of an air-conditioned car."

Most of the twenty-three conferees represented nonprofits that received donations from our host, a wealthy philanthropist. They were dedicated to protecting the environment, endangered species, human rights, and issues around gender and health.

On a number of occasions I appealed to the participants to devote some of their efforts to bringing corporations around, using RAN as an example. I was shocked at the responses.

"Executives can't be trusted."

"We stay away from the corporate world. Too corrupting."

"Too powerful. We'll lose and be punished."

"Extremely dangerous. Better not to take the risk."

"Look," I said. "Every one of you is involved in important work. But, in a way, you're applying Band-Aids. We're hemorrhaging badly, so we need Band-Aids, but unless we start curing the disease, the underlying cause, all the Band-Aids in the world won't save us. You're right to protect yourselves against corruption by corporations, but for heaven's sake, deal with them, map out a strategy."

Mona Cadena, deputy director, western region, for Amnesty International, spoke up. "We at Amnesty agree. With over 1.8 million members in about 150 countries, we know the power of corporations. In fact, we buy stock in some of the worst offenders—enough so we can attend meetings and file shareholder resolutions requiring the companies to adopt human rights policies in every country where they work."

Mona's willingness to speak out gave me heart.

Later, as we sat at a window overlooking a huge brackish lake separated from the Atlantic Ocean by a tiny sandbar, Mona talked about Tony Cruz. Amnesty's Corporate Action Network coordinator in California, he had engaged Google cofounders Sergey Brin and Larry Page and Yahoo! CEO Terry Semel and founder Jerry Yang in face-to-face exchanges at stockholder meetings, insisting that those companies stop aiding repression of free speech in China. In addition, more than forty thousand activists participated in online actions targeting the companies. "We haven't yet got either of them to take proactive stances," Mona sighed, "but we did rate an article in *Business Week* and air time on some ABC stations. We know it's worth the effort. Pressure brings results."

"RAN's done a great job," Mila Rosenthal, director of the Business and Human Rights program at Amnesty, told me over the phone when I contacted her several days later. "Their work is very challenging. They have to force management to accept specific restrictions on logging. You might think that our approach, using shareholder resolutions, would be easier and that companies would see that commitments to respect human rights will benefit everyone. But still, we get a lot of resistance. ExxonMobil is a case in point . . ."

The oil giant, the largest energy company on the planet, has accumulated a record of human rights abuses in many countries. Amnesty zeroed in on Cameroon, Chad, Nigeria, and Indonesia. "We saw how adamantly ExxonMobil resisted efforts to get them to clean up their act," Mila continued. "We had our members deluge their CEO with postcards; we organized vigils, teach-ins, and protests. On Valentine's Day, we sent cards asking them to 'have a heart for human rights.' We formed coalitions with other like-minded shareholders."

Together with the AFL-CIO, the Teachers' Retirement System of New York City, Boston Common Asset Management, Allied Industrial, Chemical and Energy Workers International Union (PACE), the Interfaith Center on Corporate Responsibility, and Walden Asset Management, they called on ExxonMobil "to adopt and implement a company-wide workplace human rights policy based on the 1998 International Labor Organization's Declaration of Fundamental Principles of Rights at Work (ILO Declaration) and prepare a report available to shareholders concerning implementation of this policy." After filing this resolution, the coalition met with corporate officials. ExxonMobil agreed to include a statement supporting the ILO Declaration in its Corporate Citizenship Report. At the 2004 annual shareholders meeting Chip Pitts, then chair of the board of

Amnesty International, warned that coalition members would hold the company responsible for its promises.[49]

"We didn't get everything we wanted," Mila admitted to me. "But we've made a good start. Our organizations learned a great deal. We will change these guys—one company at a time."

The meeting on Martha's Vineyard at first frustrated me because so many there had succumbed to corporate intimidation. Yet I also developed a greater appreciation for Amnesty and the other organizations that, like those Americans at Bunker Hill, are facing their fears. By standing up to the corporations, they inspire all of us. I knew that hearing Mona speak out must have convinced one or two of the Tories to take heart.

60

Changing Wall Street Through Financial Leverage

The MoveOn family of organizations brings real Americans back into the political process. With over 3.3 million members across America—from carpenters to stay-at-home moms to business leaders—we work together to realize the progressive vision of our country's founders. MoveOn is a service—a way for busy but concerned citizens to find their political voice in a system dominated by big money and big media.[50]

—From the MoveOn Web site

Launching a campaign in response to "the ridiculous waste of our nation's focus" over Clinton's impeachment in September 1998, MoveOn founders Joan Blades and Wes Boyd organized an online petition to "Censure President Clinton and move on to pressing issues . . ." Hundreds of thousands signed the petition in the first few days. Ever since, MoveOn has used the Internet as a free speech forum. Among its campaigns, MoveOn is fighting to:

• End genocide in Darfur, Sudan.
• Pass laws requiring a paper record at voting machines.
• Institute public financing of political campaigns and end candidates' reliance on corporate donors.
• Ban torture in U.S.-controlled facilities.
• Make solar roofs part of Public Utilities Commission's policies.
• Increase public awareness about the dangers of U.S. threats to use the "nuclear option."
• Protect Social Security.

- Prohibit further concentration of the media among a few corporations.

"People aren't apathetic—they just understand that alone it's hard to make much impact," MoveOn Executive Director Eli Pariser told me. "That's why MoveOn's about making folks heard in Washington. Together we can even the playing field against the oil and pharmaceutical companies and their allies in Washington—setting policy that serves everyone, not a few corporate bottom lines."

RAN, Amnesty, and MoveOn generate change through protests, rallies, street theater, banner hangings, newspaper ads, postcards to CEOs, shareholder resolutions, speeches, letters to editors, call-in campaigns to political representatives, massive Internet petitions, and other methods for drawing attention to their causes and for letting the corporatocracy know when its actions are unacceptable. In many respects, they owe their successes to the leadership of the African-American community.

More than any other single group, African Americans have led the nonviolent charge. This campaign started long before the Civil War and continued in modern times through the Southern Christian Leadership Conference (SCLC), the National Association for the Advancement of Colored People (NAACP), and many other civil rights movements. The story of slavery in the United States and the struggle to end it and gain equal rights and treatment for the descendents of those slaves is vast, haunting, discouraging, and inspirational all at once. While most of us know about the way this movement pioneered "civil disobedience," not so many are familiar with its leadership in employing Wall Street as a tool for transforming the corporatocracy. African Americans take credit not only for the example they set in using protests and rallies, but also for their role in recognizing the power of financial leverage. They plotted a course that has been followed by other NGOs.

In 1996 charges surfaced that Texaco employees were making

racist comments. The Rev. Jesse Jackson announced an immediate boycott of Texaco. He called his friend New York State Comptroller H. Carl McCall and asked him to join the picket lines. McCall responded: "Jesse, when you own a million shares you don't have to picket." Because McCall controlled New York's investments, he realized that he was positioned to apply pressure. He fired off a letter to Texaco Chairman Peter Bijur stating his concerns about the company's policies toward minority employees. In the end, Texaco paid a $176 million out-of-court settlement and committed to generous raises to hundreds of African-American employees.

The success of that campaign convinced Jackson to found the Wall Street Project, a financial vehicle for using stock ownership in creative, activist ways and also for raising consciousness among African-American stockholders. Employing these strategies, Jackson and his associates have convinced Coca-Cola, 7-Eleven, Shoney's, Coors, and other corporate giants to change their policies.

"When you go into a meeting as a shareholder, you now have the right to the floor," Jackson explained. ". . . We have gone from sharecroppers to shareholders."[51]

This philosophy has been adopted by other investors. Groups of socially responsible stockholders often pressure pension and mutual funds to take strong stances against corporations that have refused to adopt pro-environment or pro–human rights policies. As I traveled around the United States I frequently encountered resistance on the part of university students to various corporations; on many campuses they were especially incensed about allegations that Coca-Cola mistreats employees in other countries, including accusations that it hired jackals to intimidate and kill union organizers in Colombia. In July 2006, the $8 billion TIAA-CREF Social Choice Account ejected Coca-Cola Company from its fund. Herbert Allison, CEO of TIAA-CREF, a company that provides retirement plans in the academic, medical, and cultural fields, made the announcement at the annual meeting of CREF, the College Retirement Equities

Fund. This amounted to a divestment of 1.2 million shares of Coca-Cola. TIAA-CREF's reasons for this move centered on Coca-Cola's shortcomings in protecting worker rights at overseas bottling plants, marketing of soda products to children, and environmental issues around water usage.[52]

A very different approach that also involves financial leverage has been pioneered by a nonprofit organization that works with tribes deep in the Amazon.

61

Buying Off Third-world Debt

The Pachamama Alliance (TPA) was formed as a result of a 1994 expedition I led to the Amazon. On the last day of that trip, participants donated $118,000 to help Amazonian tribes defend their lands against oil companies. Bill Twist, the husband of Lynne Twist, the nonprofit fund-raiser who had accompanied me to Guatemala, volunteered to manage that campaign and became a very active chairman of the board. By 2006, Pachamama was raising around $1.5 million a year. It purchased two-way radios and an airplane so indigenous communities could overcome obstacles that had hampered them from communicating and meeting with one another. It hired lawyers to conduct legal proceedings against oil companies encroaching on indigenous lands. It taught workshops and produced films to empower people in the United States to become agents of change. Then it struck upon a plan that is truly groundbreaking.

"What if," Bill Twist asked one day while we were trekking together through Ecuador's Amazon jungle, "we leveraged these forests— standing, not cut—to buy off Ecuador's foreign loans?"

We sat down on a log in a sunny clearing beside a giant kapok tree, its mammoth roots slanting off from the trunk into the ground like the flying buttresses of a medieval European cathedral, and talked about the fact that the rainforests are essential for all of us; they absorb carbon dioxide, produce oxygen, impact global climate, generate fresh water, contain millions of species of plants, animals, insects, birds, and fish, and through their flora may offer cures for cancers, AIDS, and other diseases. We discussed Ecuador's external debt, one of the highest in Latin America and, at over $18 billion, equal to twice the national budget. Servicing that debt drains funds critical for health, education, housing, and other social and environmental programs.[53]

I pointed out that most of Ecuador's debt was incurred through the wiles of EHMs in order to enrich U.S. oil companies and other businesses and a few corrupt local officials. Once again World Bank and IMF policies had served the interests of the corporatocracy, at the expense of the Ecuadorian people.

"Right now," Bill observed, "the only way Ecuador can pay off that debt is by selling its crude to our oil companies. In the process the rainforests are raped." He paused as a bright blue butterfly—the size of a pancake—flew into our clearing. It hovered near Bill's shoulder and then fluttered off to a cluster of crimson bromeliads. "My idea is to use the standing forests as a resource, to send a message that they're worth more to the world than oil, a sort of debt-for-nature swap. Ecuador will protect a resource that is vital to all of us, in exchange for debt relief."

"It's a great idea," I said. "But that's an awful lot of money."

"Of course." Bill gave me a knowing smile that I have come to understand indicates that he is dead serious. A Stanford University graduate, his background in the management consulting, equipment leasing, and financial services businesses prepared him to think big.

That conversation was in 2001. For the next few years Bill devoted his personal energies to turning his idea into a reality. In August 2006, representatives of TPA signed an agreement with the Ecuadorian Ministry of Environment and the Ministry of Economics and Finance to conduct a feasibility study for a "Green Plan" in the Amazon. The agreement provides financing for sustainable development of the region, including analyzing the negative impacts of oil exploration, redefining the value of rainforests, and appraising the potential benefits of future scientific breakthroughs that are likely to increase demand for plants. Quantifying these values will enable Ecuador to bargain for conservation. For example, if a section of standing forest is valued at $1 billion, Ecuador could commit to protect that section, allowing medical and other researchers to use it in sustainable ways, in exchange for a $1 billion reduction to its foreign debt. A system of checks and balances would include obligations on the part of the creditors and watchdog organizations that they would not permit oil companies—or other threatening activities—to enter that section.

As a TPA board member I have watched this organization grow from that breakfast meeting in 1994 to a force that significantly impacts the Ecuadorian government and the oil giants. "The Green Plan is the first step," Bill told me recently. "In developing new approaches to solving the debt problem, we're creating a model that other countries can use to protect their lands from exploitation. We see this as an innovative approach to funding sustainable and equitable development."

In addition, TPA has trained nearly three hundred facilitators in five countries to teach Awakening the Dreamer symposiums aimed at empowering people to impact the world through everyday choices and actions. The goal is to have several thousand facilitators reach millions of people in the next few years. This is part of Lynne Twist's vision of the future. "We want to cure the symptoms—rainforest destruction and unfair debt—but we realize that we must also cure the disease: our shortsighted materialistic ways of seeing the world," she told me.

Lynne, Bill, and I have often discussed this idea of attacking the root cause of the crisis confronting us. Doing so requires that we answer that third question posed at the beginning of this part of the book: By what principle do we validate our actions?

The American colonists had a unifying principle. They opposed tyranny and were determined to gain freedom and liberty. In our time these continue to be guiding lights. But, given the many divergent views and customs in the world today, it seems we need a goal that is more universal. Words like *tyranny, freedom,* and *liberty* are subject to interpretation. As we saw in earlier parts of this book, there are people in Africa who view the United States as tyrannical; people in Latin America, Asia, and the Middle East who believe we support regimes that suppress their freedoms and liberty. How do we answer that third question? How do we ascertain that rather than seeking to impose our moral, religious, or philosophical values on others we intend to create something of true and lasting benefit?

62

Five Commonalities

On a sunny day in 2006, the morning after I spoke at the University of Colorado, Sarah McCune and Joseph Peha picked me up at my Boulder hotel. Students at the University of Denver, they had been instrumental in arranging for me to lecture at their school. Sarah, an international studies and political science student, had spent time in Latin America, Africa, and South Asia. Joseph was focusing on international studies, Spanish, and art. He had lived for six months in Argentina where he attended the University of Cuyo in Mendoza.

I rode up front next to Joseph. Sarah sat behind him. With the Rockies as a backdrop, I expected to settle in for a relaxing drive to Denver. Nothing could have been further from their minds. They plied me with questions about my life as an EHM and my current attitudes toward the things I had done. Then I asked how they felt about the world my generation was handing over to them.

"Apprehension," Sarah responded. "Fear. This really is an impressionable time for us. People your age say that who we become in our twenties will determine what we'll do for the rest of our lives. Words like that terrify us. We wonder what's coming next."

"It's not that we don't want to move on with our lives or grow up," Joseph added. "We just don't want to enter the rat race and spend the next forty years clawing up the corporate ladder, changing careers, ending up with a midlife crisis."

Later that evening we drove to a restaurant in Denver where we were joined by other students and Professor Robert Prince, a senior lecturer at the University of Denver who, like me, had been a Peace Corps volunteer in the sixties; for the students, he was not only an inspiring teacher but also an example of a man who walked his talk, someone they could aspire to emulate.

"These kids are amazing," Professor Rob told me. "They see what's going on in the world and they're determined to change it. I'm afraid that for the most part our educational system tries to subvert them, turn them into cogs. Guys like you and I have to give them an out, help them see that they can channel their energy into positive actions. So many brilliant minds waiting to be tapped."

Over and over that evening I heard the students talk about the broken system they are inheriting. They also expressed the hope that RAN, Amnesty, MoveOn, The Pachamama Alliance, and other NGOs inspired in them. I was deeply impressed by their determination and spirit.

Sarah, Joseph, and another friend, Eric Kornacki, drove me back to my hotel after dinner. Eric talked about the research he was conducting on a local company, the New Belgium Brewing Company in Ft. Collins, Colorado. "It's not just that I like their beer." He chuckled. "I like the way they treat people. They're at the vanguard of how business should be conducted." He glanced at his companions. "Commonalities." Then to me, "We've identified a few factors common among good organizations."

"Five," Sarah added. "Equity, transparency, trust, cooperation, and prosperity for everyone involved. In essence, the basic ingredients for democracy." They told me about the companies they were studying that are incorporating these principles into their business plans. They were finding models that ranged from a tile factory in Argentina to organic food co-ops in the Midwest.

Those University of Denver students were formulating the answer to that third question about a unifying principle. Then a couple of high school students came to me in a most unexpected place and offered insights that floored me.

63

Times of Opportunity

I was invited as a keynote speaker at the 2006 Veterans for Peace national convention in Seattle. The idea of meeting with men and women who had risked their lives for their country and now clamored for peace was intriguing. I knew that many had lost limbs and suffered other serious wounds—emotional as well as physical. What were they thinking now?

During my cross-country flight, I read the galley proofs for *The Good Remembering* by my friend Llyn Roberts, a book that reflects native wisdom from around the world. I was particularly struck by the following:

> We live in profound times of opportunity. In reading the newspaper we can feel overwhelmed by the daily crises that seem to jump from the headlines. Yet, we know that crisis and chaos can be pivotal ingredients for insight and change—they often force choices we were previously blind to. Times like these beg us to listen and also to heed the messages we receive.

That paragraph summed up my thinking about the NGOs that are convincing corporations to be good citizens and the executives who respond by taking positive actions. These are indeed "profound times of opportunity." I had a feeling that the veterans needed to hear that good news.

Once in Seattle, I mingled with the veterans, attending an evening reception, an "open mike" poetry reading, and several of their workshops. I shared a beer with a woman who had spent twenty-one years in the army and resigned in disgust when we invaded Iraq for the second time. I heard a legless man sing a lament that brought wild applause from his fellow warriors: "I sacrificed my legs so that Georgie Bushie and Dickie Cheney can pour oil-ie over their sundaes of golden caviar-ie."

I felt their frustration, anger, and determination to right a wrong they had helped perpetrate. I did not write a speech or even outline one. I wanted instead to speak from my heart. I knew that my presentation would be open to the public, but I desired above all else to talk directly to these veterans.

Once I stood before them in that vast hall and looked at their faces, I felt a deep kinship with them. Gone was my rage when as a Boston University student during the Vietnam War I tried to block them from boarding ships at the Boston Navy Yards. Gone too was the fury over their firebombing of Panama City. All I felt up there at that podium was compassion for other human beings who had been exploited by the corporatocracy. Despite any disagreements we might have harbored in the past, they were my brothers and sisters. They too had seen the folly and they now had come together as Veterans for Peace. The novelty and the power of this concept—of soldiers gathering for peace—struck me deeply.

I cannot recall the details of what I said that night. I know I urged them to understand the message in Llyn Roberts's book, that crises can pave the way for change. I implored them not to blame the Bush administration alone, to realize that the corporatocracy is much bigger than any single president. I talked about the NGOs that so courageously fight for change, and I praised the armies of RAN volunteers who commandeered the public-address systems at Home Depots across the land. I beseeched those veterans to believe in themselves and their organization and to know that they can create the type of world they wanted when they accepted their uniforms and swore to defend democracy. And then I heard myself repeat a thought I had expressed to many audiences.

"In order for my grandchildren to grow up in a peaceful, sustainable, and stable world, every child in Africa, Latin America, the Middle East, and Asia must grow up in a stable, sustainable, and peaceful world." This time as I spoke those words I realized that I was defining another part of that unifying principle.

After I left the podium and headed for the book-signing table, two young men approached me.

One of the organizers tried to brush them off. "Can't you see," she said, "there's a long line waiting for him?"

But they would not be discouraged. They introduced themselves as Joel Bray and Tyler Thompson, sophomores at Olympia High School in Olympia, Washington, and University Preparatory School in Seattle, respectively. They told me that reading *Confessions* had convinced them to take action. As we snaked our way through the crowd, one of them said that he was deeply moved by my statement earlier that evening about grandchildren. "Those are my children," he told me. "Not grandchildren. That is the most important thing for all of us to realize. Our children have no future unless all children have a future."

They came around to the back of the table and stood near my chair. They waited until I had signed all the books and finally turned my full attention to them.

"We've started a club called Global Awareness and Change [GAC]," Joel explained.

"Setting it up as two sister clubs, we hoped to be able to organize larger events between our schools and cities, and in that way reach many more people," Tyler chimed in. "After a few weeks of planning, we've already contacted hundreds of people and organizations whose goals are similar to ours, as well as getting support from more students and teachers at our schools."

"So far," Joel added, "everybody we've talked to has responded positively, enthusiastically. It seems they all want to do their part. We decided to cover many different issues in the areas of politics, ecology, sociology, and economics. But after reading your book and seeing Al Gore's movie, *An Inconvenient Truth*, we thought we should focus on the economy and the environment, and how these two are related to each other."

"We know you're very busy, but would like to e-mail you to fill you in on what we're doing." Tyler handed me a slip of paper so that I could give them my e-mail address.

Several days after I returned home from Seattle I received an e mail from Joel and Tyler. It included the following:

Mission Statement:
Global Awareness and Change (GAC) is a club that seeks to promote awareness, change, and the eventual solution of global issues. The world we live in is currently faced by many social, political, economic, and environmental problems, and we will see the effects of each of these issues in our own lifetimes. Moreover, for a solution to not only be found but also to be implemented, it is necessary to gather the help and active support of everyone in our community. The goal of GAC is to educate people about these issues while at the same time taking an active role in solving them. Together, and only this way, will we be able to reverse the effects that we ourselves have put in motion. Our ability to live is what is at stake.

I felt gratified by the urgency of these high school students. They had not been lulled by an education system that tries to divert them from critical issues by focusing on testing, homework, grades, college admissions, job searches, and the other forms of performance trauma. They had not been anesthetized by television. Or immobilized by fear. These two young men had reached a profound understanding. They knew that their "ability to live is what is at stake." They—not just their children or grandchildren—would be impacted by the horrible state of affairs my generation was leaving behind. They also realized that no solution will work unless it encompasses the entire world. And they believed that they can and will succeed.

As I reread their e-mail, I realized that the unifying principle must embrace their commitment to involve everyone in the community. It must encompass the principles advocated by the NGOs of social, environmental, and economic justice. It needs to take into account those five commonalities expressed by the University of Denver students. It has to honor the feminine insistence that children grow up feeling secure and nurtured. Instead of the moral or religious, it must emphasize the pragmatic, articulating a truly universal desire, shared by all men and women and in fact by all lifeforms. And it has to be simple, something everyone can commit to memory. I jotted words down on the back of that paper:

The unifying principle is a commitment to creating a stable, sustainable, and peaceful world for all people everywhere.

I was tempted to add something about recognizing that no child can inherit such a world unless all children do. However, this seemed self-evident. The same seemed true for the idea of "equitable." Then I thought about including plants, animals, and the environment, but decided that the words *stable* and *sustainable* address this. Best to keep it short and uncomplicated.

We commit to creating a stable, sustainable, and peaceful world for all people everywhere.

Until Denver and Seattle, I had thought of this as an important time in history. I now realized that the college and high school students and the veteran warriors who demanded an end to war—combined with all my conversations with people in the NGOs and ideas about turning imperialistic capitalism into democratic capitalism—had convinced me that this is *the* most important time in history.

We know that our society is faltering, that we are exploited, that our leaders thrive on instability and inequality, and yet we have been taught to doubt that we really do know these things. Our hesitation is summed up in one question that is asked by someone at nearly every presentation I give. It is the single most important question before us today.

64

The Most Important Question of Our Time

"Before I ask my question, I want to say that I agree with you." The woman standing at the center aisle microphone was probably in her late thirties or early forties. She had flowing auburn hair and a pleasing smile that reminded me of Meryl Streep. In her sky-blue blouse and beige slacks, she might have been a teacher, lawyer, artist, or housewife. "To change the world, we must persuade corporations to change their goals; they have got to move from serving a few rich people to focusing on making better lives for the rest of us— as well as protecting the environments and communities where we all live." She smiled sweetly. "I totally agree."

By now I was pretty sure I knew what was coming; she was about to ask the question that always came up, the question that haunted everyone. It was the final question on my list of the four we all must address.

She placed both hands on her hips and gave me a rather defiant look. "But what can I do—me personally—to make that happen?"

"There it is," I said for my own ears. I cleared my throat. "Thank you."

Back when I first began my speaking tour, I wondered whether people have always asked this question. Or is it a unique characteristic of the post-Hitler, post-A-bomb–Vietnam–Watergate–9/11–Iraq era? Have we always felt so small and helpless? Or just now?

Attempting to figure this out, I often thought about my grandfather. He owned a small furniture business in rural New Hampshire during the Depression. He died before I was born but I was raised in the shadow of his reputation. Legend held that he never made a major decision without agreement from his employees. He professed that his children could not live good lives unless the poorest members of his community lived good lives. Consequently he dedicated himself to pulling that community out of the Depression. He and other businessmen chose not to use their savings to exploit the destitute by purchasing their homes and farms for a few cents on the dollar; instead, they built an economy that offered jobs to the unemployed—to woodcutters, carpenters, street sweepers, plumbers, weavers, and upholsterers. My grandfather was never described to me as a Good Samaritan; rather his legend was that of a wise man who understood that his as-yet-unborn-grandson's future would be secure only if the futures of the grandchildren of those destitute farmers and laborers were also secure.

I also thought about my father. I suppose he could have written Hitler off as a European despot. "Killed a few million—so what? I'm not Jewish. I live across the Atlantic. I'm safe." He could have rationalized his way out of it. Or, as a language teacher, accepted a safe job as a trainer of translators. Instead, he volunteered for the Navy and headed up armed guard crews that manned the guns on merchant marine oil tankers crossing the Atlantic—an incredibly dangerous job.

I thought about the suffragettes, union organizers, civil rights workers, anti-Vietnam protesters, the young girls who stuck flowers into rifle barrels, and the students who lay down in front of tanks in Moscow and Beijing. Those times seemed long gone. Yet many of those activities happened during my adult life.

Which got me to thinking about now—and the men and women who lie on the ground before bulldozers in the forests of Oregon, the Colombian farmers who chain themselves to fences to defy corporate mercenaries trying to force them off their lands, the athletes who refuse to play in sweatshop-made uniforms, those who sing, climb buildings to hang banners, write poetry, shop only at environmentally friendly and socially responsible co-ops or privately owned local stores, and the ones—like my own daughter—who give up lucrative corporate careers to dedicate themselves to causes and lifestyles that offer more than money. They are doing all these things today.

"You know," I replied to the auburn-haired lady in the sky-blue blouse and beige slacks, "I hear that question a lot. And I'm not sure why I hear it. You and I live in a country that prides itself on being a democracy. On taking action." I told the stories of my grandfather and my father. "Please don't feel that you're alone though." I looked around at my audience. "How many share this woman's question? How many of you want to know what you can do to make things better?"

The room was a forest of hands. I turned to the woman; she gave me a relieved nod. "Why do we feel so powerless?" I asked her. "Hint, the corporatocracy has a collaborator in taking away our power."

Her brow wrinkled. Then she gave me that Meryl Streep smile. "Us."

"Right. They can't take away our power unless we allow them to."

She started to step away from the microphone. But thought better of it. "So, I repeat," she said with a gentle smile. "What can I do?"

"Take back your power. And convince everyone you know to do the same." I looked from her to the rest of my audience. "If you're tempted to say 'The problem's too big, the corporations and government too strong, I don't stand a chance,' that's just a cop-out on your part." I paused to let this sink in. "Thank God our forefathers back in the 1770s didn't say 'Oh, the King of England? He's too powerful . . . I can't do anything about him.'"

I told that audience as I have told many others that we today need to recognize that every one of the Founding Fathers and Mothers stuck their heads in nooses. They stood against the most powerful empire in history, and it happened to be their own government. They were traitors, terrorists in the eyes of the Crown; they faced hanging. Today we honor their courage, as we honor the courage of my father and other members of his generation who stopped Hitler. We honor their generosity, their willingness to make sacrifices.

We too must be courageous. And generous. We must be willing to pay more for diamonds and gold, laptops and cell phones—and insist that the miners receive fair wages, health care and insurance—and we must pay more for goods that are not produced in sweatshops but are made in places that treat their employees fairly. We must drive smaller, more fuel-efficient cars, cut back on total energy use and general consumption, and protect natural environments along with the diversity of species that inhabit them. It is imperative that we develop an awareness that every action we take and every product we buy impacts other people and the places where they live; collectively, our lifestyles today determine the future our children and grandchildren will inherit. Like those who have gone before us, we must be willing to make sacrifices—including, if necessary, the ultimate sacrifice—to ensure that we leave our progeny a world that is at least as good as the one our parents gave to us.

Individuals make a difference. I know it is easy to forget—the corporatocracy spends billions every year trying to convince us that we do not make a difference, except when we buy Product A or Brand B. But we all understand that people impact people. Remember the men and women at RAN, Amnesty, The Pachamama Alliance, MoveOn, and other similar organizations. Recall people who have impacted you personally.

Growing up in rural New Hampshire, I had no idea that African Americans were forced to ride at the back of buses in some parts of the South, until a woman named Rosa Parks showed me. Mosquitoes bred in the marsh behind our house; we were oblivious to the fact that the DDT we sprayed to control them also killed fish, birds, squirrels, and lots of other species, until Rachel Carson wrote *Silent Spring*. That book mushroomed into a global environmental movement. Eugene McCarthy started another movement—a political one—that brought down one of this nation's most powerful presidents, Lyndon Johnson. McCarthy never won the presidency but he gets a lot of credit for ending the Vietnam War. Coretta and Martin Luther King Jr. taught us about the power of dreams; they broke through race barriers not just here but also in South Africa and so many other places. My father instilled in me a deep respect for the principles expressed in the Declaration of Independence. My mother encouraged me to write editorials for my high school newspaper and listened for hours as I rehearsed for the debate team. Without the encouragement of my parents, I would not be writing this book.

I recited these things for my audience that night. Then I glanced at the woman who had stood at the microphone and was now back in her seat. "Do you have a job?" I asked. She nodded. "Are you willing to tell us what?"

"I'm a teacher."

"An amazingly privileged position," I said. "I had a third-grade teacher, Mrs. Schnare, who empowered me to stand up to a schoolyard bully and then lectured me about always defending my beliefs, as well as my body. My sophomore year in high school, an English teacher, Richard Davis, implanted in me the idea that the pen really is mightier than the sword; a year later, my history teacher, Jack Woodbury, assigned books that convinced me that the powerful are also vulnerable. 'Even monarchs,' he would say, 'are people. Their hearts break, like yours and mine. They bleed. They can be brought around—or taken down.'"

She walked slowly back to the microphone. The man at the front of the line bowed and yielded his position to her. "I guess I knew that," she said. "But sometimes it used to seem easier to forget it. Not anymore. I am a teacher. I will teach now, truly teach."

65

Today Is the Day

We are tempted these days to ask for formulaic solutions. It is what the corporatocracy has taught us to do. Follow the dotted line. If you have a headache, take the white pill; for heartburn, the pink one. Never question authority. The teacher has all the answers. Or the priest. The politician. Boss. CEO. President.

Formulaic solutions, our rigid adherence to prescribed approaches, anxiety over deviating from the norm—these preconditioned responses have swept us into deep trouble. We may flatter ourselves that we are a rational, science-based society; the sad truth is that we embrace the emperor's contention that he alone is privy to the answers. It is a lie.

A friend of mine recently suffered a serious heart attack. After a triple bypass he reported that the doctor "informed me that medical science couldn't prove my diet was the cause, but it was a real possibility. I changed my diet." We are in a similar situation on a global scale. It is symbolic of these times that our government insists that we need absolute proof that climate change is caused by man-made carbon dioxide before rewriting our environmental laws. Absolute proof. From whom?

Throughout history, men and women we now revere have questioned the status quo. We applaud people like Galileo, Joan of Arc, Molly Stark, Thomas Edison, Jonas Salk, Helen Keller, Gandhi, and the Dalai Lama. It is important to remember that all of these people were just that: people. They were individuals, like you and me. They knew fear and courage, sorrow and joy. They may have accomplished extraordinary things, but every one of them also faced obstacles that must have appeared insurmountable at times; they experimented, persevered, and (now we can say) succeeded.

There are no formulaic solutions, but there are lots of women and men to inspire us. They fill the pages of this book: from a Sudanese brother and sister to an indigenous man who became president of his country; from Peace Corps volunteers to founders of NGOs; from high school students to college professors, writers to filmmakers; they include people talking to their neighbors and ones supporting local NPR stations. Glance around. They are everywhere.

Look into the mirror. You are one of them.

You make a difference. Every day. In one way or another, you impact the folks near you. The important thing is to be aware of this and then to set about doing it consciously, in positive ways that will make the world a better place. Each day commit to creating a stable, sustainable, and peaceful world for all people everywhere.

I tell my audiences: "If you want me to map out a course of action for you, then you're asking me to do as the corporatocracy does. You don't want that. You have your own passions and talents, different from mine. There are, of course, certain steps we can take. These are simple things that we all know about. Doing as many of them as possible will help you feel good and will also head us toward a survivable future." A few examples:

To Do
- When tempted to engage in "retail therapy" instead jog, meditate, read, or find some other solution.
- Shop consciously if there is something you must have; purchase items whose packaging, ingredients, and methods of production are sustainable and support life.
- Make everything you own last as long as possible.
- Purchase at consignment and thrift stores where everything is recycled.

- Protest against "free" trade agreements and sweatshops.
- Write letters telling Monsanto, De Beers, ExxonMobil, Adidas, Ford, GE, Coca-Cola, Wal-Mart, and other labor exploiters and environment destroyers why you refuse to purchase from them.
- Write letters praising Home Depot, Kinko's, Citicorp, Starbucks, Whole Foods, and other companies that cooperate with RAN, Amnesty International, and other NGOs.
- Cut back on oil and gas consumption.
- Downsize your car, home, wardrobe, everything in your life.
- Send money to nonprofits, radio stations, and other organizations that promote just causes.
- Volunteer your time and energy to such organizations.
- Support local merchants.
- Encourage stores to buy from local growers, producers, and suppliers.
- Shop at your local farmers' market.
- Drink tap water (get the water company to do a better job if necessary, but avoid buying bottled water).
- Vote for enlightened school boards, commissions, ordinances, and politicians.
- Run for office.
- Insist that those who use your money—banks, pensions, mutual funds, companies—make socially and environmentally responsible investments.
- Speak out whenever forums present themselves.
- Volunteer to talk at your local school about your favorite subject (beekeeping, weaving, tennis, anything) and use it to challenge students, to wake them up.
- Discuss externalities, the costs of pollution, poor working conditions, public subsidies, corporate exemptions, and other environmental, social, and political factors that should be included in the prices we pay for goods and services but are not (discussed in Chapter 54); let people know that when we do not pay for these very real expenses we rob future generations.

- Encourage "taxes" on externalities—higher prices for gas, clothes, electricity, etc., as long as the difference pays to right social and environmental wrongs.
- Offer study groups at local libraries, bookstores, churches, and clubs.
- Expand this list and share it with everyone you know.

All the items listed above impact corporate and political leaders. To break the stranglehold this empire has on our planet we must remove power from the seventh characteristic of empires, the emperor, the corporatocracy. Only through transforming their vehicles of control, the corporations, will we succeed in manifesting the world we wish to leave to our children. It is our right and our duty to demand that corporations become good citizens, that they desist from operating imperialistically, and that instead they embrace the laws of democracy.

Let your actions—the ways you spend your money and cast your votes—send strong messages that those charged with running our organizations need to dedicate themselves to creating a stable, sustainable, and peaceful world.

"Are you asking me to pay more for my T-shirts? Not shop at Wal-Mart? To buy from places where unions drive the prices higher?" These are questions I often hear, usually followed by, "I work hard, I've got kids. I can't afford to make such sacrifices."

"I'm asking you," I respond, "not to sacrifice your children's futures. Make sure the brands you buy are made by environmentally and socially responsible companies. Wal-Mart does not meet those criteria—at least not yet. Wear fewer T-shirts if necessary. Keep them longer. Remember too that sometimes you actually pay more for the sweatshop brands. Nike products aren't cheap. Be sure to let the 'good' companies and stores know why you patronize them and let the 'bad' ones know why you don't."

This last is critical. We must work together to send a new message across our planet; those impacted by our actions need to hear our reasons and feel our passions. The corporatocracy prospers from deception and secrecy. We must expose their lies.

Think of the stories of assassination and corruption you read earlier in this book, the ones that made your skin crawl. When you do not shop and live consciously, you ensure that these stories will continue to unfold; you support the EHMs and jackals.

As a boy growing up in New Hampshire, I wished that I had been born in the 1700s so I could have participated in the Revolution. Now I give thanks that I am alive today. I know that you and I have launched ourselves on perhaps the greatest adventure our country has ever known, and one of the most exciting in world history.

I like to make a special appeal to people over fifty years old. "Many of you no longer need to worry about being fired," I say. "Your children have left the nest. So, this is your time to make a real difference. Stick your neck out. Mentor the young. Shake up the boardrooms. Take action—and enjoy it."

And to the young I say, "Some of you can work for corporations and inspire change from within. Others will only be corrupted by the process, and should instead work from the outside, for NGOs or other such organizations. You alone know what is best for you. Above all, understand that success is not defined by the size of your house, or by cars and yachts—it comes when you feel good about yourself."

I encourage everyone to join activist organizations. Throughout our history civil movements, like the Sons of Liberty during the American Revolution, have been essential to our democracy. Never have they been more needed than today. Lists are provided in Appendices A and B. You can find others on the Internet by searching for words that describe your deepest passions and deciding which most appeal to you. Participate in their e-mail campaigns, rallies, and demonstrations, donate ten dollars or ten thousand dollars, volunteer to answer telephones—or simply get yourself added to their lists, be counted, and commit to learning more.

We possess all the resources we need for a world that is stable, sustainable, and peaceful. The corporatocracy has provided them for us. The education, communications, financial, and transportation networks, the minerals and other resources, the scientific information and technological advances are here to serve us. We can save future children from dying of hunger and disease, provide basic amenities, close the gap between poor and wealthy, and we can see to it that the corporations pay their fare share to the communities where they operate. But the key is that you and I have to stand up and be counted!

In addition to deception and secrecy, the corporatocracy thrives on lethargy. It counts on us to remain passive, to accept its advertisements as gospel, to buy unconsciously and allow it to continue destroying our planet. This must stop. Every one of us must shake ourselves awake. Taking action is the only way to ensure that our children and grandchildren, our nieces and nephews and their children, will inherit a world that is not torn apart in hatred and suffering, not ravaged by war and terrorism.

You personally have a great deal of power; it is essential that you allow your passions to rise up, channel them in ways that complement your talents, and take action. The course you choose must come from your heart, not from the dictates of anyone else. You simply need to step forward.

Am I optimistic? Absolutely. How can I not be, given what I know about the thousands of organizations that are successfully fomenting change, all the people working for corporations who want an excuse to do the right thing, and the millions of unsung heroes who donate their time or money to good causes? How can I be anything other than optimistic given what I know about the power you and I have?

Over the past one hundred years we Americans have pledged ourselves to what we called "progress." We visualized huge cities where automobiles replaced horses and electricity lit our homes and ran mammoth factories, and where we could enjoy fresh produce in the middle of a northern winter. We applied ourselves to tasks aimed at realizing these and similar visions every day. We talked about our dreams and produced books, movies, and TV shows glorifying them. We encouraged everyone to join in this process. Caught up in it, we became so preoccupied that we allowed a few men to exploit us and the world. They dreamed of empire and they used their media networks to convince us that their empire was a democracy, a champion of the oppressed, a promoter of a healthy planet. Subtly, without us noticing, our vision was transformed into a sort of nightmare.

We allowed it to happen and we can reverse it. Our true vision, we now realize, was about pulling ourselves out of poverty, living healthier, more dignified lives. Wanting to rid ourselves of the pollution caused by streets jammed with horses and buildings that lacked sanitation systems, desiring greater comfort and more nutritious diets, we embraced visions that appeared to satisfy our needs—and did for a while. Now we see that we were duped by the corporatocracy into employing methods that were selfish and destructive. The visions they foisted on us excluded billions of people; they damaged habitats and the species living in them; they threaten us, our offspring, and the very survival of the planet as we know it.

Today our country exhibits all seven of those characteristics of an empire that were defined in the Prologue of this book. This is not what we intended. It is not what we want. It is, in fact, contrary to our most basic beliefs. We desire something more important than materialistic consumption and the comforts afforded by our modern cities, cars, factories, and shopping malls. Our dream is about life. It is about enjoying peace, stability, and a sustainable planet, about adults dedicated to passing the ideals we most cherish on to our children.

One of those children recently identified the essence of both the problem we humans have created and the solution to that problem. Sayre Allyn Herrick heard my graduation address to her school, Hartsbrook High School in Hadley, Massachusetts, in 2006, during her junior year. The next fall she wrote the following essay:

I saw the entire world for the first time in second grade, laid out on a paper map. The ocean was blue and the countries were yellow, green, and pink. This way of looking at our planet has shaped the perceptions of people for hundreds of years.

Just once, I would like to catch a glimpse of the world free from any human perception except my own—to see our globe suspended in dark space the way it must look from the window of a shuttle. I want to see that the borders and names imprinted on maps are our own creation. In recognizing the impermanence of the man-made boundaries that separate us, we can reveal how truly united we all are on this planet.

What we have been shown or told to be true can stay with us forever. Yet, I think it is our task as an evolving world community to take even the most fundamental preconceptions, recognize them for what they are, and realize their impact on us. Only then can we begin to take the actions necessary for the survival of future generations.

The hour has now arrived for us to take those actions. We have acquired everything we need to realize a new vision. All the resources, the networks, and systems are in place. In recent years we have also found that we have the will. We—you and I—possess the necessary tools.

Today is the day for us to begin to truly change the world.

Appendix A

Organizations Described in This Book

Amnesty International
www.amnesty.org

Cinema Libre Studio
www.cinemalibrestudio.com

Democracy Now!
www.democracynow.org

Dream Change
www.dreamchange.org

Ecova-mali
(*founded by Gregory Flatt, Cynthia Hellman, and Siré Diallo
to promote sustainable development in Mali*)
www.ecovamali.org

Educating for Justice
(*founded by Jim Keady and Leslie Kretzu,
filmmakers who lived like Nike workers in Indonesia*)
www.educatingforjustice.org
Sweat, the film depicting conditions of Nike workers:
www.sweatthefilm.org

Global Awareness and Change Club (GAC)
(*founded by high school students Joel Bray and Tyler Thompson*)
At www.dreamchange.org, see "Dream Change Projects"

Global Dialogue Center, The
www.globaldialoguecenter.com

MoveOn
www.moveon.org

Pachamama Alliance, The
www.pachamama.org

Rainforest Action Network
www.ran.org

Entry Points for Living Democracy

By Frances Moore Lappé
Author of *Diet for a Small Planet* and
Democracy's Edge: Choosing to Save Our Country by Bringing Democracy to Life

Tens of thousands of citizen initiatives nationwide are transforming the very meaning of democracy into a living practice. Linking and learning with them, we each can find satisfying entry points to help break the dominant cycle of destruction. In my 2006 book *Democracy's Edge* I strive to capture the lessons they are teaching. John Perkins kindly welcomed me to share with his readers some of the organizations and resources highlighted in that book. The following list is abridged to reflect the nature of John's book. For a more extensive compilation, please see *Democracy's Edge*.

Also, please visit www.democracysedge.org for additional leads. Many have newsletters and other publications. Some have training programs. Reach out and be inspired! I also welcome you to search the American News Service (my 1990s newswire) for our online archive of 1,600 still-relevant stories of citizens tackling our biggest problems—from health care to reforming prisons—at www.smallplanetinstitute.org/ans.php.

National and International Environmental and Social Issues

Association of Community Organizations for Reform Now (ACORN)
Tel.: (877) 55ACORN
Web site: www.acorn.org

Bioneers
Tel.: (877) BIONEER
Web site: www.bioneers.org

The Gamaliel Foundation
Tel.: (312) 357-2639
Web site: www.gamaliel.org

Industrial Areas Foundation (IAF)
Tel.: (312) 245-9211
Web site: www.industrialareasfoundation.org

National People's Action (NPA)
Tel.: (312) 243-3038
Web site: www.npa-us.org

National Training and Information Center (NTIC)
Tel.: (312) 243-3035
Web site: www.ntic-us.org

Pacific Institute for Community Organizations (PICO)
Tel.: (510) 655-2801
Web site: www.piconetwork.org

Working for a More Democratic Political System

Center for Responsive Politics
Tel.: (202) 857-0044
Web site: www.opensecrets.org

Center for Voting and Democracy
Tel.: (301) 270-4616
Web site: www.fairvote.org/irv

Clean Elections Institute, Inc.
Tel.: (602) 840-6633
Web site: www.azclean.org

Common Cause
Tel.: (202) 833-1200
Web site: www.commoncause.org

InstantRunoff.com
Tel.: (312) 587-7060
Web site: www.instantrunoff.com

League of Independent Voters/League of Pissed-Off Voters
Tel.: (212) 283-8879
Web site: www.indyvoter.org

League of Women Voters
Tel.: (202) 429-1965
Web site: www.lwv.org

Public Campaign
Tel.: (202) 293-0222
Web site: www.publicampaign.org

Public Citizen
Tel.: (202) 588-1000
Web site: www.citizen.org

Working Families Party
Tel.: (718) 222-3796
Web site: www.workingfamiliesparty.org

Working for a More Democratic Economy

The Alliance for Democracy
Tel.: (781) 894-1179
Web site: www.thealliancefordemocracy.org

American Independent Business Alliance (AMIBA)
Tel.: (406) 582-1255
Web site: www.amiba.net

As You Sow Foundation
Tel.: (415) 391-3212
Web site: www.asyousow.org

Bi-Mart
Tel.: (800) 456-0681
Web site: www.bimart.com

Business Alliance for Local Living Economies (BALLE)
Tel.: (415) 348-6284
Web site: www.livingeconomies.org

Center for Working Capital
Tel.: (202) 974-8020
Web site: www.centerforworkingcapital.org

Citizens Trade Campaign
Tel.: (202) 778-3320
Web site: www.citizenstrade.org

Clean Clothes Connection
Tel.: (207) 947-4203
Web site: www.cleanclothesconnection.org/search.asp

Coalition for Environmentally Responsible Economies (CERES)
Tel.: (617) 247-0700
Web site: www.ceres.org

Co-Op America
Tel.: (800) 584-7336
Web site: www.coopamerica.org

Corporate Accountability International
Tel.: (617) 695-2525
Web site: www.stopcorporateabuse.org

The Corporation
Web site: www.thecorporation.com

Domini Social Investments
Tel.: (800) 762-6814
Web site: www.domini.com

Dow Jones Sustainability World Index (DJSI World)
Zurich, Switzerland
Tel.: (+41-1) 395-2828
Web site: www.sustainability-index.com

Ecological Footprint Quiz
Web site: www.myfootprint.org

E. F. Schumacher Society
Tel.: (413) 528-1737
Web site: www.schumachersociety.org

Fair Labor Association
Tel.: (202) 898-1000
Web site: www.fairlabor.org

Fair Trade Resource Network
Tel.: (202) 234-6797
Web site: www.fairtraderesource.org

GreenMoney Journal
Tel.: (800) 849-8751
Web site: www.greenmoney.com

Greenpeace, Inc.
Tel.: (800) 326-0959
Web site: www.greenpeaceusa.org

IdealsWork.com
Web site: www.idealswork.com

Institute for Local Self-Reliance
Tel · (612) 379-3815
Web site: www.ilsr.org; www.newrules.org

Interfaith Worker Justice (IWJ)
Tel.: (773) 728-8400
Web site: www.iwj.org

International Labor Organization
Tel.: (202) 653-7652
Web site: www.us.ilo.org

Justice Clothing
Tel.: (207) 941-9912
Web site: www.justiceclothing.com

National Center for Employee Ownership (NCEO)
Tel.: (510) 208-1300
Web site: www.nceo.org

National Cooperative Business Association
Tel.: (202) 638-6222
Web site: www.ncba.coop

Natural Step
Tel.: (415) 318-8170
Web site: www.naturalstep.org

No Sweat Apparel
Tel.: (877) 992-7827
Web site: www.nosweatapparel.com

Program on Corporations, Law and Democracy (POCLAD)
Tel.: (508) 398-1145
Web site: www.poclad.org

ReclaimDemocracy.org
Tel.: (406) 582-1224
Web site: reclaimdemocracy.org

Redefining Progress
Tel.: (510) 444-3041
Web site: www.rprogress.org

Social Accountability International (SAI)
Tel.: (212) 684-1414
Web site: www.cepaa.org

Social Investment Forum
Tel.: (202) 872-5319
www.shareholderaction.org

Sustainable Connections
Tel.: (360) 647-7093
Web site: www.sconnect.org

TransFair USA
Tel.: (510) 663-5260
Web site: www.transfairusa.org

Trillium Asset Management
Tel.: (800) 548-5684
Web site: www.trilliuminvest.com

Unionwear
E-mail: resource@unionwear.com
Web site: www.unionwear.com

United Nations Global Reporting Initiative (GRI)
Amsterdam, Netherlands
Tel.: (+31-0-20) 531 00 00
Fax: (+31-0-20) 531 00 31
Web site: www.globalreporting.org

United Students Against Sweatshops (USAS)
Tel.: (202) 667-9328
Web site: www.studentsagainstsweatshops.org

United Students for Fair Trade
E-mail: linam@gwu.edu
Web site: www.usft.org

Verité
Tel.: (413) 253-9227
Web site: www.verite.org

Walden Asset Management
Tel.: (617) 726-7250
Web site: www.waldenassetmgmt.com

White Dog Café
Tel.: (215) 386-9224
Web site: www.whitedog.com

Workers Rights Consortium (WRC)
Tel.: (202) 387-4884
Web site: www.workersrights.org

Working for a More Democratic, Sustainable Approach to Food

American Community Garden Association
Tel.: (877) 275-2242
Web site: www.communitygarden.org

American Corn Growers Association
Tel.: (202) 835-0330
Web site: www.acga.org

Community Food Security Coalition
Tel.: (310) 822-5410
Web site: www.foodsecurity.org

EarthSave International
Tel.: (800) 362-3648
Web site: www.earthsave.org

Food First/Institute for Food and Development Policy
Tel.: (510) 654-4400
Web site: www.foodfirst.org

Global Resource Action Center for the Environment (GRACE)
Tel.: (212) 726-9161
Web site: www.gracelinks.org

Heifer International
Tel.: (800) 422-0474
Web site: www.heifer.org

Local Harvest
Tel.: (831) 475-8150
Web site: www.localharvest.org

National Campaign for Sustainable Agriculture
Tel.: (845) 361-5201
Web site: www.sustainableagriculture.net

National Cooperative Grocers Association
Tel.: (251) 621-7675
Web site: www.ncga.coop

National Farm to School Program
Tel.: (323) 341-5095
Web site: www.farmtoschool.org

National Gardening Association
Tel.: (800) 538-7476
Web site: www.kidsgardening.com

Organic Consumers Association
Tel.: (218) 226-4164
Web site: www.organicconsumers.org

Reclaiming the Media

Alliance for Community Media
Tel.: (202) 393-2650
Web site: www.alliancecm.org

Allied Media Projects
E-mail: info@alliedmediaprojects.org
Web site: www.clamormagazine.org/allied/about.html

Center for Digital Democracy
Tel.: (202) 986-2220
Web site: www.democraticmedia.org

Center for International Media Action
Tel.: (646) 249-3027
Web site: www.mediaactioncenter.org

Center for Media & Democracy (Publisher of *PR Watch*)
Tel.: (608) 260-9713
E-mail: editor@prwatch.org
Web site: www.prwatch.org

Fairness and Accuracy in Reporting (FAIR)
Tel.: (212) 633-6700
Web site: www.fair.org

Media Access Project
Tel.: (202) 232-4300
Web site: www.mediaaccess.org

MediaRights
Tel.: (646) 230-6288
Web site: www.mediarights.org

Media Tenor
Tel.: (212) 448-0793
Web site: www.mediatenor.com

Microcinema International
Tel.: (415) 864-0660
Web site: www.microcinema.com

Openflows Networks, Ltd.
Tel.: (416) 531-5944
Web site: openflows.org

Reclaim the Media
E-mail: universaldeclaration@reclaimthemedia.org
Web site: www.reclaimthemedia.org

Third World Majority
Tel.: (510) 682-6624
Web site: www.cultureisaweapon.org

Interactive Media and News Sources

AlterNet
Web site: www.alternet.org

Coalition of Immokalee Workers/Radio Conciencia
Tel.: (239) 657-8311
Web site: www.ciw-online.org

Common Dreams News Center
Web site: www.commondreams.org

Free Press
Tel.: (866) 666-1533
Web site: www.freepress.net

Free Speech TV
Tel.: (303) 442-8445

Guerrilla News Network/GNN.tv
Web site: www.guerrillanews.com

Hometown Utilicom (public Internet utility)
Tel.: (610) 683-6131
Web site: www.hometownutilicom.org

Independent Media Center
Web site: www.indymedia.org/en/index.shtml

In the Mix
Tel.: (800) 597-9448
Web site: www.pbs.org/inthemix

The Meatrix
Web site: www.themeatrix.com

Pacifica Radio
Tel.: (510) 849-2590
Web site: www.pacifica.org

Thin Air Radio
Tel.: (509) 747-3807
Web site: www.thinairradio.org

Tompaine.com
Web site: www.tompaine.com

TruthOut
Web site: truthout.org

Education

Big Picture Schools
Tel.: (401) 781-1873
Web site: bigpicture.org

Center for Collaborative Education
Tel.: (617) 421-0134
Web site: www.ccebos.org

Coalition of Essential Schools
Tel.: (510) 433-1451
Web site: www.essentialschools.org

Educators for Social Responsibility
Tel.: (617) 492-1764
Web site: www.esrnational.org

Forum for Education and Democracy
Tel.: (740) 448-3402
Web site: www.forumforeducation.org

Institute for Student Achievement
Tel.: (516) 812-6700
Web site: www.studentachievement.org

KIDS Consortium
Tel.: (207) 784-0956
Web site: www.kidsconsortium.org

School Mediation Associates
Tel.: (617) 926-0994
Web site: www.schoolmediation.com

School Redesign Network
Tel.: (650) 725-0703
Web site: www.schoolredesign.net

YouthBuild USA
58 Day Street
Somerville, MA 02144
Tel.: (617) 623-9900
Web site: www.youthbuild.org

Promoting Public Dialogue

Conversation Cafés
New Road Map Foundation
Tel.: (206) 527-0437
Web site: www.conversationcafe.org

Meetup, Inc.
Tel.: (212) 255-7327
Web site: www.meetup.com

National Coalition for Dialogue and Deliberation
Tel.: (802) 254-7341
Web site: www.thataway.org

September Project
E-mail: info@theseptemberproject.org
Web site: www.theseptemberproject.org

Study Circles Resource Center
Tel.: (860) 928-2616
Web site: www.studycircles.org

Justice and Legal Issues

Justice Policy Institute
Tel.: (202) 363-7847
Web site: www.justicepolicy.org

Men Against Destruction-Defending Against Drugs and Social Disorder
(MAD DADS)
Tel.: (904) 388-8171
Web site: www.maddads.com

National Association for Community Mediation
Tel.: (202) 667-9700
Web site: www.nafcm.org

National Youth Court Center
Tel.: (859) 244-8193
Web site: www.youthcourt.net

Sentencing Project
Tel.: (202) 628-0871
Web site: www.sentencingproject.org

Time Dollar USA
Tel.: (202) 686-5200
Web site: www.timedollar.org

Appendix C

Recommended Reading

Cohen, Ben, and Mal Warwick. *Values-driven Business: How to Change the World, Make Money, and Have Fun.* San Francisco: Berrett-Koehler, 2006.

Derber, Charles. *Regime Change Begins at Home.* San Francisco: Berrett-Koehler, 2004.

Eisler, Riane. *The Real Wealth of Nations: Creating a Caring Economics.* San Francisco: Berrett-Koehler, 2007.

Farmer, Paul. *Pathologies of Power: Health, Human Rights, and the New War on the Poor.* Berkeley: University of California Press, 2005.

Floyd, Esme. *1001 Little Ways to Save Our Planet: Small Changes to Create a Greener, Eco-friendly World.* London: Carlton Books, 2007.

Garrison, Jim. *America as Empire: Global Leader or Rogue Power?* San Francisco: Berrett-Koehler, 2004.

Goodman, Amy, with David Goodman. *The Exception to the Rulers: Exposing Oily Politicians, War Profiteers, and the Media That Love Them.* New York: Hyperion, 2004.

Hammel, Laury, and Gun Denhart. *Growing Local Value: How to Build Business Partnerships That Strengthen Your Community.* San Francisco: Berrett-Koehler, 2007.

Henderson, Hazel, and Daisaku Ikeda. *Planetary Citizenship: Your Values, Beliefs and Actions Can Shape a Sustainable World.* Santa Monica, CA: Middleway Press, 2002.

Henry, James S., and Bill Bradley. *The Blood Bankers: Tales from the Global Underground Economy.* New York: Four Walls Eight Windows, 2003.

Hiatt, Steven, editor, with an introduction by John Perkins. *A Game as Old as Empire: The Secret World of Economic Hit Men and the Web of Global Corruption.* San Francisco: Berrett-Koehler, 2007.

Kabat-Zinn, John. *Coming to Our Senses: Healing Ourselves and the World Through Mindfulness.* New York: Hyperion, 2005

Korten, David. *When Corporations Rule the World.* San Francisco: Berrett-Koehler, 2001.

Lappé, Frances Moore. *Democracy's Edge: Choosing to Save Our Country by Bringing Democracy to Life*. San Francisco: Jossey-Bass, 2006.

Mander, Jerry, and Edward Goldsmith, eds. *The Case Against the Global Economy and for a Turn Toward the Local*. San Francisco: Sierra Club Books, 1996.

Palast, Greg. *The Best Democracy Money Can Buy*. New York: Plume, 2004.

Roberts, Llyn. *The Good Remembering: A Message for Our Times*. New York: O Books, 2007.

Rodriguez, Felix I., and John Weisman. *Shadow Warrior: The CIA Hero of a Hundred Unknown Battles*. New York: Simon and Schuster, 1989.

Rossi, M. L. *What Every American Should Know About the Rest of the World*. New York: Plume, 2003.

Stiglitz, Joseph E. *Globalization and Its Discontents*. New York: W. W. Norton, 2003.

Twist, Lynne. *The Soul of Money: Transforming Your Relationship with Money and Life*. New York: W. W. Norton, 2003.

Zinn, Howard. *People's History of the United States: 1492 to Present*. New York: Harper Perennial Modern Classics, 2005.

Notes

Part 1: Asia

1. According to World Bank and IMF-IFS statistics; see Giancarlo Corsetti, Paolo Pesenti, and Nouriel Roubini, "What Caused the Asian Currency and Financial Crisis," *Elsevier*, May 7, 1999, www.sciencedirect.com/science/article/B6VF1-3XJSW8X-1/2/77bdde4277268f51bc3e813dec579a79, Table 23 (p. 335) and Table 27 (p. 337).

2. Associated Press, "Indonesia Admits 'Support' by U.S. Gold Company to the Military," *The New York Times*, Dec. 30, 2005, www.nytimes.com/2005/12/30/international/asia/30indo.html.

3. Amy Goodman, with David Goodman. *The Exception to the Rulers: Exposing Oily Politicians, War Profiteers, and the Media That Love Them* (New York: Hyperion, 2004), p. 1.

4. "Thirty Years After the Indonesian Invasion of East Timor, Will the U.S. Be Held Accountable for Its Role in the Slaughter?" *Democracy Now!* December 7, 2005; www.democracynow.org/article.pl?sid=05/12/07/1519244.

5. Jane Perlez, "A Cautious Reformer as Indonesia's Next President," *The New York Times*, Sept. 22, 2004, www.nytimes.com/2004/09/22/international/asia/22indo.html.

6. Melissa Rossi, *What Every American Should Know About the Rest of the World* (New York: Plume, 2003), p. 32.

7. NPR, "Interview: Sidney Jones on the Tsunami Easing Peace Process with Aceh Rebels," *Morning Edition*, Dec. 27, 2005, nl.newsbank.com/nl-search/we/Archives?p_action=doc&p_docid=10EC735E901BD (downloaded Aug. 14, 2006).

8. Ibid.

9. Jane Perlez, "U.S. Takes Steps to Mend Ties with Indonesian Military," *The New York Times*, Feb. 7, 2005, www.nytimes.com/2005/02/07/international/asia/07indo.html.

10. *Democracy Now!*, www.democracynow.org/article.pl?sid=05/11/23/152214.

11. Michael Sullivan, "The Green Heart of Sumatra," *Morning Edition*, NPR, Aug. 14, 2006, www.npr.org/templates/story/story.php?storyId=5611866.

12. Steve Bailey, "'The Bribe Memo' and Collapse of Stone and Webster," *The Boston Globe*, March 15, 2006, p. E1. See also www.boston.com/business/globe/articles/2006/03/15/the_bribe_memo_and_collapse_of_stone__webster/.

13. Associated Press, "Indonesia Admits 'Support' by U.S. Gold Company to the

Military," *The New York Times*, Dec. 30, 2005, www.nytimes.com/2005/12/30/international/asia/30indo.html.

14. Jane Perlez, "U.S. Gold Mining Company Says Indonesia Detains 4 Officials," *The New York Times*, Sept. 23, 2004, www.nytimes.com/2004/09/23/international/asia/23CND-INDO.htm; and Jane Perlez and Evelyn Rusli, "Spurred by Illness, Indonesians Lash Out at U.S. Mining Giant," *The New York Times*, Sept. 8, 2004, www.nytimes.com/2004/09/08/international/asia/08indo.html.

15. Joseph E. Stiglitz, *Globalization and Its Discontents* (New York: W. W. Norton, 2003), p. 232.

16. Jane Perlez, "China Competes with West in Aid to Its Neighbors," *The New York Times*, Sept. 18, 2006, p. A1, www.nytimes.com/2006/09/18/world/asia/18china.html.

Part 2: Latin America

17. Felix I. Rodriguez, *Shadow Warrior: The CIA Warrior of a Hundred Unknown Battles* (New York: Simon and Schuster, 1989).

18. See my *Confessions of an Economic Hit Man* (San Francisco: Berrett-Koehler, 2004).

19. Ibid.

20. Paul Richter, "The U.S. Had Talks on Chávez Ouster," *Los Angeles Times*, April 17, 2002.

21. "Lucio Gutierrez: Ecuador's Populist Leader," BBC News World edition, Nov. 25, 2002, news.bbc.co.uk/2/hi/americas/2511113.stm.

22. "Indigenas Achar liberan a ocho petroleros," Reuters, December 16, 2002.

23. Associated Press, "Lawmakers Remove Ecuador's President," April 20, 2005, www.foxnews.com/story/0,2933,154069,00.html.

24. "Bechtel Abandons Water Suit Against Bolivia," Earth Justice, www.earthjustice.org/urgent/print.html?ID=107. Maude Barlow, Tony Clarke, *Blue Gold: The Fight to Stop the Corporate Theft of the World's Water* (New York: New Press, 2003), pp. 91, 107, 124–25, 138, 152, 154–55, 177, 186.

25. Alma Guillermoprieto, "A New Bolivia?" *New York Review of Books*, Aug. 10, 2006, p. 36, www.nybooks.com/articles/19210.

26. Quotes from Wikipedia, en.wikipedia.org/wiki/Evo_Morales (accessed June 28, 2006).

27. Juan Forero, "Ecuador's New Chief Picks Cabinet; Leftist in Economic Post," *The New York Times*, April 22, 2005, p. A4.

28. Juan Forero, "Presidential Vote Could Alter Bolivia, and Strain Ties with U.S.," *The New York Times*, Dec. 18, 2005, sect. A, p. 13.

29. Paulo Prada, "Bolivian Nationalizes the Oil and Gas Sector," *The New York Times*, May 2, 2006, p. A9, www.nytimes.com/2006/05/02/world/Americas/02bolivia.html.

30. "Evo Morales Nationalizes Gas Resources in Bolivia," *Democracy Now!*, May 5, 2006, www.democracynow.org/article.pl?sid=06/05/05/1432216.

31. Quoted from "Hello President," Hugo Chávez's regular TV and radio program,

April 10, 2005, no. 218, Radio Nacional de Venezuela, Caracas. Translated and observed by BBC World Monitoring, April 13, 2005.

32. Associated Press, "War Crimes Tribunal Dispute Threatens Aid," *The New York Times*, July 1, 2003, www.npwj.org/?q=node/1307.

33. Raúl Zibechi, "Brazilian Military Getting Ready for Vietnam-style U.S. Invasion," *Brazzil* Magazine, July 22, 2005, www.brazzil.com/content/view/9344/76. See Professor Zibechi's monthly column at americas.irc-online.org/.

Part 3: The Middle East

34. James S. Henry, *The Blood Bankers: Tales from the Global Underground Economy* (New York: Thunder's Mouth Press, 2005), pp. 307–10; Jim Garrison, *America As Empire: Global Leader or Rogue Power?* (San Francisco: Berrett-Koehler, 2004), pp. 93–95.

Part 4: Africa

35. BBC News, "The Chagos Islands: A Sordid Tale," Nov. 3, 2000, news.bbc.co.uk/2/hi/uk_news/politics/1005064.stm (accessed Aug. 28, 2006).

36. BBC News, "Country Profile: Seychelles," news.bbc.co.uk/2/hi/africa/country_profiles/1070461.stm (accessed Aug. 28, 2006).

37. For more information, see Larry Rohter, "Pinochet Entangled in Web of Inquiries," *The New York Times*, Feb. 7, 2005, p. A7, www.nytimes.com/2005/02/07/international/07chile.html.

38. Both quotes from "Nobel Peace Laureate Wangari Maathai and Son of Executed Nigerian Activist Ken Wiwa Discuss Oil and the Environment," *Democracy Now!*, Sept. 20, 2005, www.democracynow.org/print.pl?sid=05/09/20/1330227.

39. A general summary of "The Seychelles Case," including the names of most of the mercenaries involved (Jack is listed under his legal name, not as Jack Corbin, an alias) is available under "The Truth Commission Files" at www.contrast.org/truth/html/seychelles.html.

40. BBC News, "The Chagos Islands: A Sordid Tale," Nov. 3, 2000, news.bbc.co.uk/2/hi/uk_news/politics/1005064.stm (accessed Aug. 28, 2006).

41. BBC News, "Diego Garcia Islanders Battle to Return," Oct. 31, 2002, news.bbc.co.uk/2/hi/africa/2380013.stm (accessed Aug. 28, 2006).

42. Simon Robinson and Vivienne Walt, "The Deadliest War in the World," *TIME*, June 5, 2006, pp. 40–41, www.time.com/time/magazine/article/0,9171,1198921,00.html.

43. Ibid., p. 39. Parenthetical definition included in original.

44. Cynthia McKinney, "Covert Action in Africa: A Smoking Gun in Washington, D.C.," April 16, 2001, www.house.gov/mckinney/news/pr010416.htm; House Committee on International Relations, *Suffering and Despair: Humanitarian Crisis in the Congo: Hearing Before the Subcommittee on International Operations and Human Rights*, 107th Cong., May 17, 2001.

45. Robinson and Walt, "The Deadliest War in the World," p. 39.

46. For more information, see Joan Baxter, "Mali's David v. Goliath GM Struggle," *BBC News*, Dec. 7, 2005, news.bbc.co.uk/2/hi/africa/4445824.stm.

Part 5: Changing the World

47. David C. Korten, *When Corporations Rule the World* (San Francisco: Berrett-Koehler, 1995). See Joel Bakan, *The Corporation: The Pathological Pursuit of Profit and Power* (New York: Penguin, 2004) and *The Corporation*, DVD, directed by Mark Achbar and Jennifer Abbott (Zeitgeist Films, 2004).

48. Dr. Riane Eisler, *The Real Wealth of Nations*, Ch. 10, p. 9, galley proofs.

49. Quote from and more information at Amnesty International Web site, www.amnesty.org.

50. MoveOn, www.moveon.org, accessed July 31, 2006.

51. Quotes from Thomson Gale, "Black History: Jesse Jackson," www.gale.com/free_resources/bhm/bio/jackson_j.htm (accessed Aug. 27, 2006); "On the Issues: Rev. Jesse Jackson on Civil Rights," www.ontheissues.org/Celeb/Rev_Jesse_Jackson_Civil_Rights.htm (accessed Nov. 1, 2006); "How Jesse Jackson's Focus on the Financial Markets Could Make a Difference," LookSmart, www.findarticles.com/p/articles/mi_m1365/is_n3_v29/ai_21227720 (accessed Nov. 1, 2006).

52. Cal Manjowski, "TIAA-CREF Drops Coke from Social Choice Account," Reuters, July 18, 2006, reuters.com/misc/topnews&storyID=2006-0, www.indiaresource.org/news/2006/1080.html.

53. Central Intelligence Agency, *The World FactBook*, www.cia.gov/cia/publications/factbook/geos/ec.html.

Index

351